AT WORK

Spirituality Matters

Journal of
Management, Spirituality & Religion
An international refereed journal

The remarkable explosion of scholarship in the study of Spirituality and Religion highlights the important role they play in shaping any organisational context. In short, issues of spirituality and religion underlie every act of managing resources and people.

Audience. JMSR serves scholars of business, spirituality and religious studies. In doing so, JMSR seeks to include, without prejudging any, a mix of interests and concerns.

Standard. JMSR is an academic, double blind refereed journal. The primary criteria for publication in JMSR include relevance, merit, and academic rigour.

Editors. JMSR is co-edited by Yochanan Altman, Jerry Biberman, Louis W. (Jody) Fry, and Jonathan Matheny.

For more information about the journal please contact
Yochanan Altman at y_altman@hotmail.com

Subscriptions and Back Issues. JMSR published two issues in Volume 1 in 2004, three issues in Volume 2 in 2005 and four issues per year starting with Volume 3 in 2006. To order back issues or purchase an annual subscription, please contact the following: Philosophy Documentation Center, 701 Charlton Ave, Charlottesville, Virginia 22903. http://www.pdcnet.org/. Rates for 2007 (4 issues) are: $450 for institutions and $180 for individuals.

The Journal of Management, Spirituality and Religion
is indexed in
Cabell's Directory of Publishing Opportunities in Management.

ISSN   1476-6086   WWW.JMSR.COM

AT WORK

Spirituality Matters

Editors:

Jerry Biberman,
University of Scranton

Michael D. Whitty,
University of Detroit Mercy

UNIVERSITY OF SCRANTON PRESS
Scranton and London

Some of these articles first appeared in two special issues on "Spirituality in Organizations" published in the *Journal of Organizational Change Management* ("Spirituality in Organizations," Parts I and II, Jerry Biberman and Michael Whitty, guest editors, Vol. 12, Numbers 3 and 4, 1999, MCB University Press, Bradford, UK). Further information on the *Journal of Organizational Change Management* and MCB University Press may be found at www.emeraldinsight.com/info/journals/jocm/jocm.jsp

Library of Congress Cataloging-in-Publication Data

At work : spirituality matters / editors, Jerry Biberman, Michael D. Whitty.
  p. cm.
ISBN 978-1-58966-130-1 (pbk.)
1. Religion in the workplace. 2. Management--Religious aspects.
3. Employees--Religious life. 4. Spirituality--Social aspects. 5. Quality of work life. I. Biberman, Jerry, 1949- II. Whitty, Michael D., 1942-
BL65.W67A85 2007
201′.73--dc22

2007021543

Distribution:
University of Scranton Press
Chicago Distribution Center
11030 South Langley Avenue
Chicago IL 60628

DEDICATION

In memory of Rev. George J. Schemel, S.J., founder and director of the Institute for Contemporary Spirituality at the University of Scranton, and founder and for 12 years director of the Jesuit Center for Spiritual Growth at Wernersville, PA.

CONTENTS

∎

OVERVIEW

■

Jerry Biberman and Michael Whitty

Spirit matters—in management, economics, and in business in general. Just as the contributing authors have broken new ground in their teaching, training and consulting, the articles in this reader offers educators the opportunity to incorporate various aspects of spirit into their teaching and scholarship, and offers leaders the opportunity to incorporate spirit into their work environments.

Since the publication of *Work and Spirit,* (Biberman and Whitty, 2000), spirituality, religion and work have increasingly emerged as a recognized field of scholarship and teaching in academia—particularly in business, health settings, and schools. Management, Spirituality and Religion is now a recognized interest group of the Academy of Management, special issues on spirit and work have been published in several scholarly journals, a journal devoted entirely to the subject (the Journal of Management, Spirituality and Religion) is in its third year of publication, and a handbook on the subject is now in its second printing.

We are hopeful the diverse collection of viewpoints presented in this reader will advance the dialogue on the possible meaning and value of workplace spirituality. Our intention is to provide a broad representation of the academic scholarship in the field of spirituality in management/organizations. No attempt has been made to exclude the overlap between many other closely related fields such as consciousness in business and religion in business. If fact, we have found much of the scholarship to be highly interdisciplinary in its focus. Medicine and psychology may yet prove to be the most initially convincing paradigms for new integral approaches to reinventing work. Individually healthy work lives beget a truly healthy workplace.

Many of the articles in this reader first appeared in the *Journal of Management, Spirituality and Religion*, an international refereed journal (edited by Jerry Biberman and Yochanan Altman) and in special issues of the *Journal of Organizational Change Management* (then edited by David Boje and published by MCB Press). We are grateful to these two journals for allowing those articles to appear in this reader.

The articles that appear in this reader on work and spirituality join the many articles that are now appearing in various scholarly journals across many disciplines. This interdisciplinary scholarship has appeared not only in the various business disciplines but also in the sciences, the social sciences, and the humanities. Moreover, academic studies and books reflect a renewed interest in the topic of spirituality and work as it applies to all the professions, institutions of modern life, and the future visions for the global society of tomorrow.

We have divided our selections into four main selections. This introduction will give a short introduction to-and description of-each of the articles contained in the four sections of the reader. Each section contains a diverse mix of views and approaches to a subject that can be and is approached from a vast number of often very different directions. We make no final case for any particular approach. We hope that you will find this reader useful in your teaching, consulting, and research. It can be utilized as a supplementary reader in management, organizational behavior, business ethics, business social responsibility, organizational development, business policy, or a course in spirituality at work.

Located at the beginning of three sections of the reader are three poems by Tom Brown—"Glow," "Embers," and "Dawn"—from his e-book *The Anatomy of Fire*. The complete book can be accessed online at http://www.thomaslbrown.com/

The elements of this topic—work and spirituality—are as old as time but equally timely for the new millennium. It will take more than one academic reader on spirituality to begin to explore these topics. The diverse approaches of our authors ensure a uniquely rich list of references and sources for further study and research. This collection of essays is interdisciplinary, attacking this vast topic of work from different vantage points. These path-breaking essays set the standard for a post-economic world. It is fitting we open this special issue with something affirming of human evolution toward a higher consciousness. We may not make it in our academic lifetimes, but the goal is worth shooting for.

Theoretical Perspectives

It has only been within the last decade that serious academic interest has been evident regarding the possible relevance of spirituality to organizations. Now, with the popular business literature awash with pop psychology for business leaders and their organizations, the world of academia recognizes the importance of visionary organizational theory and a deepened view of basic core values. Both mainline consultants and opinion leaders in the popular business culture realize the need for a higher purpose for organizational life than solely acquiring money and power. They have turned, often, to spiritual business philosophy.

This readers' sample of theoretical perspectives on spirituality reveals the diverse approaches to this new discipline of organization theory. The dominant theme is that the search for deeper meaning in work often leads to a spiritual insight or path, and sometimes a renewal or transformation of the work organization itself. New management theory is coming from the fields of organizational psychology, humanistic psychology and a new business philosophy based on environmental management.

Charles Fornaciari and Kathy Lund Dean boldly review the state of spirituality, religion and work research reminding the reader at the onset that much has been done in various disciplines of the social sciences and the humanities prior to serious interest from the business disciplines. The established fields of philosophy, religious studies and transpersonal psychology have pioneered many dynamic and varied empirical approaches to research in this evolving interdisciplinary field. Fornaciari and Dean are focused on detailed discussion and implications for research methodologies already fairly well established in the inquiry traditions of education, psychology and theology. This essay argues for a greater integration of business and organizational studies of spirit and religion with those of the social sciences. As pragmatic business professors they also want more quantitative /science and less philosophy or purely qualitative research.

Thierry Pauchant takes quite the opposite approach to work and spirit by interviewing one of the leading philosophers of human consciousness, Ken Wilber. With just these first two papers the reader will get a sense of the range of perspectives and approaches available to the study of spirit and religion in work and organization.

Wilber is looking at the big picture as philosophers and thought leaders are supposed to do. He may posit more theory than can be measured by the traditional quantitative models of business school, but he does offer spiritual psychology for leadership, a needed sobering observation on current political culture, and a peek at the possible future of human consciousness.

If anything, future editions of this reader and similar works should strive to expand the boundaries of debate and interdisciplinary exchange. Someday the walls of the ancient disciplines will break down into a new way of seeing, learning and understanding.

As a step in this direction, David S. Steingard and Dale E. Fitzgibbons synergistically combine Burrell and Morgan's classic work on sociological paradigms and organizational analysis with the interdisciplinary work of philosopher Ken Wilber to envision a spiritually integral theory of management. They envision and describe new possibilities for management research and application arising from their proposed holistic spiritually integral theory of management.

Len Tischler presents one very reasonable starting point for understanding the growing interest in business spirit—Maslow's notion that we have a basic need for self-transcendence. Tischler posits the notion that the long-term socioeconomic advance of modern society has allowed for an ever more conscious effort at self-actualization and self-transcendence. Thus, Tischler argues, both the modern individual and the evolving organization seek higher-order needs much in line with Maslow's hierarchy of needs. This is a good starting point for the scientific mind—the behaviorists and the mainstream academics who may have their doubts about the possibility of spirit impacting the workplace. The worlds of organizational psychology, self-actualization, and spiritual philosophy are bridged by the work of humanistic psychologists such as Maslow. Tischler shows us the academic roots of the new interest in higher-order consciousness as the next step in human evolution (once basic human needs are met). Tischler believes conscious evolution can be applied to organizations.

As if to prove the point on the diversity of assumptions surrounding spiritual values and work, Dan Butts raises the challenge to researchers of the necessity of considering the macroeconomic and political aspects of organizational power. Butts suggests that it is not enough to find personal meaning in work, or for the organization to be a jazzed-up, winning team. The long-term impact on the total society and the planet must be factored into a complete and far-seeing spirituality of work. Few business writers have included these considerations. This short essay invites symposia between organizational theory, business social responsibility, political economy, and a desirable political philosophy for the future. Where do we begin? Maybe with theories of socioeconomic evolution which mold human behavior and consciousness, or maybe by linking the needs of the human community and planet earth with organization vision and goals.

David Boje calls for a new worldview for business and economics. He calls it "festivalism" to distinguish it from the systems of the past and present. Boje believes it is possible and desirable to cultivate the core value of harmlessness or nonviolence toward work and economics. He believes production and consumption can be more balanced and humane with the principle of harmlessness or "ahimsa." Boje provides a vision for an alternative to our current economic system, an alternative that seems to contain the implicitly selfless, spiritual values implied in most of the visionary essays selected for this reader. Maybe the next step will be to connect the personal, inner work which has motivated much of the early literature in the field of spirituality and work to the cosmological vision of global thinkers, philosophers, and political economists who are attempting to shape the global future. In the end, reinventing the individual, the organization, and the total environment will be integral to the spiritual future of work.

The Individual Within Organizations

The academic interest in workplace spirituality actually has most of its roots in the vast and longstanding literature of consciousness, self-actualization, and self-transformation. The selections contained in this category reflect the renewed belief in the importance of healthy spirituality to individuals within organizations. This has been increasingly accepted by business leadership and most organizational theorists. Stephen Covey's *Seven Habits of Highly Effective People* is a current, mainstream example of the popularity of this insight. Business higher education has long stressed self-motivation, stewardship, and work as vocation and duty. The case for spirituality as a vital part of individual and organizational health is seen as the key to connecting the cry of the human heart for meaning in work with the soul in organization, which is addressed in our third segment of articles.

Nancy Day looks at the practical effects of religiosity on workplace behaviors such as physical and mental health, coping with stress, concern for others, creativity, commitment, ethical behavior, prejudice, intelligence and personality. She argues for more research into individual outcomes that may affect organizational functioning. A useful review of past research from psychology and management literature offers a correlate between work habits, skills and satisfaction with a values based religious framework. Recommendations for future research call for theory based conceptualizations with well articulated measures conducted in organizational samples.

While appreciating the positive aspects of the impact of religion on work, Day also notes the historic dark side of religion—bigotry and bias in the workplace; quite the opposite of the corporate diversity model. Day also reminds the reader not to subscribe to the myth of automatic progress. The challenge of integrating old time religion with the new spirituality of consciousness is still in its academic infancy.

While some of the scholars of this newly developing field suggest that a sweeping paradigm shift is underway, the essay by Gerald Cavanagh identifies longstanding ways that spirituality enables business people to gain a more integrated life perspective on their work and career. Cavanagh documents the growing interest in this topic among professors, professionals, and business leaders. He argues convincingly that spirituality is a vital asset to individuals, organizations, and society. Simply put, it helps people treat themselves and others properly. That, Cavanagh argues, is why more managers and firms are encouraging spirituality in the workplace. Cavanagh offers a strong case for bridging current ethical concerns in the here and now world of business to the higher aspirations of the best in world religion and spirituality. His agenda for business schools includes service learning, justice, spirituality, and faith. He observes that religiously oriented universities may provide a model for integrating spirituality and service into their mission. In this essay the reader can see the interrelationship of spirituality and religion as it plays itself out in work and higher education.

Abbass Alkhafaji discusses the issue of spirituality in the workplace from the point of view of a Muslim. He describes the conflict throughout history between the approaches of rationalists (mind embodied) and traditionalists (soul embodied), and contrasts both approaches with the messages of the divine prophets that call for reforms and a balance of the soul, mind, and body. He then explores how these issues apply to the role of management and to his own individual spiritual practice.

Ultimately, our beliefs and scholarship must be grounded in our teaching and consulting. Andre Delbecq provides a personal reflection on how his beliefs have affected his teaching and scholarship. Delbecq suggests that our deeply held values, often spiritual or religious, provide a foundation for our professional lives. Delbecq believes that his service and sense of mission has been grounded in his spiritual convictions. He believes our core values strengthen our teaching and provide meaning to our working lives. We believe similar essays could be written by faith-based scholars from any of the great spiritual traditions.

Grace Ann Rosile has a very down-to-earth approach to demonstrate the value and practicality of a major theme in almost all schools of spirituality namely, connectedness. Rosile shows how appreciation of the natural world can improve individual and organizational effectiveness. Rosile shows how raising horses and loving animals provide profound lessons for all aspects of our life. She provides "horse sense" that any business person can understand and apply to their tasks or organization. Rosile offers us a simple, credible metaphor for wholeness in our personal and professional existence as well as the life of the organization. When spirituality is clearly and simply connected to the natural world and to our part in that natural world, we come to see that basic spirituality is just good "horse sense."

Organizational and Societal issues and Applications

Many of the following contributors realize the necessity of societal changes as a precursor to macro-organizational changes. Only with a paradigm shift on a global level in economics and business philosophy and values can the assumptions which drive business organization be modified or unleveled to the realms of higher consciousness. Most of the academic writers seem to hold great faith in spiritual evolution creating a new consciousness in human society. Clearly, more interdisciplinary work needs to be done on the relationship of political economy, global economics and politics, and cultural values as they affect and govern organizational values. Social justice, cosmology, and business ethics need to join the dialogue as well.

John Young and Jeanne Logsdon are pioneer scholars of validating integral sensemaking for executives and organizational leaders. Young and Logsdon contrast integral sensemaking with the mental-rational approach that has characterized management practice. They apply the spirit based integral consciousness in the organizational context to leadership, strategy formulation, organizational culture, ethical culture and human resource management. While Young and Logsdon compare and contrast the differences between transactional and transformative styles of executive thinking and process as good post-modernists are apt to do, it is possible that the continuing evolution of consciousness will produce an integral management which is non-dual-embracing both sensemaking and modernity. With Young and Logsdon we see the frontier of organizational psychology touching the theory of evolution to higher states of human consciousness. Maybe integral sensemaking will take this new field beyond modernism and post-modernism to a non-dual new paradigm for work and spirit—worklife.

Jerry Biberman, Michael Whitty, and Lee Robbins use the story of *The Wizard of Oz* as a metaphor to describe how balance and spirituality in an organization can lead to the organizational transformation generally sought by most authors in the new field of spirituality and work. While most writers address spirituality on the individual level, this article addresses spirituality on the macro-organization level by suggesting specific steps organizations can take to promote balance and spiritual values. The authors demonstrate how the ingredients for transformation are already available within organizations. Awareness, courage, heart, and will are the keys to success in achieving the paradigm shift sought and predicted by many of the authors in this reader. *The Wizard of Oz* is a metaphor for the human journey through life. If that is so, in terms of basic virtues and life's negative qualities as well, then perhaps, argues Biberman, Whitty, and Robbins, this morality tale can be applied to organizational life as well. To inspire the reader, the authors have focused on positive trends in new work values which offer hope to those seeking a deeper meaning in work than provided by the dominant value system of greed, excessive competition, and alienation from our fellow work and the world around us. The authors also hope that the use of metaphors and storytelling proves a useful complement to the tidal wave of popular and academic studies currently available to businesses and to higher education. It may take something simple and well understood by all—such as the folk story of *The Wizard of Oz*—to reach the mainstream work culture with the good news. Systems that work in a balanced way with all aspects of human potential and our conscious evolution will best serve the future holistic, sustainable, global economy. Nothing less meets our human destiny and the needs of the planet.

Sandra King, Jerry Biberman, Lee Robbins, and David Nicol provide a brief history of the rising interest in spirituality in the workplace on the external, organizational, and individual levels. These authors argue for its legitimacy as a relevant and worthwhile part of work life. They are bringing this theme into their classrooms in various different ways using many diverse approaches and techniques. Their surveys show many academics and many leading firms on the same trend line of integrating spirituality into management education and in the constantly changing world of business organizations.

Sandra Waddock provides a concrete application of Butt's thesis. Waddock calls for a basic modification of the competitive systems imbalance and the supremacy of raw, exploitative economics as king in the absence of community or spirit. She boldly suggests that a more humane workplace community will require far more collaboration and interconnectedness than the current hypercompetitive norms. Waddock believes connectedness and a healthy interdependence are truly part of a communitarian organizational spirituality, that we are in this together, and should always be fully factored into the broader human work culture. Waddock adopts Ken Wilber's integrative framework to argue that we seek deeper meaning in work, and that organizations are more successful if they address humankind's search for meaning in community and spirit. Waddock's work contributes to the dialogue seeking the restoration of human community at work and capitalism with a human face.

The Possible Future

Large systems and organizational process have been undermined through culture pathologies, addictions, and shadow. This is the modern paradigm-toxic stress and inequity in the name of profit. In the light of this reality, a growing school of scholars, consultants, business journalists, and visionary business leaders have taken the road less traveled. On this yellow brick road we have encountered many cultural, political, and even technological obstacles. But, we as a business civilization in a new century are overcoming much of this, inch by inch, day by day. It is a process of cultural and societal growth into higher consciousness. Breakthrough points appear on the horizon despite the shadow of this present moment in business history. We are invited to heal the organizations within which we live. A basic workplace spirituality can be the common grounds for the new work community. Working people and human evolution itself are constantly seeking meaning, purpose, and a sense of contribution to work life. These needs are best served and deepened when a spiritual paradigm frames the intentions of all stakeholders. Real human nourishment is provided by the soulful organization. Reframing the meaning of work has a support of the servant leaders worldwide who see that a life of service best fits the basic human need for relevance, recognition, meaning, and self-transcendence. The concluding essay is representative of a growing literature, which advocates and predicts a period of fundamental and continuous change in human organizational values.

Jerry Biberman and Mike Whitty report a significant trend in business theory and practice which indicates a possible spiritual future for work. Their essay cites a representative selection of popular business titles and some early academic work which reinforce each other with arguments for the practical benefits of spirit-based core values for organizations. Biberman and Whitty believe the early part of the twenty-first century will witness a paradigm shift in underlying business philosophy. They forecast these megatrends in business and economics to result in a post-modern spiritual future for work.

Perhaps this reader will contribute, in some small way, to a paradigm shift in societal values toward a more soulful organizational ethos and ethics in the new century. Conscious evolution is contributing to this jump time in human and organizational transformation. We are all leaders in this jump time of organizational change of heart.

Most of the contributors to this collection come from the perspective of identifying or advocating an oncoming paradigm shift in business values. In the "Another View" piece which follows, David Boje describes the wide range of paradigms and metaphors used in the study of what he calls "Spiritual Capitalism." We share the view that more scholarship is needed to demonstrate the importance of spirituality to organizations, visionary leadership and global economics. We also appreciate the distinctions made by Boje with regard to the study of spirit in organizations. The mainstream business press is awash with the managerialist and free market/fundamentalist perspective on spirituality and religion. This collection makes valuable contributions to the humanist, ecologist and affirmative postmodernist application of spirituality to the workplace. More work needs to be done by the skeptical postmodernists to be sure that we are not simply returning to Calvinism and the predatory capitalism which both spirituality and religion seek to transcend. Can spirituality give capitalism and its organizations a human face? For the sake of the common good, we hope so. The field of spiritual/religiosity capitalism may contribute ultimately to the reinvention of work giving it new transcendent meaning for future humanity.

Special Thank you

We wish to thank Jeffrey L. Gainey, Director and Patricia Mecadon, Production Manager of the University of Scranton Press, the publisher of this book.

ANOTHER VIEW:

APPROACHES TO THE STUDY OF SPIRITUAL/RELIGIOSITY CAPITALISM

David M. Boje

My preface to *Work & Spirit*, (Biberman and Whitty, 2000), created such controversy that I am glad to be invited to write one for this reader. I would like to start with State of the Field, and then provide revison to the preface, and concluding comments.

ANTE-PREFACE

Here is my ante, about debates, disturbing trends, and what might be done. First, Conceptual tensions and debates in spirituality/religiosity:

1. **Spirituality Religiosity Dualism** There is debate over the relationship between spirituality and religiosity. Some spirituality writers just ignore religiosity or treat it as a hopeless corrupted and failed project. Others admit that within each religiosity is a core of spirituality practice, but do not venture beyond it. There are attempts to work out spirituality and religiosity theory that see it as progress over earlier forms, which are variously described as ego-centric, ethno-centric, etc. My thesis is that developing critical postmodern spirituality/religiosity theory might help research into how both religiosity and spirituality affect the practice of business ethics.

2. **Quantitative Qualitative Dualism** There is tension between those who practice the quantitative arts and those who see positivism as in league with shallow research or worse, a veil that legitimates current

versions of Social Darwin spirituality and religiosity. I read the claim made that a new field such as *Spirit & Work* ought to move away from qualitative work, so the field will be respected among its social science elders.

3. **Theory Practice Dualism** The espoused theory of spirituality and religiosity is estranged from business practices of late modern capitalism. The business practices have retreated and de-evolved back to the Dark Ages of Vampirism, sweatshop, and slaughterhouse. Meanwhile spirituality and religiosity theory espoused theory that purports to be an enlightenment consciousness of transcendence for leaders, business ethics consultants, and human resource managers.

From a critical postmodern theory perspective, there are several things about these debates and theoretical trends that disturb me:

1. **Managerialism** Too much emphasis on spirituality for the executive suite, not enough on bottoms-up liberation from forms of oppression and exploitation that stem from a managerialist view of spirituality. It as if "reality" of material global conditions is denied completely. There is an important emergence of worldwide consciousness that is thoroughly overlooked in this field: the emergence of a peace consciousness in the worldwide peace movement, as well as the anti-globalization, and the anti-sweatshop, and slaughterhouse reform movements; these are counterforces to predatory capitalism, loss of freedom, and postmodern war.

2. **Progress Myth** There continues to be faith in the co-evolution theory of the sort that says that science is improving the evolution of Nature and that human spirituality is evolving progressively towards higher levels of global consciousness. To those of us in critical postmodern theory, this is nothing more than the old progress myth. As I look around I see more postmodern wars, more global supply chains linking sweatshops of misery to Wal-Mart, and as a Jain, I am amazed at the complete lack of scholarship about slaughterhouse capitalism. Critical postmodern theory has learned to spot the progress myth has seen late modern capitalism continually appropriate each postmodern move into its enterprise, and as come up with concepts and methods that can be helpful to management, spirituality, and religion. (MSR)

3. **Beyond Good and Evil** It is disturbing that Nietzsche, Bataille, and others who advanced a "critical spirituality" and a "critical religiosity" are not part of the dialogue and debate.

What we should be doing in *Spirit & Work*:

1. Develop a dialectic spirituality/religiosity theory. This would allow for executive suite spirituality and an appreciation of the ways workforces suffer their vampirism. Managerialism sees spirituality from the view of the owners, and sometimes the shareholders, but does not look at the dialectics of resistances to managerialism, and its spiritualities of legitimation. One can begin with Hegel to see how a dialectic spirituality theory could be formed, then to Marx for its revision and to Debord for its culmination in the spectacle.

2. Drop the dualities. People at work are integrating fragments of this or that spirituality with this or that fragment of religiosity.

3. Instead of evolution of consciousness, look also at its de-evolution, and how there is only the Eternal Return of one tyrant and one empire after another, each proclaiming spirituality maturity, as Nietzsche foretold.

ABRIDGED VERSION OF THE PREFACE

This anthology taps an emergent postmodern management paradigm that emphasizes "spiritual/religiosity capitalism," but as in the 1st edition, continues to marginalize critical postmodern spirituality theory.

The new edition testifies that "Spiritual/religiosity capitalism" is still all the rage, and there is plenty of quantitative research, optimistic predictions for Integral and other nouveau spiritualities, and the promise of realignment with spirituality and religiosity. My thesis is there is not much critical theory, or critical postmodern theory. My challenge to future editions of this book: create more critical review of knowledge and practices of spiritual/religiosity capitalism. I have suggested that it is time for a much more "critical spirituality/religiosity theory."

I would like to briefly list the paradigms and metaphors being applied in this anthology to the study of spiritual/religiosity capitalism as affirmative or skeptical.

The modernist paradigm has both a "humanist" and "managerialist" focus. Managerialists espouse a functionalist and enlightenment worldview in which even spirituality has its function in making business more profitable. There are other paradigms from which writers look to indigenous spiritual practices to revitalize ecology to erect "spiritual capitalism" in place of predatory capitalism enterprise

(Karliner & Karliner; Mokhiber & Weissman, 1999). For example, Steingard and Fitzgibbons (1995) argue that global capitalism is a spiritually flawed discourse that is not ecologically sustainable. Butts (1997) is outraged at the selfishness, greed, and mean-spirited, winner-take-all scapegoating (class warfare) inflicted on the working class and other disfranchised social groups. And, Walck (1995) is cautious about spirituality, reminding us that our global discourse ignores the "spirituality" of the poor. Christian spirituality played a major role in native genocide, and continues to play a role in the current war in Iraq. It therefore makes sense to look at alternative paradigms to see both the good and evil of any spirituality movement. What I would like to do is arrange several of the paradigms into a map (see Figure One).

Six of the many paradigms in the study of spiritual capitalism are paired as follows: affirmative and skeptical postmodern, fundamentalist and ecological, and managerialist and humanist (See Figure One). Each

Figure 1: Paradigms and metaphors in the study of spiritual capitalism.

offers different metaphors to spirit. To some spirit is the metaphor of love, festival, transcendence, and self-development (Marcic, 1997). But to other paradigms, spirit is the metaphor of the "psychic prison" and the "instrument of domination" or the privileging of rich over poor class in Herbert Spencer's "Social Darwinism." Höpfl (1994: 20–31), for example contends that organizations imitate religious forms and invoke even the "Holy Spirit" to exploit through demands for submission, obedience and control. She adds "management evangelists and various other prophets of management have engaged in an unreflective or opportunistic rhetoric of change management."

For the affirmative postmodernists, spirit is simply "love" and "sense making" at work. For the skeptical postmodernists, spirit can by a form of "psychic prison" or an "instrument of domination." For the managerialists spirit is a form of "control," a way to increase "performativity" through greater commitment, and something "leaders" do with their sense of vision and mission. To the ecologist, spirit is the "Gaia," the living nature of Mother earth and the cosmos. Journal of Organizational Change Management (JOCM) writers have posited a relation between environment and the spiritual value of the land as well as the spiritual, not just economic needs of citizens (Bullis & Glaser, 1992; Stead & Stead, 1994: Upadhyaya, 1995). Christa Walck (1996) for example writes about organizations being seen through the metaphor of "spiritual places." However to the religious fundamentalist, spirit is the promise of the "after life," or next life and to some it is still a very "Social Darwinian" notion of the blessedness of being born rich and the curse of the poor threatens the survival of the human species. Between these six paradigms, there are metaphors that are between two or more paradigms (e.g. spectacle, culture, transcendental). Spirit is a way to reinvigorate "culture" with a more enlightened capitalism for the affirmative postmodernists. And "culture" is a way to invoke higher levels of functional performance, control and leadership for the managerialist paradigm. Between affirmative postmodernist and ecologist paradigms is the sustainability movement. And between the humanist and ecologist paradigms is "transcendental and "festival" metaphors of spirit. And between the skeptical postmodernist and fundamentalist paradigms are the metaphors of spectacle and religious fetish. My point in displaying this array of spirit metaphors and paradigms is to give the reader some idea of the many worldviews that are doing work in the study of spirit in the workplace and in the theater of global capitalism. With this map, I can now say something about the various writings on spirit in JOCM and in this anthology. This book does something important that the mushrooming lists of books on spiritual capitalism are not doing.[i] That is, Gerald Biberman and Mike Whitty have brought together a rich array of paradigms and metaphors on spiritual capitalism.

While there is much that is affirmative and appreciative in the functionalist, managerialist, ecological, and humanist approaches to spiritual capitalism, there are paradigms that are critical of the nouveau spirituality-based philosophies of business. In particular the new books and articles of JOCM, as well as other journals and teaching seminars may offer the aura of spiritual transformation of work and society, while masking the material conditions and their important needs.[ii]

Cavanagh (1999), in my view, takes a refreshingly critical view of the spirituality movement. He approaches the skepticism of the critical postmodernist. He see spirituality growing in emphasis as a backlash to the downsizing craze (as did Burack, 1999), the number of 1960s baby-boomers who are now writing, and our imminent change to a new millenium. Cavanagh is skeptical about mixing the New Age movement in spirituality with the good old time religions. He also questions how "both Evangelical Christianity and the spirituality in business movements" legitimate a "person-centered individualism." And given the diversity of spiritual practices, from humanist, fundamentailist, to New Age ecologist in a complex organization, there can be hegemonic consequences as some spiritual practices gain power in the workplace over others.

---

[i]See for example, Servant Leadership (Greenleaf, 1977; Melrose, 1995), Spirit at Work or in the Workplace (Sproul, 1980; Hawley, 1993; Scherer & Shook, 1993; Conger, 1994; Gozdz, 1995; Schechter, 1995; Guillory, 1997), Leading with Soul (Bolman & Deal, 1995), The Soul of a Business (Chappell, 1993), Soul in the Workplace (Briskin, 1996; Canfield & Hansen, 1996; Renesch & DeFoore, 1996), Managing with the Wisdom of Love (Marcic, 1997), The Fourth Wave (Maynard & Mehrtens, 1993) and spiritual leadership books by Covey (1989, 1994).

[ii]There are two journals devoted just to spirit at work (*Spirit at Work* and *Business Spirit*). The 1998 Academy of Management meeting overflowed with spiritual capitalism. Cavanagh (1999) comments that the1998 theme was "What matters most?" and hosted seven symposia (six were showcase sessions) that explicitly discussed spirituality and/or religion.

Some Conclusions

I conclude this preface by asking for more rigor in the way we theorize, research, and teach spirituality, lest this become a passing fad and do more harm than good. For me, more rigor includes qualitative research, not premature embracing of only positivism.

I still contend this anthology represents a healthy debate among the paradigms and metaphors in Figure One, though I hoped for more critical spirituality scholarship. As Biberman, Whitey, and Robbins (1999) remind us, "without spirituality the normative purpose of business is profit." Worse, it is only the surplus value extraction machine of vampire capitalism.

I have asserted that "critical spirituality/religiosity" theory, research, and practice could bring balance to an otherwise predatory capitalism, that a tolerance for qualitative research is needed by quantitative, that espoused managerialist enlightenment consciousnesses does not match ethical practice, and that we need a spirituality dialectical theory, and more Nietzsche.

There is a dualism between religiosity and spiritualism theory that could be deconstructed to focus on how both are not unified concepts. Self-reflection and self-criticism can be constructive to both religiosity and spirituality.

— Namasté

REFERENCE

Barrett, Frank J.
 1995 "Finding voice within the gender order." Journal of Organizational Change Management; 08:6: 8–15.
Biberman, Jerry & Michael Whitty
 2000 *Work and Spirit: A Reader of New Spiritual Paradigms for Organizations.* (Scranton, PA: University of Scranton Press).
Biberman, Jerry & Michael Whitty
 1997 "A postmodern spiritual future for work." Journal of Organizational Change Management, Vol. 10, #2: 130–138.
Bullis, Connie & Hollis Glaser
 1992 "Bureaucratic Discourse and the Goddess: Towards an Ecofeminist Critique and Rearticulation." Journal of Organizational Change Management; 05:2.
Butts, Dan
 1997 "Joblessness, pain, power, pathology and promise." Journal of Organizational Change Management, Vol. 10, #2: 111–129.

Höpfl, Heather
1994 "The Paradoxical Gravity of Planned Organizational Change." Journal of Organizational Change Management; 07:5 1994: 20–31.

Kaplan, Kathy L.
1995 "Women's voices in organizational development: questions, stories, and implications." Journal of Organizational Change Management; 08:1: 52–80.

Louis, Meryl Reis
1994 "In the Manner of Friends: Learnings from Quaker Practice for Organizational Renewal." Special Issue, "Spirituality in Organizations." Journal of Organizational Change Management, Vol. 7, #1: 42–60.

Marcic, D.
1997 Managing with the Wisdom of Love: Uncovering Virtue in People and Organizations, Jossey-Bass, San Francisco, CA.

Spirit Hawk
1995 "Three women's stories of feeling, reflection, voice and nurturance: from life to consulting." Journal of Organizational Change Management, Vol. 8 Issue 6: 39–57 - Gender and Voices Special Issue.

Stead, W. Edward & Jean Garner Stead
1994 "Can Humankind Change the Economic Myth? Paradigm Shifts Necessary for Ecologically Sustainable Business." Journal of Organizational Change Management; 07:4: 15–31.

Steingard, David S. & Dale E. Fitzgibbons
1995 "Challenging the juggernaut of globalization: a manifesto for academic praxis." Journal of Organizational Change Management; 08:4: 30–54.

Upadhyaya, Punya
1995 "The sacred, the erotic and the ecological: the politics of transformative global discourses." Journal of Organizational Change Management; 08:5: 33–59.

Walck, Christa L.
1995 "Global ideals, local realities: the development project and missionary management in Russia." Journal of Organizational Change Management; 08:4:69–84.

Walck, Christa L.
1996 "Organizations as places: a metaphor for change." Journal of Organizational Change Management; 09:6:26–40.

Weber, Max (Darth)
1958 The Protestant Ethic and the Spirit of Capitalism. NY: Charles Scribner's Sons.

THEORETICAL
PERSPECTIVES

Glow

■

by Tom Brown

The human race
Now runs in place,
Exclaiming, "Little
We don't know!"

Yet mark its path,
Count all it hath;
One truth's been lost:
We are born to glow.

We started out from land untamed,
From boundless rock and root.
Only man could see
Past trunks of trees,
Through river's roar;
Creating, we did grow.

On farms, in mines,
From seas to timberlines,
We shovelled, cast, and cut,
Our progress never slowed.

Till now.
We've trounced this planet's wealth
And claimed it as our own.

And every house and every car,
Each creature comfort known —
Yes, every shoe and every phone —
Shouts our presence home.

We've made the world
Reflect ourselves:
Our wishes ceaseless flow.
The human mind,
Stretched enterprise-wide,
Hungers still to grow.

Then doubt not that —
From infant wiggle
To elder amble slow —
Within each breast
The spark *is* there.
We are born to glow.

The human mark,
How we most shine,
Exceeds accounting line.
Accrue? Create?
Don't hesitate.
We are born to glow.

On mankind's cake
Our time is marked
By candles,
The progress show.

Each new Age
Inspires a wish —
Each wish a gift —
'Cross wax alit,
It blows and blows.

But wax snuffed out
Is not the flame
Tomorrow yearns to know.

What was the wish?
What was the wish?
We are born to glow.

—from *The Anatomy of Fire: Sparking a New Spirit of Enterprise*
by Tom Brown © 2000 by MANAGEMENT GENERAL
http://www.mgeneral.com

1

.

Diapers to Car Keys: The State of Spirituality, Religion and Work Research[1]

Charles J. Fornaciari and Kathy Lund Dean
Florida Gulf Coast University and Idaho State University

The a priori "newness" of research in the spirituality, religion and work (SRW) field has been generally accepted, even though the domain of SRW credibly overlaps with well-established inquiry traditions, such as education, psychology, and theology. Because of this multi-disciplinary nature of SRW, we asked: How truly new is research work in this domain? Following the philosophy of science literature, this paper explores five hypotheses related to the research methodologies in all peer-reviewed empirical work published within the SRW domain during the initial years of its popular emergence, 1996–2000. Chi-square and text analysis (N=26) revealed mixed results with respect to hypothesized norms, and that many dynamic and varied empirical approaches are already in use within more established fields. Findings also suggest that work in the SRW domain may be further along than generally thought in the literature. Detailed discussion and implications for SRW research methodologies conclude the paper.

Key Words: *Research Methods, Spirituality, Religion, Work*

---

[1] An earlier version of this paper was presented at the 2003 Annual Meetings of the Academy of Management: Seattle, Washington.

Much has been written in both the academic literature as well as in the popular press about the new domain of spirituality and religion at work (SRW). The a priori "newness" of SRW has been generally accepted (Biberman and Whitty, 1999; Dehler and Neal, 2000; Gunther, 2001), even though the domain of SRW work credibly overlaps with a variety of well-established inquiry traditions including psychology, theology, education, and anthropology (Pauchant, 2001; McGee, 2001). Because of this cross- and multi-disciplinary nature of SRW, we asked the question: How truly new is research work in this domain? Where, perhaps, has the empirical groundwork already been laid for SRW researchers within the management discipline?

The argument has been made that SRW research constructs resist traditional quantitative and positivist methods (Fornaciari and Lund Dean, 2001; Lund Dean, Fornaciari, and McGee 2002); others (Gibbons, 2000; Mitroff and Denton, 1999) have pointed to the lack of empirical work in the SRW field. We were, then, curious how past empirical work in this domain fits with current efforts.

It is well established (c.f., Arba, 1998; Daft and Buenger, 1990; Denzin and Lincoln, 2000; Eisenhardt 1989; Yin, 1989) that most new research in emerging fields is theory building and tentative. This study identified five characteristics from the philosophy of science literature as representative of a field that is theory building and tentative, ranging from the prevalence of qualitative methods over quantitative approaches to exploratory versus conclusive findings. Thus, in addition to the research questions identified in the first paragraph, we were also interested in discovering whether early SRW empirical work fits philosophically with a field that is in its infancy.

Issues such as those identified above are always important to any field, but they often become more important during foundational eras because early work within a discipline typically defines the paradigm under which it will operate for a significant period. Once established, paradigms are difficult to change (Kuhn, 1970), and failure to establish an appropriate research paradigm for a discipline may hamper its development, or even worse, permanently marginalize it (Daft and Buenger, 1990; Mills, 1959). These concerns are well reported within the SRW domain (c.f., Gibbons, 2000; Lund Dean, Fornaciari, and McGee, 2002) and are even heightened due to the recognition of its unique characteristics, such as questions concerning the topic's legitimacy as a field of research within the management discipline; acknowledgement that many of its concepts resist the trappings of modern day normal science; discussions about what constitutes an appropriate SRW domain; and internal debates over whether SRW research should ever adopt a single paradigm.

This study seeks to understand the state of early SRW research. Utilizing an extensive database search, we retrieved articles from a variety of disciplines within the SRW domain of interest, and examined their empirical methods to see how closely they fit with the characteristics of an immature research field. Chi-square analysis revealed mixed results. Qualitative analysis revealed that many dynamic and varied empirical approaches are already in use within more established fields that struggle with many of the same empirical issues as does SRW, and that these approaches appear to be accepted as legitimate within these fields. These findings also suggest that work in the SRW domain of interest may be further along than generally thought in the business and management related literature. Implications for future SRW research methods are discussed.

RESEARCH HYPOTHESES

Gibbons (2000) states:

> "In Spirituality at Work texts, one tends to encounter definitions of spirituality that are abstract, universal, and conclusive ... this level of abstraction and the universality of its application afford little practical help with understanding the phenomenon, or how the search might be conducted, or about the variety of belief systems that guide this research" (pp. 113–114).

The lack of clear measurements, or struggles with isomorphism (Kerlinger, 1976), is emblematic of a research domain that is in its infancy (Miles and Huberman, 1994, pp. 5–8). Consequently, much of the effort among scholars in young fields is not geared towards testing or verification of existing theory. Instead, the effort focuses on beginning to understand the phenomenon that is being explored, i.e., to build theory. In short, the goal is not to answer questions, but rather to discover what the appropriate questions are.

Typically, in new domains, investigators employ qualitative inductive approaches such as grounded theory (Glaser and Strauss, 1967), ethnography (Tedlock, 2000) and case study research (Eisenhardt, 1989;

Yin, 1989) to help develop theory and measures. These methodologies usually gather data directly from the source using techniques such as in-person interviews, focus groups, thick description, observational recording, semiotics, narrative, and discourse (Denzin and Lincoln, 2000; Hedrick, 1994).

The above discussion closely reflects what is thought to be occurring in the SRW domain. As would be expected, Gibbons (2000) notes that most of the doctoral work in the SRW field is focused on measurement development. He also notes that leading scholars such as Neal, Lichtenstein, and Banner (1999) are calling for more use of ideographic approaches (techniques that employ data generated outside the confines of the written word, such as symbolism) to spur its development. Other SRW scholars such as Lips-Wiersma (2001), Lund Dean, Fornaciari, and McGee (2002), and McGee (2001) have also echoed the call for increased use of non-nomothetic research techniques that respect the deeply particularized nature of SRW research matter.

This suggests the study's first two hypotheses:

H1: Published empirical research during the SRW domain's founding years will employ qualitative methods more frequently than quantitative methods.

H2: Published empirical research during the SRW domain's founding years will employ primary data collection techniques more frequently than secondary data techniques.

A common trade-off of ideographic approaches compared to their nomothetic brethren is that they often sacrifice generalizability for deep understanding of a particular case or situation (Denzin and Lincoln, 2000; Miles and Huberman, 1994; Uzzell, 2000). Ideographic research lowers sample size to investigate deeply, while nomothetic research sacrifices depth to achieve large-sample generalizability. Since this study's first two hypotheses posited that emerging fields such as the SRW domain would typically employ ideographic approaches to begin formulating initial research questions, research constructs, and measurement tools, the third hypothesis follows from those arguments:

H3: Published empirical research during the SRW domain's founding years will employ small sample sizes more frequently than large sample sizes.

Finally, Denzin and Lincoln note that ideographic methodologies:

> "... Stress the socially constructed nature of reality, the intimate relationship between the researcher and what is studied, and the situational constraints that shape inquiry. Such researchers emphasize the value-laden nature of inquiry. They seek answers to questions that stress *how* social experience is created and given meaning" (2000, p. 8, emphasis in original).

Thus, implicit within ideographic methodologies is the non-positivist understanding that there is more than one way to describe and understand a phenomenon. The lived experience of spiritual and religious life at work, whether on an individual, group, or on an organizational level of analysis, would demand working, hypothetical understanding in place of nomothetic, generalized understanding. This, along with the previous discussion, suggests the fourth hypothesis:

H4: Published empirical research during the SRW domain's founding years will display exploratory results discussions more commonly than conclusive results discussions.

The final research question asks which type of studies will be more prevalent in the SRW research domain: longitudinal or cross-sectional studies? Here the discussion is not so clear. We are again brought back to the issue of ideographic versus nomothetic approaches. Although qualitative methods are normally used for theory and measure development (see Hypothesis 1 argument), qualitative traditions also tend to focus on constructing deep understandings of pre-interpreted realities-difficult in a new field. Quantitative traditions tend to focus on establishing cause-and-effect relationships, or exploring why a particular phenomenon is occurring. This then would suggest that cross-sectional studies might dominate a field in its early years.

Another more practical concern may lie with the nature of academic publishing, especially in a new discipline. Longitudinal studies, by definition, take time, and their pursuit is often perceived as a riskier career strategy, especially for junior faculty members. The incentive may be for producing a quantity of quick "hits" to gain promotion, recognition and tenure (Arba, 1998). This factor may be exacerbated by how work is being produced in the SRW domain: Gibbons (2000) noted that much of the new construct measures within SRW appear to be produced by doctoral students. Doctoral students (soon to be junior faculty) have more to gain in quickly establishing a research stream and a reputation in an emerging discipline than more established faculty members.

The other side of that argument is that it may be that most SRW scholars are those who have already achieved promotion and tenure, and are consequently more willing to experiment with less certain research projects. This would coincide with Delbeq's (2000) assertion that many more senior than junior managers within organizations feel a spiritual obligation in their work. Can we extend, then, Delbecq's observation to conclude that senior academics have both the motive and the opportunity to engage in longitudinal SRW research? While theory suggests that either approach may predominate, we believe that the need to explore causation within what many believe is a new phenomenon, as well as the operational practicalities of shorter-term research projects imply that cross-sectional research will dominate. This suggests the fifth hypothesis:

H5: Published empirical research during the SRW domain's founding years will employ cross-sectional approaches more commonly than longitudinal approaches.

METHODS

This paper seeks to explore methodological approaches employed by all the peer-reviewed empirical work published within the SRW domain during the initial years of its popular emergence. For the purposes of this paper, we defined the period from 1996 to 2000 as the first five years of the SRW domain. This frame was chosen to coincide with the initial approval by the Academy of Management's board of directors of the Management, Spirituality and Religion (MSR) interest group in December 1999 and the group's first officially sanctioned participation on the Academy program during the August 2000 meetings in Toronto, Canada.

Since the Academy typically approves new interest groups only after there is an indication that a new domain or field has begun to establish itself to a point where its future is somewhat certain (among other things, members seeking to create a new interest group must demonstrate its potential by submitting a petition with a specified minimum number of signatures as well as submitting samples of existing research that exemplify the domain), we picked the five years leading up to MSR's first participation at the Academy meetings as the founding years.

After determining the period for study, we then set out to identify all research articles that met the study's selection criteria. To be included in the present study, a candidate article must have met all three separate criteria. First, as indicated previously, it must have been published in any peer-reviewed journal between 1996 and 2000. Second, it must be an empirical study, i.e., it must involve a systematic investigation of some problem where the proposed answer is checked through observation, testing, or experimentation (Dewey, 1933; Kerlinger, 1976). Finally, it had to demonstrate a relevance to the SRW domain. To determine relevance, candidate articles were compared against the Academy of Management's MSR domain statement, which we believe to be the most cogent and accepted definition of this emerging field:

> The domain of this special interest group is the study of the relationship and relevance of spirituality and religion in management and organizations. Major topics include: theoretical advances or empirical evidence about the effectiveness of spiritual or religious principles and practices in management, from approaches represented in the literature including religious ethics, spirituality and work, and spiritual leadership, as well as applications of particular religions and secular spiritualities to work, management/leadership, organization, and the business system; and evaluation studies of the effectiveness of management approaches that nurture the human spirit in private, non-public or public institutions. (Academy of Management, 2002)

Candidate articles were initially searched for and screened using one of two methods. First, we conducted an extensive database search (see Appendix 1 for a list of databases used) to determine if any published articles matched keywords relevant to the SRW domain from both the organization and spirituality/religion perspectives for all articles published between 1996 and 2000. Four terms (including word forms), *organization, management, business*, and *work*, were used for the organization component of the search, while five terms (including word forms), *faith, God, spirituality, religion*, and *whole person*, were used for the spirituality/religion aspect of the search. Each term from the organization side was joined with each term from the spirituality/religion side to produce twenty separate Boolean "and" searches on each database (e.g., we searched on organization AND

God as well as business AND religion). Where possible, searches were conducted using the broadest possible results pages, e.g., if given the choice, "title, abstract, keywords, and full text" was chosen over the "title and abstract" results option.

The second search method was achieved by physically examining all issues of leading empirical management journals (*Academy of Management Journal, Journal of Management, Administrative Science Quarterly, Journal of Organizational Change Management, Journal of Management Education, Strategic Management Journal, Organization Science, and the Journal of Management Inquiry*) to determine whether they had published articles relevant to the SRW domain.

All candidate articles obtained using both methods were then examined to determine whether they met the criteria of domain-relevant, peer-reviewed, and empirically based. To be included in the study, an article needed to obtain unanimous agreement by the present study's authors that it met all the selection criteria.

Articles meeting the selection criteria were then hand-coded on six separate constructs that reflect the hypotheses and record the research methodologies employed:

1. Does the article employ primary or secondary, or a combination of data?
2. Does the article use cross sectional, longitudinal, or a combination of data?
3. Does the article use a large or small sample size (and total sample size)?
4. Does the article uses quantitative, qualitative, or a combination of data?
5. What research methods were used in the article?
6. What was the article's descriptive/narrative tone: conclusive or exploratory?

The coding procedures for the first five criteria used were straightforward assessments of common research concepts. In the interests of space, we skip discussions of them here (more in depth discussions of these concepts are available in almost any book on research methods and design, e.g., Creswell, 2003; Denzin and Lincoln, 2000; Kerlinger, 1976; Reichardt and Rallis, 1994). We do wish to note, that for the purposes of this paper, we defined a study as employing a large sample size if the total number of subjects exceed 30–the point at which most populations begin to exhibit normal distribution characteristics (Sheskin, 1997, p. 76).

For the sixth construct above, we did a text analysis of the language used in the Discussion and Conclusions sections of each article for coding either conclusive or exploratory. Each article had at least one section for Discussion or Conclusions; as a general rule the articles we analyzed had both. When a study was coded as conclusive, the authors had used definitive language and/or had reported discrete and quantitative results. Some conclusive authors recognized limitations of their studies (i.e., secondary data source issues, small sample size, confounding contextual issues, etc.) but nonetheless supplied readers with definite conclusions. Examples of this include:

- Measured or measurable "final" results and implications:
  – "Church hospitals were operating at an average efficiency of .81 and secular hospitals were operating at an average efficiency of .76" (White and Ozcan, 1996).
- Claims of generalizability:
  – "This is the problem faced by any organization as it attempts to become a spiritual organization" (Konz and Ryan, 1999).
- Verbiage was certain:
  – "Two basic facets of the values domain were hypothesized and verified: value modality and life area" (Sagie and Elizer, 1996).

Correlatively, if authors did not draw definitive conclusions based upon their study, we coded the work as exploratory. When this was the case, the authors recognized limitations with their studies, and subsequently chose not to include in the Discussion and/or Conclusions sections generalizations or more widely applicable findings. Examples of this include:

- Recognition of limited scope of the study:
  – "This study attempted to provide a more integrated look at occupational stress and coping issues with a particular visible racial/ethnic group, African American professionals, in a particular type of setting, predominantly White work environments" (Holder and Vaux, 1998).

- Outcomes could be attributable to factors other than those hypothesized and tested:
  - "Such approaches may supplant systematic training, not because they do the same job better, but because they are more in line with changing cultural expectations of employees" (Beech, Cairns, and Robertson, 2000).
- Verbiage was conditional:
  - "In conclusion these results provide initial support for a surrender style of coping as a distinct approach from other styles of religious coping.... Implications from this study await future research and replication" (McDonald and Gorsuch, 2000).

Two independent researchers coded all articles. In the relatively few cases of disagreement (4 out of 126 coding events, for an inter-rater reliability of 97%), final coding was based on a consensus discussion between the coders. Finally, all research hypotheses were explored using descriptive statistics and Chi-square tests.

RESULTS

Over 10,000 articles were initially identified as being possible candidates for inclusion in the current study due to the expansive nature of electronic database searching. Most articles were quickly excluded for a variety of reasons, e.g., lacking relevance to the SRW domain, being published in the popular press, or not being empirical. Though exact counts were not taken, it is estimated that fewer than ten articles met most of the primary selection criteria but were excluded because they either failed to appear in a peer-reviewed journal or their topic did not fit within the SRW domain. The search ultimately produced 26 articles that met the three primary criteria of: published in peer-reviewed journals from 1996 to 2000; empirical in nature; and relevant to the SRW domain. These 26 articles formed the basis of the current study and are summarized in Appendix 1.

All five research hypotheses were investigated using Chi-square tests to determine whether the distribution of the results were statistically significant in one direction or another. The results are presented in Table 1.

Table 1: Hypotheses Results

Hypothesis	Variable	n	% of Total	Chi-square
1	Qualitative measures	8	30.77%	14.85*** (2 d.f.)
	Quantitative measures	17	65.38%	
	Both measures	1	3.85%	
2	Primary data	20	76.92%	21.15*** (2 d.f.)
	Secondary data	5	19.23%	
	Both types of data	1	3.85%	
3	Small samples	4	15.38%	12.46*** (1 d.f.)
	Large sample	22	84.62	
4	Exploratory findings	9	34.62%	9.77** (2 d.f.)
	Conclusive findings	15	57.69%	
	Mixed findings	2	7.69%	
5	Cross-Sectional data	23	88.46%	35.62*** (2 d.f.)
	Longitudinal data	2	11.54%	
	Both types of data	1	3.85	

*** = p<0.001   ** = p<0.01

Hypothesis 1 suggested that more studies within the early years of the SRW domain would be qualitative, as opposed to quantitative, in nature. In the total sample of 26 published studies, 8 (30.77%) employed qualitative measures, 17 (65.38%) employed quantitative measures, and 1 (3.85%) employed both types. Chi-square results ($v2$=14.85, d.f.=2, p <0.001) indicate a significant distribution skewed towards quantitative studies. Hypothesis 1 is not supported.

Hypothesis 2 suggested that most early SRW studies would employ primary data instead of secondary data. Of the 26 studies in the sample, 20 (76.92%) studies used primary data, 5 (19.23%) used secondary data, and 1 (3.85%) used both primary and secondary data. The chi-square results ($v2$=21.15, d.f.=2, p<0.001) indicate a significant skewed distribution towards primary data. Hypothesis 2 is supported.

Hypothesis 3 suggested that more early SRW studies would employ small sample sizes versus large samples. Four (15.38%) studies employed small sample sizes while the remaining 22 (84.62%) studies used large samples. Chi-square results ($v2$=12.46.15, d.f.=1, p<0.001) indicate that early SRW studies are significantly skewed towards large sample sizes. Hypothesis 3 is not supported.

Hypothesis 4 posited that early SRW studies would more commonly exhibit exploratory findings versus conclusive findings. From the sample of 26 studies, 9 (34.62%) described exploratory findings, 15 (57.69%) described conclusive findings, and 2 (7.69%) described both exploratory and conclusive findings. The Chi-square results ($v2=9.77$, d.f.=2, p<0.01) indicate that early SRW research results are significantly skewed towards conclusive findings. Hypothesis 4 is not supported.

The study's final hypothesis posited that more studies within the early years of the SRW domain would be cross-sectional instead of longitudinal. Twenty-three (88.46%) of the 26 studies were cross-sectional, 2 (7.69%) studies were longitudinal, and 1 (3.85%) was both cross-sectional and longitudinal. Chi-square results ($v2=35.62$, d.f.=2, p <0.001) indicate a significant distribution skewed towards cross-sectional studies. Hypothesis 5 is supported.

DISCUSSION

While only two of the five proposed hypotheses were supported, it is perhaps more interesting in the context of this study to have such results in lieu of support for proposed hypothetical relationships! *All* Chi-square tests had significant results, but three of the five tests were skewed significantly in the opposite direction from the hypothetical relationship expected. Thus, results generally indicate that authors of empirical papers published in peer-reviewed journals are in the field, gathering cross-sectional primary data from a huge variety of sources, while using large sample sizes to come to definitive conclusions about their investigations.

Survey instruments were the most prominent data-gathering method but many other techniques were employed as well, and a variety of levels of researcher-subject involvement are evident. It was impressive to us that even for extremely involved techniques such as interviews and ethnography, researchers utilized large numbers of respondents to generate what we have to believe was a massive amount of data. We were humbled by some of the researchers' obvious commitment to creating and implementing a study with integrity to the deeply personal subject matter.

"Snapshot" or cross-sectional studies were significantly more common than longitudinal ones, although we cannot know from the studies examined whether the motivations we suggested for a majority of cross-sectional work were in fact true. The great majority of studies examined "causation," or, they attempted to explain with a reasonable mix of variables some observed phenomenon. This is consistent with our proposed explanation of why cross-sectional studies might be more prevalent in the SRW domain. It is impossible to know, on the other hand, the professional demographics of the studies' authors to ascertain how senior they may be, and to ascertain their levels of risk propensity for their work. What may be more important is to note the very few longitudinal studies in the sample, and to suggest that longer-term organizational impacts of SRW may best be explored using a longitudinal research design.

The significant majority of studies employed quantitative analyses, again with a large variety of analysis tools employed. Both common and sophisticated techniques were present in these studies, which is very encouraging when one considers the spectrum of journals and disciplines represented. These methods appear to be accepted as legitimate within each field as implied by the peer-review and journal publication process, and offer templates and ideas that may not have been previously considered for use within the management research domain.

Although not statistically significant, raw numbers indicated that almost a third of the studies employed qualitative methods, from case study to interviews to focus groups. This, too, is encouraging as McGee (2001) convincingly made the argument that SRW constructs may require more interactive involvement between researcher and respondent, relationships that qualitative methods engender. The mix of quantitative and qualitative studies appears to indicate that researchers are mindful of the different and dynamic ways available to explore SRW questions.

Related to the above discussion about quantitative vs. qualitative methods is the significant dominance of findings that were coded as conclusive. Almost 60% of the studies examined used language and/or statistics to indicate conclusive findings. A positivist characteristic of nomothetic research, it could be that drawing authoritative conclusions even within the SRW rubric is a research methodological habit that is supported and repeated by the institutions of academic legitimacy-peer review and journal publication. These are the lifeline of prolonged academic careers. Findings are important, and the emphasis on conclusiveness may be related to the proposal that exploring causation in the SRW domain was a critical motivation for many of the studies.

There is a lot of good news to be gleaned from our study for the SRW domain. Methods were diverse and dynamic. The research designs examined were almost without exception soundly created and implemented. The journal reviewers and editors across disciplines appear to be open to studies within the SRW domain, and we may be getting better at considering these types of empirical efforts as the literature gets larger. The question remains unanswered, however, as to whether their receptiveness is based on the papers' strong methodologies or their SRW content, or a combination of the two.

Beyond the good news, this study also provides insights into the larger-scale concerns expressed earlier (c.f., Gibbons, 2000; Lund Dean, Fornaciari, and McGee, 2002) about the current state of paradigm development within the SRW domain. As noted in the introduction of this paper, Kuhn (1970), Daft and Buenger (1990) and others have cautioned about the potential for stagnation when a field adopts a single dominant paradigm. There is often a great deal of learning to be had by not locking into a single paradigm too quickly. This study's findings, while displaying many collective tendencies towards traditional positivist research paradigms, also show that indeed the SRW paradigm is not yet fixed-even where the results where significantly in the direction of positivism, there existed numerous studies that were non-nomothetic. In other words, the results demonstrate both youth and adolescence simultaneously within the domain.

Taken from another perspective, Merton (1973) notes that the field of sociology underwent three distinct phases during its development: differentiation from antecedent disciplines; the quest to establish institutional legitimacy and academic autonomy; and reconsolidation with selected other social sciences. Clearly, the range and variety of articles analyzed in this study indicates that the SRW field likewise is experiencing a similar developmental path as it seeks both differentiation and legitimation.

Going forward, how does SRW research avoid the problems attendant to locking into a paradigm too early by simply settling upon traditional positivist research methodologies? There is a longstanding perception that the most demanding empirical management journals will not publish non-nomothetic research. Indeed, it may be daunting to non-positivist researchers to note that the first qualitative study published in the "modern" Academy of Management's journals was Isabella's (1990) supermarket study—a relatively recent publication date. However, Tom Lee, editor of the *Academy of Management Journal*, recently discussed alternatives to positivist research studies (Williams, 2002). He indicated that, contrary to popular assumption, qualitative and ideographic research studies are welcomed by top management journals if the appropriate methodology is rigorous and the studies are interesting. He also noted that authors of studies utilizing alternative methodologies would help the reviewing process greatly by suggesting reviewers who are familiar with the methodology(ies) employed in the study when submitting a manuscript. The onus then falls squarely on SRW researchers to engage and implement well-conceived research, and to be familiar with those who have successfully used research models upon which new studies are based.

SRW research entails risk: constructs such as "love," "God," and "spirit" must never be taken lightly, and creating variables for quantitatively-appropriate analysis that respect the nature of those constructs is extremely difficult. It is troublesome, in some respects, to consider that so many of the studies we looked at indicated definitive findings and conclusive implications. Because of this, we echo the recommendation (Lund Dean, Fornaciari, and McGee, 2002; Lund Dean, 2003) that researchers include both quantitative as well as qualitative data in their studies, to respect SRW understanding that defies nomothetic modelling.

IMPLICATIONS AND FUTURE DIRECTIONS

This study provided an initial overview of the published empirical research in the Spirituality, Religion, and Work domain during its founding years. Despite the significance of the findings, several potential areas for improvement are evident. One area is based on the method used to select articles for inclusion within the current study. While the study's researchers examined well over 10,000 articles using online databases and manual searches, there exists the possibility that some articles may have been missed due to not being published within the leading management journals (as defined by the researchers) or not being indexed within the online databases available to the researchers. Other methods could have been potentially employed to identify articles for inclusion within the current study, for example examining the bibliographies of various SRW publications, both theoretical and empirical, for potential empirical articles published between 1996 and 2000.

Another concern reflects the criterion to only include empirical articles published within academic journals. In some ways, this guarantees that articles are of sufficiently "high quality" as judged by the time-honored tradition of peer-reviewing. However, potentially significant SRW research may have been excluded from the study during its early critical years. For example, by definition Mitroff and Denton's (1999) groundbreaking book is excluded from this study, as are several unpublished doctoral dissertations from some of the domain's current leading researchers (e.g., Beazley, 1997; Trott, 1996).

A final concern represents the time frame selected for the study, both in length and in period selected. Arguments could certainly be made for extending the study forward to include 2001 and 2002, as well as the study's five year time frame described as its "founding years." However, Hambrick's (1990) study of the adolescence of the strategic management discipline utilized a six year period, and like him, we argue that the time frame we chose represents a fairly dramatic and well-defined period of activity within the domain. As Table 2 indicates, with the exception of 1997, where only one empirical study was published, there is a slow but steady increase in the number of empirical articles appearing within the SRW domain, with 2000 representing a dramatic increase in the number of articles published. This evidence, along with the Academy of Management's legitimation of the MSR interest group for its 2000 meetings, suggests that 1996–2000 does indeed represent the initial formative years of the SRW domain.

We believe this study suggests several important avenues for future research. A natural follow-on would be to examine the methodological approaches used during the SRW domain's adolescence, say for example from 2001 to 2006. One interesting question arising from this is, will a diversity of methods continue to be employed during the adolescence as advocated by many, or will their fears come true with the field ossifying around time-worn quantitative approaches? Further,

Table 2: Frequency of Empirical Studies Published in SRW

Year	Articles Published
1996	4
1997	1
1998	4
1999	5
2000	12

as suggested above, the founding years of the field could be examined using more inclusive and less restrictive selection criteria to attempt to understand the total empirical overview of the field rather than only the journal-published empirical work.

Another fascinating question may be to determine which articles from 1996 to 2000 will become the seminal works in the field, perhaps through a bibliographic analysis of future publications or by a future social sciences citation index search. Finally, the articles in this study present an interesting opportunity to map out their theoretical and empirical foundations by examining their citations and bibliographies. Perhaps one of the greatest challenges facing the SRW domain is attempting to construct a coherent knowledge base of a discipline that is inherently fragmented. The articles examined within this study, for better and for worse, represent the collective, published peer-reviewed empirical work of our domain during its founding years; any attempt to build coherence based on their sources will surely provide interesting results for future projects.

REFERENCE

Academy of Management (2002). Management, Spirituality, and Religion. Divisions and Interest Groups. Retrieved December 12, 2002 from http://www.aomonline.org/aom.asp?ID=1&page_ID=15#.

*Ashmos, D., and Duchon, D. (2000) Spirituality at work: A conceptualization and measure, *Journal of Management Inquiry,* 9(2), 134–145.

Arba, J. (1998) *Should Psychology be a Science?* Westport, CT: Praeger.

*Barnett, T., Bass, K., and Brown, G. (1996) Religiosity, ethical ideology, and intentions to report a peer's wrongdoing, *Journal of Business Ethics,* 15, p1161.

Beazley, H. (1997) Meaning and Measurement of Spirituality in Organizational Settings: Development of a Spiritual Assessment Scale, Unpublished doctoral dissertation George Washington University: Washington, DC.

*Beech, N., Cairns, G., and Robertson, T. (2000) Successful innovations or token gestures?, *Personnel Review*, 29(4), 460–473.

Biberman, J., and Whitty, M. (Guest Eds.) (1999) Spirituality in organizations, part I, *Journal of Organizational Change Management*, 12(3).

Daft, R., and Buenger, V. (1990) Hitching a ride on a fast train to nowhere: The past and future of strategic management research, In Fredrickson, J.W. (Ed), *Perspectives on Strategic Management*. New York: Harper Business, 81–103.

Dehler, G., and Neal, J. (Guest Eds.) (2000) Spirituality in contemporary work: Its place, space, and role in management education, *Journal of Management Education*, 24(5).

Delbecq, A. (2000) Personal communication.

Denzin, N. and Lincoln, Y. (2000) *Handbook of Qualitative Research, 2nd ed*, Thousand Oaks, CA: Sage.

Dewey, J. (1993) *How We Think,* Boston: Heath, 106–118.

Eisenhardt, K. (1989) Building theories from case study research, *Academy of Management Review*, 14(4), 532–550.

Eisenhardt, K. (1991) Better stories and better constructs: The case for rigor and comparative logic, *Academy of Management Review,* 16(3), 620–627.

Fornaciari, C., and Lund Dean, K. (2001) Making the Quantum Leap: Lessons from Physics on Studying Spirituality and Religion in Organizations, *Journal of Organizational Change Management*, 14(4), 335–351.

Gibbons, P. (2000) Spirituality at work: Definitions, measures, assumptions, and validity claims, in J. Biberman and M. Whitty (Eds.) *Work and Spirit: A Reader of New Spiritual Paradigms for Organizations*. Scranton, PA: University of Scranton Press, 111–131.

Glaser, B., and Strauss, A. (1967) *The Discovery of Grounded Theory*. Chicago, IL: Aldine.

Gunther, M. (2001) God and business *Fortune* June 26, Retrieved December 26, 2002 from http://www.fortune.com/fortune/careers/articles/0,15114,371129,00.html.

Hambrick, D. (1990) The adolescence of strategic management, 1980–1985: Critical perceptions and reality, in Fredrickson, J.W. (Ed), *Perspectives on Strategic Management*. New York: Harper Business, 237–261.

*Harold, B. and Jones, J. (1997) The Protestant ethic: Weber's model and the empirical literature, *Human Relations,* 50(7), p. 757.

* Haroutiounian, A., Ghavam, S., Gomez, S., Ivshin, E., Phelan, S., Freshman, B., Griffin, M., and Lindsay, C. (2000) Learning and being: Outcomes of a class on spirituality in work, *Journal of Management Education*, 24(5), 662–681.

*Harpaz, I. (1998) Cross-national comparison of religious conviction and the meaning of work, *Cross-Cultural Research,* 32(2), 143–170.

Hedrick, T. (1994) The qualitative-quantitative debate: Possibilities for integration, in Reichardt, C., and Rallis, S. (Eds.), *The Qualitative-Quantitative Debate: New Perspectives.* San Francisco: Jossey-Bass, 45–52.

*Holder, J., and Vaux, A. (1998) African American professionals: Coping with occupational stress in predominantly white work environments. *Journal of Vocational Behavior,* 53(3), 315–333.

* Howard, N.C., McMinn, M.R., Bissell, L.D., Faries, S.R., and VanMeter, J.B. (2000) Spiritual directors and clinical psychologists: A comparison of mental health and spiritual values, *Journal of Psychology and Theology*, 28(4), 308–320.

Isabella, L. (1990) Evolving interpretations as a change unfolds: How managers construe key organizational events, *Academy of Management Journal*, 33(1), 7–42.

*Kamya, H. (2000) "Hardiness and spiritual well-being among social work students: Implications for social work education" *Journal of Social Work Education*, 36(2), 231–240.

*Kennedy, E., and Lawton, L. (1996) "The effects of social and moral integration on ethical standards: A comparison of American and Ukrainian business students" *Journal of Business Ethics*, 15, 901.

*Kennedy, E., and Lawton, L. (1998) Religiousness and business ethics, *Journal of Business Ethics*, 17, 163.

Kerlinger, F. (1976) *Foundations of Behavioral Research, 3rd ed.* Fort Worth, TX: Holt, Rinehart and Winston.

* Keyes, M., Hanley-Maxwell, C., and Capper, C. (1999) 'Spirituality? It's the core of my leadership': Empowering leadership in an inclusive elementary school, *Educational Administration Quarterly*, 35(2), 203–237.

* Knotts, T., Lopez, T., and Mesak, H. (2000) Ethical judgments of college students: An empirical analysis, *Journal of Education for Business*, Jan/Feb, 158–163.

*Konieczny, M., and Chaves, M. (2000) Resources, race, and female-headed congregations in the United States, *Journal for the Scientific Study of Religion*, Sept, 261–271.

*Konz, G., and Ryan, F. (1999) Maintaining an organizational spirituality: No easy task, *Journal of Organizational Change Management*, 12(3), 200–210.

*Li, E., Feifer, C., and Strohm, M. (2000) A pilot study: Locus of control and spiritual beliefs in alcoholics anonymous and SMART recovery members, *Addictive Behaviors*, 25(4), 633–640.

Lips-Wiersma, M. (2001) Furthering management and spirituality education through the use of paradox, Workshop presented at the 2001 Annual Meetings of the Academy of Management, Washington, DC.

Lund Dean, K. (2003). Systems thinking's challenge to research in spirituality & religion at work: An interview with Ian Mitroff, *Journal of Organizational Change Management* in press.

Lund Dean, K., Fornaciari, C., and McGee, J. (2002) Research in Spirituality, Religion, and Work: Walking the Line between Relevance and Legitimacy, *Journal of Organizational Change Management*, 16(4), 378–395.

*McDonald, A.W. and Gorsuch, R. (2000). Surrender to God: An additional coping style?, *Journal of Psychology and Theology*, 28(2), 149.

McGee, J. (2001) "Research methods for spirituality and management" J. McGee (session chair). Workshop presented at the 2001 Annual Meetings of the Academy of Management, Washington, DC.

Merton, R.K. (1973) *The Sociology of Science; Theoretical and Empirical Investigations*. University of Chicago Press: Chicago, IL.

Miles, M., and Huberman, A. (1994) *Qualitative Data Analysis: An Expanded Sourcebook, 2nd ed.* Thousand Oaks, CA: Sage.

*Milliman, J., Ferguson, F., Trickett, D., and Condemi, B. (1999) Spirit and Community at Southwest Airlines: An Investigation of a spiritual values based model, *Journal of Organizational Change Management,*12(3), 221–233.

Mills, C. (1959) *The Sociological Imagination.* New York: Oxford University Press.

Mitroff, I. and Denton, E. (1999) *A Spiritual Audit of Corporate America: A Hard Look at Spirituality, Religion, and Values in the Workplace.* San Francisco: Jossey-Bass.

*Neal, J. (2000) Work as service to the divine, *American Behavioral Scientist*, 43(8), 1316–1333.

Neal, J., Lichtenstein, B., and Banner, D. (1999) Spiritual perspectives on individual, organizational, and societal transformation, *Journal of Organizational Change Management*, 12(3).

*Niles, F. (1999) Toward a cross-cultural understanding of work-related beliefs, *Human Relations*, 52(7), 855–867.

Pauchant, T. (2001) Spirituality at work: The need for biographical inspirations, J. McGee (session chair). Workshop presented at the 2001 Annual Meetings of the Academy of Management, Washington, DC.

* Ram, M. (1999) Managing professional service firms in a multi-ethnic context: An ethnographic study, *Ethnic and Racial Studies,* 22(4), 679–701.

Reichardt, C. and Rallis, S. (Eds.) (1994) *The Qualitative-Quantitative Debate: New Perspectives.* San Francisco: Jossey-Bass.

*Sagie, A., and Elizur, D. (1996) The structure of personal values: A conical representation of multiple life areas, *Journal of Organizational Behavior,* 17, 573–586.

Sheskin. D. (1997) *Handbook of Parametric and Nonparametric Statistical Procedures,* Boca Raton, FL: CRC Press.

*Sidani, Y., and Gardner, W. (2000) Work values among Lebanese workers, *The Journal of Social Psychology*, 140(5), 597–607.

Tedlock, B. (2000) Ethnography and ethnographic representation, in Denzin, N. and Lincoln, Y. (Eds.) *Handbook of Qualitative Research, 2nd ed.* Thousand Oaks, CA: Sage, 455–486.

Trott, D. (1996) Spiritual Well-Being of Workers. Unpublished doctoral dissertation. University of Texas, Austin, TX.

Uzzell, D. (2000) Ethnographic and action research, in Breakwell, G., Hammond, S., and Fife-Shaw, C. (Eds.), *Research Methods in Psychology, 2nd ed.* Thousand Oaks, CA: Sage, 326–337.

*Wallace, R. (2000) Women and religion: The transformation of leadership roles, *Journal for the Scientific Study of Religion,* Dec, 497–508.

*West, W. (1998) Developing practice in a context of religious faith: a study of psychotherapists who are Quakers, *British Journal of Guidance & Counselling,* 26(3), 365–375.

*White, K., and Ozcan, Y. (1996) Church ownership and hospital efficiency, *Hospital & Health Services Administration*, 41(3), 297–310.

Williams, P. (2002) "Meet the AMJ Editor" Caucus presented at the 2002 Annual Meetings of the Academy of Management, Denver, CO.

Yin, R. (1994) *Case Study Research: Design and Methods, 2nd ed.* Thousand Oaks, CA: Sage.

Note: References preceded by * are the subject articles of the study.

Appendix 1: Electronic Resources Used in the Study

Database used	General Description
ABI/INFORM (now in ProQuest)	Business and management work; academic literature as well as popular press and newspapers.
Cambridge Scientific Abstracts (includes ATLA Religion Database; ERIC; Linguistics and Language Behavior Abstracts; PsycINFO; Social Services Abstracts; and Sociological Abstracts)	A comprehensive social science database that includes research work in religion, education, language, psychology, social services, and sociology fields.
EBSCO*host* Academic Search Elite	Full text for nearly 1,850 publications, including nearly 1,300 peer-reviewed journals and abstracts for 2,900 journals. This database offers information in nearly every area of academic study including: social sciences, humanities, education, computer sciences, engineering, physics, chemistry, language and linguistics, arts and literature, medical sciences, ethnic studies and more.
ERIC	The comprehensive database for research in education literature.
JSTOR	An online database covering over 320 scholarly journals in 26 disciplines including arts and sciences, business (46 titles), ecology and botany, general science, and language and literature.
Lexis-Nexis Academic	Provides full-text documents from over 5,600 news, business, legal, medical, and reference publications.
MERLIN	A cooperative cataloguing effort including most of the state of Missouri university libraries; it includes all hardcopy and electronic sources for all libraries within that system.
PsychLit (now PsychINFO)	The comprehensive database for research in psychology literature.

2

■

Integrating Spirituality at Work: An Interview with Ken Wilber

Thierry C. Pauchant
HEC Montreal and Consulting Faculty
Accompanied by members of the Academy of Management, Management,
Spirituality and Religion Interest Group (MSR)$^\heartsuit$: Joel Bennett, Margaret
Benefiel, Andre Delbecq, Dale Fitzgibbons, Thomas Goddard, Khalsa
Gurudev, Jim McGee, Judi Neal, Lee Robbins, David Steingard, David Trott
and John Young

During the Academy of Management meeting in Denver, Colorado (August 2002), a team of members of the Academy's Management, Spirituality and Religion Interest Group (MSR) interviewed Ken Wilber at his downtown Denver apartment. Known as a leading voice in spirituality and the founding father of the Integral Institute, Ken Wilber presents in this interview some of his views on the challenges of integrating spirituality in organizations, in terms of management practice, research and education$^\diamond$.

$^\heartsuit$ We wish to thank Kariann Aarup for her help in the transcription of this interview and the SSHRC for financial assistance.
$^\diamond$ An introduction to Ken Wilber's work is available in Wilber (1996), in a more extended form in Wilber (1995; 2000; 2001) and in synthetic form in Pauchant et al. (2002, pp. 18–26, 201–211).

MSR: *Many people disagree today on the meaning of spirituality. You have proposed different definitions. Perhaps we could start this interview with these definitions and proceed from there?*

Ken Wilber: Yes. This is a good place to start. There are at least four definitions of spirituality. I will present each one in turn.

The most common definition is that spirituality is the highest level of any of the developmental lines, the upper reaches. We could say, for example, when talking about cognition, that the higher reach is trans-rational. Notice that in this definition, it is not supposed that cognition is itself spiritual. Only the higher levels of cognition—trans-verbal, trans-rational, and so on—are considered a spiritual or a meditative or a contemplative type of cognition. To take another example, in the realm of moral development, we could think of post-conventional morality, or world-centric morality, as being spiritual. Conversely, using the model proposed by Lawrence Kohlberg, we do not think of ego-centric or ethno-centric morality as being spiritual, although they are moral responses as well, in their respective stages of human development.

A second definition, also very common, is that spirituality is an altered state or a peak experience, which can be experienced at pretty much any stage of development. I tend to divide these states of consciousness into four major types: waking state, dreaming, deep sleep and ever-present, non dual, consciousness. Some of these states of consciousness include the experience of formless absorption, feelings of oneness with radical emptiness prior to manifestation. Others include experiences of luminescent light, bliss, love, transcendence and so on. Still other states of consciousness can include the experience of oneness with the entire world or with the natural world.

Many people consider these states to be spiritual. This is because you can literally have an experience of nature mysticism or deep mysticism through them. The empirical evidence available indicates very strongly that you can be at any level or stage of development and have altered states or peak experiences, as Abraham Maslow called them. Any person tends to interpret these experiences given the mental apparatus that that person has achieved. Thus, a person can interpret these peak experiences in magic terms, mythic terms, rational terms, and so on.

A third definition of spirituality is to consider it as a developmental line. In this case, we can speak about spirituality as developing much like cognition, or affect, or any other line of development. There is something intuitively appealing about this definition because we can all say that a given person is either highly spirituality developed or not. Most of us know what this means. But, beyond this, it is very hard to come up with a precise definition of a spiritual line, i.e. one that does not steal characteristics from another line. In other words, it is very hard to say that a development is just "spiritual" and not also in part affective, emotional, interpersonal, moral, cognitive and so on. If you take James Fowler's research, for example, which I think is wonderful, you will find this ambiguity. If you give his test to people and you test these people as well with Lawrence Kohlberg's procedure, you will get positively correlated scores between the two. This suggests that these tests are not really different developmental lines at all, i.e., spiritual on one hand and moral on the other.

The fourth definition of spirituality is a little bit vague and nebulous but seems to be one of the most practical. In this case spirituality is not a level of development, or a state, or a line of development. It is simply an attitude that you can assume at whatever level or wave or state you are at. This tends to be an attitude of openness or care or a loving attitude. But this attitude is itself limited to the level you are at. It gets a little bit dicey in terms of what you actually mean when saying that someone is being spiritual at a lower level of development and when you otherwise do not think that this person is very spiritual at all. For example, can we say that a caring person at the ego-centric stage or the ethno-centric stage of development is really "spiritual"?

And yet, many people are more comfortable bringing spirituality into business when using this definition, as opposed, for example, to bringing a religious belief system. Now obviously, many people are doing both in a sense. But for many, spirituality has nothing to do with a church or a synagogue. Spirituality for them is more a matter of your own awareness or your own consciousness and what you bring moment to moment to bear. The attitude is basically an attitude of awareness, of being sensitive and perceptive, moment to moment. A certain awareness is brought to bear on a situation and is also going to play out on how people will interact. This is a very human aspect of spirituality and yet a very profound one as well.

MSR: *How can one integrate spirituality at work from these different*
perspectives?

Ken Wilber: Well, the way to bring spirituality into the market-place
depends, in part, on the definition you use. If you use the first definition,
i.e. spirituality as the upper reaches, the only way to bring it into a
business setting is to transform individuals. We want these individuals
to reach the higher reaches of development. That is a noble thing to
do but this is also very difficult to achieve. It is very hard to get an
adult human being to transform. I have been trying on myself for 30
years! Empirical evidence suggests that it takes about five years for
an individual to develop one stage. And this is even more difficult
with a collection of individuals, which constitutes an organization. This
development is indeed possible but very hard to achieve. It is at once
discouraging and realistic.

To bring the second aspect of spirituality—as an altered state—in
business settings is, in a certain sense, easier than with the previous
one. Here, you can take someone at any stage of development and use
various types of techniques or methods to help him or her to get an
altered state experience or a peak experience. This can be a very life-
changing, very profound, sometimes very disruptive experience. There
are very powerful techniques to do this.

Using the third definition of spirituality—as a developmental
line—can make intuitive sense. But the difficulty of developing an
independent metric scale for spirituality is a very serious one. And yet,
many people are actually introducing several developmental lines into
business or leadership training: the emotional line, the interpersonal
line, what they call the spiritual line, the physical line, the cognitive
line, etc. This allows one to say to a business leader or a manager that
if they are very well developed in one or several areas, for example the
cognitive and interpersonal lines, they still need to develop other areas,
such as the moral and the spiritual ones. This is very helpful as this
can orient the kind of training to pursue. In some cases you may have
people that are spiritually well developed and not doing too well in
others areas. This aspect is particularly important when you attempt to
measure the effects of meditative or contemplative practices. Empirical
evidence suggests that some people who are very highly developed in
meditation techniques are not well developed interpersonally or morally,

for example. This is one of the mysteries of the psyche. It appears that the different developmental lines are in some sense intertwined but relatively independent as well. In this area, we need a lot more research, to better understand the relationships existing among these different developmental lines. It is often easy to find someone who is really highly developed in one line and pathological in one or two others! This becomes very problematic when you belong to a tradition where you need to submit to a Guru for developmental reasons and when that Guru is going to abuse you sexually or otherwise.

I think that the fourth definition of spirituality—an attitude of care—is a good place to start in business settings. It just starts where people are. For instance, it is where you are right now. You can talk about love as a developmental need, or love as a meditative state, but right now there is a certain "is-ness" about your own existence, a certain presence about what is happening. And that presence might be known as God or the Spirit, so you can till that soil of being present to the present and whatever unfolds is going to be spiritual.

In this fourth definition, spirituality is not really a set of beliefs or a set of doctrines. It is a practice. It is something that you actually do. It is much more like judo or riding a bike or baking a cake. It is something you actually do. It is actual, physical, it involves the whole body, and many people resonate with this. The proof of the pudding is the actual, the product of your actions, the tasting and that is exactly what it means, and business people like this. So you bake the cake and you taste the cake. In this definition, spirituality is something you do, with your mind and your body, in actual practice, moment to moment. It is a muscle you have to exercise and when you do it, this muscle gets bigger and stronger, if you exercise on a daily basis.

One of the reasons I use examples of practices like judo or baking a cake to describe spirituality is to get people to realize that, at least for certain aspects of it, spirituality is just a way of being. It is a practice that one can do. It is not a belief structure. You do not have to believe in Yahweh, in Mohammed, in Jesus, or in Buddha. All those beliefs are interesting enough. If you want to use them as part of a richer spiritual tradition, this is fine. But that is probably not something that you want to bring to the workplace.

If you wish to bring spirituality into a particular business organization, you will have to find ways that do not require people to agree with your metaphysical claims or religious belief system. This is where it becomes delicate and dicey. My sense about spirituality, taken as the fourth definition, is there is something about presence right now, something that has to be cultivated. This presence is very profound and very deep and is the basic thread that leads right to full consciousness anyway. If a team or a group of managers want to discover this presence, they can, for example, stop every 15 minutes during their work and be present to the present.

And out of the four aspects of spirituality I have talked about, three of them are 100 per cent immediately available to everybody. The only one that is not directly available is, of course, the higher level or stage of development. I do not think that business people are offended by that. They do not have much trouble in understanding that there exist stages of meditative development which are very advanced. Also, they can understand that the goal is not to rank people high or low in their spiritual development. Rather the interesting thing is for each person to realize how one can go higher in his or her own development. Thus a good place to start in business is sharing these types of ever-present experiences that people have naturally.

MSR: What are the major difficulties you have encountered when introducing spirituality at work?

Ken Wilber: Particularly in today's world, anything that has to do with higher and lower stages or levels of development is just almost impossible to deal with. The business groups that I have been working more directly with have no trouble with applying the all-quadrants, all-lines, all-states model to business. But as soon as you delve into the developmental part—the all-levels model—problems start. It is obviously a very sensitive issue as people start to evaluate themselves and others as being at a higher or lower level of development.

For that reason, almost all approaches start by first introducing the quadrants. In business management, nobody has any trouble with the quadrants as there is no implication of judgment. And the introduction of the quadrants tends to bring an immediate clarification to the situation at hand. For example, people can start to realize that it is probably the lower-left quadrant—a cultural problem—which is mostly responsible for the jamming of an assembly line in Kuala Lumpur, and not only a technical problem, which would be in the lower-right quadrant of the model. The quadrants help them to realize, for instance, the clash existing between a collective meaning that emphasizes profit maximization and another that emphasizes team membership, as well as their relations to the realities in the other quadrants. That can help enormously. But, at some point, you have to introduce the levels.

MSR: Which strategies can be used to introduce the levels of development without embarrassing people?

Ken Wilber: Different people are using different strategies. One strategy is to introduce the quadrants by proposing that the right-hand quadrants represent the facts of a situation, the material entities that one can see, touch, etc., and that the left-hand quadrants represent the interpretation of these facts. Using the quadrant approach, people can start to realize that they can all agree on the facts but not necessarily on their interpretations. After that, using Don Beck's Spiral Dynamics model for example, you can introduce different ways of interpreting facts. But, in this strategy, these different ways are not presented as lower and higher levels of development. Rather they are presented as different types, as different but equivalent ways to interpret facts. Equipped with these models, people can then attempt to find ways to reconcile both the facts and their interpretations or at least deal with the situation in a more integrated way.

Another strategy for addressing the issue of levels of development is to use Robert Kegan's seven languages of transformation or Daniel Golman's emotional intelligence techniques. They are simple ways of getting around the problem of dealing with levels, while still preserving some of their essence. Robert Kegan's material, using a lot of examples, is pretty straight-forward for business people.

Another strategy has been used at Notre Dame University where they offer a Masters level course in integral leadership. They present first the quadrants and then the lines. They call the quadrants Personal Meaning, Individual Behavior, Business Systems and Processes, and Organizational Culture and Shared Meanings. They also present six major developmental lines, including the physical, the emotional, the cognitive, the interpersonal, the moral and the spiritual lines of development. People intuitively understand what those mean and they start to realize that you can be either more or less developed in these lines. They understand, for example, that someone can be highly developed at the cognitive but less at the interpersonal level. Then the staff at Notre Dame introduces some empirical evidences on the different levels of development. The terminology they use is deliberately not offensive, with terms that everybody agrees with, such as ego-centric, ethno-centric, world-centric, etc. One of the things they have realized with this approach is that it is very difficult to find a leader who is integral. So they attempt to have the management team cover all the bases, so to speak, instead of waiting five to ten years for the transformation of a person.

Whatever the strategy, when introducing the levels of development, it has to be done very carefully. You have to be very cautious with the terminology you use. You need to present carefully the empirical evidences. And you have to make sure that you are factoring out the gender factors, the ethnic factors, the cultural factors, and so on.

MSR: Focusing either on the quadrants or on the levels will lead to different conceptions of integral development. Is it the reason why you advocate focusing on both?

Ken Wilber: Yes. There are two different types of integral development. The first type consists of integrating the quadrants the best one can at the level of development one is at. This is horizontal health. The idea is to get some sort of balance between the I, the We, the It and the Its of the quadrants. We all know people that are unbalanced. There is too much emphasis on the I, for example, leading to narcissism; or there is too much emphasis on the We, being afraid of one's autonomy; or one does not take care enough of the It, such as one's body, his physical health, and so on. The second type of development consists of transforming the level of consciousness one is at, to higher levels of care and compassion. This is vertical health.

If we practice truth in advertising while integrating spirituality in business organizations, we have to be real clear about what it is we are going to do, i.e. translation and/or transformation. The first thing that I look at is horizontal health. Can I help an individual, a group or an organization to become the healthiest they can be at whatever stage in life they are? It is a way to help them to translate in a more effective way and in different areas or quadrants where they are in that moment. A lot of us, and particularly in my generation, felt that we needed to be engaged in transformation. Transforming everything was the ultimate goal. We have to scale back what we can actually do. When we look at kids, who are at earlier stages of development, we do not necessarily want them to develop right away a higher level; we just want to help them to become better at the level they are.

When talking about development, some of the core business teams we have at the Integral Institute use a terminology that comes from medieval torture techniques: The first, second and third degree tortures. The first degree torture consists of describing what you are going to do; the second degree is when you show the instruments you are going to use; and the third degree consists of actually applying them on your victim.

Our business consultants offer three degree of tortures to our clients. The first degree consists of describing the actual situation in terms of our model and using different scales of measurement, such as offered by Daniel Goleman, Robert Kegan, Jane Loevinger and others. This conceptual map helps people to diagnose the situation and decide on what they want to do. The second degree consists of choosing potential tools an individual, a team or a business, who wishes to become more integral, could use. The third degree is actual, real, profound life transformation.

MSR: *The first two degrees of torture are less transformational and more translational. Do you ask people their permission when you involve yourself in the third degree?*

Ken Wilber: Of course. But what happens is that most of the changes you can make in a business situation, when you do leadership or management consulting, occur by simply helping people to see the present situation, diagnose it in a way that makes sense for them and then recommend changes that only require translation. For example, if you have three sub-cultures in a company, one that emphasizes effectiveness, another membership and a third one existential meaning, they need to understand these value differences before anything else. A team is not only a collection of individuals working on an assembly line, for example, which is the conception from the lower-right quadrant. From a lower-left perspective, a team shares common meanings, grounded in similar levels of value development. From a management perspective, we give people tools and processes they can use in order to constitute real teams who can work together in a more integral fashion. Most of the changes that we facilitate come from the first and second degree of torture. And this can alleviate 60 to 80 per cent of the tensions in a team or an organization.

And, of course, some are looking for deeper changes. It is almost always a leader who expresses this need. In these cases, we explore with them the methods of human transformation which could be appropriate: meditation, yoga, a type of psychotherapy, a type of spiritual practice, journaling, dialogue, growth group, etc. Using the Loevinger scales, we have found that some meditation practices can help people to grow up two stages in four to five years. But this is very hard to accomplish and we warn people of that difficulty. The easier way is to hire a person with the desired level of consciousness, without waiting four to five years for that person to develop. Now hopefully all of us, in some ways, are involved in our own transformative growth; and this is going to happen whether we intentionally want it or not. Life acts as a great teacher, through pain, suffering, illness, joy, surprise, death of a loved one, and so on.

It is possible that ten thousand years from now, what we call the level of autonomous and integrated self will be common in the general population. It could be then negotiated by kids of eight or nine years old. And many more subtle levels of consciousness are likely to be known. One hundred thousand years ago, the common development one had to achieve was ego-centrism. And now that stage is negotiated by infants. Life, indeed, acts as a great teacher.

MSR: You are the founding father of the Integral Institute. What type of work is the Institute doing to bring spirituality into business organizations?

Ken Wilber: Right now one of the primary activities we are involved in is working with Core Teams. Core Teams are groups of seven or eight people that are working in one particular area with the task of producing a major theoretical statement about this area. It may be integral art, integral business, integral medicine, integral education, and so on. We have about two dozen of these Core Teams. This is primarily what we want to do in the next three to five years: We wish to make major theoretical statements, just to get the conversation started.

Also, one of the things that has been really gratifying and very promising has been using the abstract theoretical framework—because this is what it is—and taking it into the real world. We wish to see what works and what does not work, in an attempt to adjust the framework. We are going to learn an enormous amount from people who are actually doing this practical work. The generic answer so far is that first degree torture is a system that almost anybody can use to sort and analyze what is happening in an organization. But it is in the second and third degree that you really bring about change and that is very interesting.

My sense is that the most important thing in the short run, more important than helping people transform, is to find those people who already have access to some kind of second-tier level of development or higher consciousness. Of course, this is difficult to do as the different lines of development do not always match up. We often find people who have a cognitive grasp of integral issues and values, for example, but who do not really live them, behaviourally, interpersonally or morally. However, we try to do what we call two-to-two matching and two-to-one matching: we bring people who are second-tier together as well as mixing second-tier people with first-tier. In this way, we attempt to develop a conversation on integral issues and get some development going.

MSR: *What are the critical elements that require research efforts at this point?*

Ken Wilber: We need to develop more metrics that people could use to help judge transformation. You are never going to nail that process down because the whole point about the great river of life is that it does not matter how many snapshots you take of it, you are never going to get it, except by just jumping in and starting to swim. However, what we do need is better metrics when people want to know how far down the river they have travelled as well as measuring some of the effects of their efforts. We hope that better metrics, better measurements, qualitative as well as quantitative, would help people who wish to use these instruments. Some feel that this effort at measurement is pigeonholing and they really do not want to know, and this is fine. In any case, these instruments should not be used without the consent of the people involved or against their will.

I am very suspicious of statements that affirm that only five or eight levels of development exist. All the instruments we have today are based on only one way of looking at the river of life. And that way is sliced according to one type of question that has been asked or observations that have been made. For example, if you ask a person to describe his conception of the world, you get a reading of cognitive development; if you ask another what she thinks one should do in a certain circumstance, you get a reading of moral development; if you ask another person what are her deepest concerns right now, you get levels of meaning development; or if you ask another person what he values, you get a reading of value development.

All of these, developed by great researchers such as Maslow, Loevinger, Kohlberg, Graves, Kegan, Piaget, Fisher, Gilligan and many others, are all valid to the extent that they all have supporting tests. But they are but one slice of the great river of life and you have to be very careful when using them. They are indeed only a step in consciousness.

The tests have also to be comprehensible by the people who use them. One of the most useful in business is the one used in Spiral Dynamics, based on the work of Claire Graves. People intuitively understand what the values mean, when they are described. For example, they understand what it means to be ego-centric or power hungry, or to be fundamentalist. Unfortunately, that test is very simple and its answers can be faked easily, diminishing its usefulness. In my opinion, the best test we have so far is Loevinger's measures of self development. It is impossible to fake and is very accurate for what it does. However, it is impossible to use it in the field as it takes two hours to complete and as people have difficulty understanding its constructs. Other people are also using Kegan's model. It is very straight-forward and people in business understand why the complexity can go, literally, over their head.

MSR: *Do you hope that these metrics will help to bring about a more ethical society?*

Ken Wilber: It is the hope! If you actually look at the developmental markers that we use in society, these markers are very crude. For example, one of the most often used markers in the world is the age of people: you are not allowed to vote until you are 18 or 21. The assumption made, in our democracies, is that this marker guarantees to some extent that voters will be able to use some judgment. But if you have a democracy built on an extremely conventional mythic membership and fundamentalist orientation, the orientation that causes wars, then it could become legal to gas gays and execute Jews. It is essential to remember that Hitler was elected democratically. The crude developmental markers that we use today in our democracies do not guard us against such tragedies. Better metrics could help us to get less crude measures of development.

These are very delicate issues. But they are also the decisions we have to make all the time anyway. They are based on this sort of intuitive understanding of higher and lower development. It is the single common nightmare that anybody who has achieved some degree of moral development encounters: the higher levels are where most of the values that we cherish come from; and yet the numbers of people who have achieved the higher levels are so few in number! At present, it is evaluated that 70 per cent of the world's population is at the ethno-centric level or lower. It is one of God's little jests that everyone starts at square one and needs to go up the developmental process, from ego-centric to ethno-centric, from ethno-centric to world-centric and so on.

MSR: *In your opinion, what should be the minimum level of moral development achieved by our leaders?*

Ken Wilber: We just do not want people making decision who are at the ethno-centric level of moral development or lower. Leaders and executives need to be, at minimum, at the post-conventional, world-centric level. We have to find a way to make those judgments, which will not be easy, and we have to try to stop people below these stages of development from becoming in charge of things. We know what happens when these people take charge.

In addition, there are studies showing that when you put people together in a group, the average response of the group is two stages lower than the average level of the stages that people are at in the group. There exists, under certain circumstances, a certain mob mentality. Thus, part of the difficulty is looking not only at the level of development of individuals, such as a leader, but at the level of development of collectives as well. Also, part of the difficulty when bringing spirituality into a group is to be clear on the type of spirituality one wishes to integrate. But if we are talking about a generic type of spirituality, such as an attitude of openness, transparency and caring, the hope is that this spirituality can act as a framework in which some of the potentially ugly aspects of group dynamics can be held in check. The presence of a leader who could hold that space could also help in avoiding horde mentality or mob rule. Also, presumably, if you get a spiritual or meditative group, it is a little harder to pull people down.

A very brilliant solution in governance for avoiding ugliness is the constitution of the United States. This constitution is a moral stage five document, according to Kohlberg's scale. When it was first written, probably less than ten percent of the population was at that moral stage. What is brilliant in this document is that it does not restrain the thinking at the individual level. At the individual level, each one can adopt the stage or level of morality that one wishes or can achieve. Rather, the document proposes that you have to behave, in your public behaviour, according to moral stage five norms. The founding fathers have basically institutionalized in society the right-hand quadrant's behaviour by proposing a non-ethnocentric, non-egocentric set of rules.

If human beings start down the spiral of ugliness, often all they need is for somebody to give permission to act as low as possible. This is generally what happens to businesses when they get stressed. People start moving down that spiral and the whole group circles in on itself. It is a very delicate thing when human beings get together.

MSR: Might this spiralling process provide some explanations as to why religions have been the source of many wars in the world?

Ken Wilber: Historically, religious people were progressing upward in the developmental process. Religious beliefs have united people based on something other than blood lines. The original tribes of five to six thousand years ago were based on a kinship lineage. There existed no way to communicate or interact across tribes, not just because of the lack of common languages, but because there existed different blood lines. The mythical process consisted of convincing every person in these tribes that each believer of the chosen god was a descendent of that god. So members of different tribes became brothers and sisters, whereas they were or not blood related. Mythology in that sense was a way of binding these ego-centric tribes together into an ethno-centric culture. This was a very important and necessary process of development. Religion, then, got an A+.

Of course, ethno-centric tribes declared wars on other ethno-centric tribes, who believed in other gods. Most of the early forms of religion were based on forms of mythic or ethno-centric membership. Many believers in these religions could not collectively bring about a post-conventional, world-centric view. These religions have thus developed an us versus them mentality, that is those who will be saved and those who will damned. This is a D-.

Today, in our post-conventional world, we are struggling with moving up from an ethno-centric view to a world-centric view, which brings about another type of spirituality. For some of us, the thought that one could attack anybody for their beliefs, race, gender or religion, is physically nauseating. This dilemma is also the one confronted by every child that is born, having to go up the developmental process. Since everyone is born at square one, everybody goes through a period of ego-centric and ethno-centric prejudices on the way to higher stages of development.

So it is understandable that to talk about spirituality and religion in business makes people really nervous. They do not know exactly what god you mean or what you want to do to them if they do not believe in your god. The ethno-centric view has been the dominant form of religious experience and has lead to some very ugly things, including wars or the Spanish inquisition; and 70 per cent of the world population is still at that ethno-centric stage. Of course, we wish to introduce some sort of post-conventional, trans-personal, world-centric spirituality. This type of spirituality is not only the core of the inner conditions of the great religious traditions; it is also our own highest potential for our evolutionary future.

MSR: What are the evidences that different spiritual practices can contribute to the unfolding of a post-conventional spirituality?

Ken Wilber: We have, at the Integral Institute, a core team called the Human Change Project. We also call it the Encyclopedia of Transformation. The purpose of that team is to gather and compare the current knowledge on human transformation. Nobody had really offered a good theory of transformation. A lot of research has been done, for example, on meditation using a number of scales, but there does not exists at the present time any solid critical review of that work. We do not know how human beings transform. It is the ultimate mystery. What we do know is that you wake up one morning with world-centric cognition or higher.

Any PhD student will tell you that before starting research on a topic you need to perform a literature review. This is what the Human Change Project team will do. First, the team will itemize any technique anywhere in the world claiming to lead to a transformation of human beings. Second, the team will gather evidence on how these techniques have really transformed people. And third, based on this review, the team will assess each technique and recommend further research projects on the techniques which seem worthwhile.

The case of the Transcendental Meditation (TM) technique is very interesting in that regard. There are at least two thousand scientific studies done by field researchers using the TM technique. Roger Walsh, who is a very good statistician and a great meditation practitioner, has gone through much of that literature. He has found that about a third of the research is deeply flawed, a third ambiguous and the last third very solid. TM is a very precise technique with a very predictable response in human beings, which explains, in part, why so many tests have be made on this technique. In Zen, for example, you could wait five years before practitioners would have a similar experience.

Some of the results uncovered on TM are very encouraging. In the US adult population, less than two per cent have reached Loevinger's autonomous and integrated stages. However, after four years of TM meditation, that percentage goes up to 34 per cent in TM practitioners! That is quite astonishing. Of course, this does not mean that TM should be practiced by everybody nor than other spiritual techniques will show similar effects. While we need more research on these techniques, other types might be better at helping with openness or being present or other abilities. However, the TM results are very encouraging. They suggest that vertical transformative change can occur through the practice of a spiritual technique, a change that has not been demonstrated to occur with anything else, including psychotherapy.

MSR: ***While you are stressing here the use of spiritual techniques,***
you are also critical toward them in your writing. Could you
say more on this subject?

Ken Wilber: Broadly speaking, there exist two major types of spiritual
practice. The first one is oriented towards the object of awareness. That
object can be a prayer, an image, a mantra. If you are involved in that
type of practice, you actually have to stop your activities for doing your
spiritual practice. For example, you can use a bell every 15 minutes
during a meeting and engage in your spiritual practice for some time.
Some of the Core Teams at the Institute are doing that. The second
type of spiritual practice has to do with the subject of awareness. If you
are practicing that type of spirituality, you do not need to stop your
activities for doing your practice. You are witnessing basically 24 hours
a day. Whatever is happening, moment to moment, is spiritual practice.

Beyond any technique, all knowledge ultimately is knowledge of the
knower itself, which is presently looking out through your eyes and
listening with your ears. That knower is God or Spirit. So the idea is
not how we can know some object, but how can we directly cognize
that Seer. This is the spiritual path or the fourth definition of spirituality
I have proposed at the beginning of this interview. The quadrants, the
levels, the lines, etc. that I have proposed are just objects, and that is
fine. But there is something in you which is aware of all those objects
around you. And all of this is arising in your awareness. As we engage
in a spiritual practice, we find ways to get more and more in touch with
that spirit in which everything is arising.

REFERENCE

Beck, E. and Cowan, C.C. (1996) *Spiral Dynamics. Mastering Values, Leadership and
Change. Exploring the New Science of Memetic,*. London: Blackwell Publishers.
Fowler, J.W. (1995) *Stages of Faith. The Psychology of Human Development and the
Quest for Meaning.* San Francisco: Harper.
Goleman, D., Boyatzis, R. and McKee, A. (2002) *Primal Leadership. Realizing the
Power of Emotional Intelligence.* Boston: Harvard Business School Press.
Kegan, R. (1994) *In Over Our Heads: The Mental Demands of Modern Life,* Boston:
Harvard University Press.
Kegan, R. and Lahey, L.L. (2002) *How the Way We Talk Can Change the Way We
Work: Seven Languages for Transformation.* New York: John Wiley and Sons.

Kohlberg, L. and. Ryncarz R.A (1990) Beyond justice reasoning: Moral development and consideration of a seventh stage, in C. E. Alexander and E. J. Langer (Eds.) *Higher Stages of Human Development: Perspectives on Adult Growth*. New York: Oxford University Press, 191–207.

Lovinger, J. (1998) *Technical Foundations for Measuring Ego Development*. Mahwah, NJ: Lawrence Erlbaum Publishers.

Maslow, A.H. (1993) *The Farther Reaches of Human Nature*. New York: Arkana.

Pauchant, T.C. (2002) *Ethics and Spirituality at Work. Hopes and Pitfalls of The Search For Meaning in Organizations*. Wesport, CT: Quorum Books.

Walsh, R. (2000) *Essential Spirituality. The 7 Central Practices to Awaken Heart and Mind*. New York: John Wiley and Sons.

Wilber, K. (1996) *A Brief Theory of Everything*. Boston: Shambhala.

Wilber, K. (1995) *Sex, Ecology, Spirituality. The Spirit of Evolution*. Boston: Shambhala.

Wilber, K. (2000) *A Theory of Everything. An Integral Vision for Business, Politics, Science, and Spirituality*. Boston: Shambhala.

Wilber, K. (2001) *The Eye of the Spirit. An Integral Vision for a World Gone Slightly Mad (3^{rd}ed.)* Boston: Shambhala.

3

■

Towards a Spiritually Integral Theory of Management

David S. Steingard and Dale E. Fitzgibbons
St. Joseph's University and Illinois State University

Novel epistemological, ontological, and metaphysical foundations of the burgeoning spirituality in management "movement" suggest a fundamental revisioning of the extant management disciplines. First, we examine the roots of management knowledge by revisiting Burrell and Morgan's (1979) classic work on sociological paradigms and organizational analysis. Their subjectivist-objectivist/sociology of regulation-sociology of change, four-quadrant paradigm framework has become a seminal work in organizational studies. Second, we explore the interdisciplinary work of philosopher Ken Wilber (1998), whose integral four-quadrant, holonic paradigms nicely complement Burrell and Morgan's efforts. Third, as inspired by the vanguard ideas and practices of the spirituality in management movement, we synergistically combine these two bodies of knowledge to produce a spiritually integral theory of management. Such a holistic theory may serve as an intellectual and methodological grounding for the new spirituality in management movement. In conclusion, we envision new possibilities for the future of management research and application in light of praxiological advancements offered by a spiritually integral theory of management.

Key Words: *Spirituality, Integral Management, Ken Wilber*

This paper seeks to integrate three bodies of knowledge into a coherent framework for management—a spiritually integral theory of management. Over the last 10 years, management as a discipline has experienced fundamental rumblings of profound change. Qualitative, feminist, postmodern, critical, cross-cultural, ecological, spiritual, and other theoretical and methodological challenges have called into question many of the fundamental assumptions of the field. This pluralism has brought with it a plethora of possibility for the future of the field. These influences have interrupted the positivistic hegemony of management construed as a purely scientific field of inquiry and application. Management is no longer solely concerned with the application of empirically validated methodologies aimed at rationalizing and optimizing bureaucratic functionalism—its obsessive malaise of scientific "physics envy" (Bygrave, 1989: 16) is attenuating. The halcyon days of objectified planning, motivating, and controlling have given way to values, socially responsible business, spirituality, chaos, self-organization, learning, appreciative inquiry, inner development, new science, and other approaches to management informed by a variety of methodological approaches. Fragmented and dis-integrated, management is perhaps in some type of identity or mid-life crisis, unsure of its destiny. Thus, our paper explores the possible manifestation of management as it matures and evolves into the 21st century.

To ground our vision of integral management, we attempt to integrate three extant perspectives: 1) the pioneering work of Burrell and Morgan (1979) in "sociological paradigms and organizational analysis"; Ken Wilber's "integral philosophy" (Wilber, 1998)[1]; and the burgeoning discipline of spirituality in management (Ashmos and Duchon, 2000; Delbecq, 2000; Mitroff & Denton, 1999; Bolman & Deal, 1995).

As perhaps the most comprehensive and classic reconciliation of disparate paradigms about organization and management theory, Burrell and Morgan (1979) provide the foundation for our analysis. They classify and distill a diversity of intellectual approaches to organizational theory into a useful four-quadrant matrix. Essentially, their matrix identifies and clarifies the multiple paradigmatic nature of organizational analysis and has served as the touchstone for

---

[1] For an accessible and somewhat comprehensive overview see Wilber (1996).

organizational researchers for the last twenty years. In Hegelian terminology, we view this matrix as the thesis, the starting point, in assessing the evolution of organizational analysis. To this foundational analysis, we introduce and explicate the integral philosophy of Ken Wilber (1998) to form a new synthesis of a "spiritually integral theory (and practice) of management." Now, let's take a deeper look into each perspective.

BURRELL AND MORGAN'S MATRIX

Burrell and Morgan (1979) did us a commendable service by charting the paradigmatic domains of social science and its intersection with the nature of society. In their groundbreaking book, they detail a four-quadrant classification scheme organized on two different continua (see Figure 1).

The first continuum characterizes the "subjectivist-objectivist" nature of social science. Within this continuum are four underlying assumptions. First, the ontological assumption asks, "To what extent is reality a function of individual consciousness (subjective) or imposed on it from without (objective)?" Second, the epistemological assumption focuses on the question of, "Is knowledge acquired (objectivist) or does it have to be personally experienced (subjectivist)?" Third, the

Figure 1: Four sociological and organizational paradigms (Burrell and Morgan, 1979)

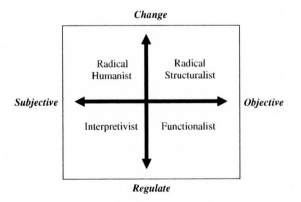

assumption about human nature is framed by the question, "Does human nature respond to social stimuli in a deterministic fashion (objectivist) or does it creatively engage the environment in which it finds itself (subjectivist)?" The fourth and final assumption questions, "What kinds and types of research methods are appropriate if one is conducting an ideographic (subjectivist) or nomothetic (objectivist) analysis?" (1–9). The second continuum characterizes the "regulation-change" dimension of society and organizations. On the one hand, "Is society stable, orderly and somewhat predictable (regulation)?" Or, on the other hand, "Is society principally a contentious arrangement of elements in a constant state of flux and disintegration (change)?" (10–20).

When these two continua are arranged in a 2 x 2 matrix, they produce four paradigmatic quadrants that represent the "map" of organizational theory and analysis. Burrell and Morgan have labelled these quadrants: functionalist, interpretivist, radical humanist, and radical structuralist to describe the meta-theoretical assumptions that compose the worldview of the researcher or theorist working in each (21–37). For example, the functionalist researcher starts from an objectivist perspective while being deeply rooted in the sociology of regulation. This body of work includes many of the early sociologists (e.g., Comte, Spencer and Durkheim) as well as the subsequent work of Mead, Simmel, Parsons and Merton. The interpretivist also starts from an assumption of regularity but attempts to understand the social world at the level of subjective experience. Here we find the early sociologists Dilthey, Weber and Husserl resting firmly on the German idealism of Kant. Similarly, the less-known radical humanist paradigm is concerned with the origins of consciousness but from a subjectivist perspective. So while we again find Kant's work acting as the foundational assumptions we now see the works of Hegel, Ficthe and the "early" Marx represented. Lastly, we see the radical structuralists' interest in change but from a firmly objectivist perspective. This paradigm is underpinned by the later work of Marx and many of the Russian and Mediterranean "Marxists" who followed (e.g., Kropotkin, Bukharin, Lukacs, Gramsci and Althusser). This 2 x 2 matrix now acts as a domain map that allows researchers to more easily position and understand their own and others' work.

Figure 2: The Four Quadrants, Great Nest of Being, and Levels of Consciousness (Wilber, 1998)

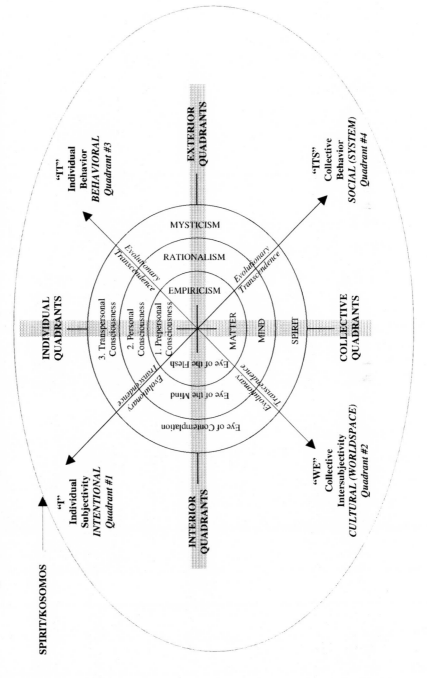

KEN WILBER'S INTEGRAL PHILOSOPHY

Figure 2 depicts a layered model[2] of integral philosophy based on three of Wilber's (1998) key ideas: the four quadrants (64–5); the "Great Nest of Being" (8); and the three levels of consciousness or knowing: prepersonal consciousness/body/eye of the flesh (empiricism); personal consciousness/mind/eye of the mind (rationalism); and transpersonal consciousness/eye of contemplation/spirit (mysticism) (Wilber, 1998: 18; 2000: 210–213).

The four quadrants map out a unique, emergent hierarchy of the evolution of the universe or Kosmos—"the patterned nature or process of all domains of existence, from matter to math to theos, and not merely the physical universe, which is usually what 'cosmos' and 'universe' mean today" (Wilber 2000: 45). Such a hierarchy is actually a "holarchy," which "transcends but includes" (Wilber, 1998: 9) preceding evolutionary stages.

The upper half of the four quadrants represents the individual or the micro, the lower half represents the collective or the macro (Wilber 2000: 127). The right half represents the exterior view, "what they [holons in that quadrant] look like from the outside" and the left half represents the interior view, "what they [holons in that quadrant] look like from within" (127). The upper left quadrant is the "I" or personal subjectivity quadrant, containing a holarchy of "interior awareness" (Wilber, 1998: 69), or the "intentional" Wilber (2000: 127) dimension of human consciousness. The lower left quadrant is the "We" or intersubjective awareness (73) quadrant, basically the collective amalgamation of all of the "Is" individual awarenesses—that comprises the "cultural (worldspace)" (Wilber, 2000: 127). The upper right quadrant represents the "It" or "behavioral" characteristics of human beings— "Behavior can be seen, it is empirical. . . . " (Wilber, 2000: 127). The lower right column encompasses the "ITS" or "social (system)" in which individual "IT" (human beings) act communally (Wilber, 2000: 127).

---

[2] The concentric circles each has four different facets of the same level and don't correspond to a single quadrant. Varied terminology is employed here to enrich the descriptive power of the model. For example, transpersonal consciousness employs mysticism that is the same as utilizing the eye of contemplation. And, when operating at this level, spirit is the realm that is primary (but not exclusive, as all levels transcend and enfold as evolutionary transcendence proceeds).

Overlaying the four quadrants are the three stages of consciousness (Wilber, 2000: 210–213) arranged in an unfolding holonic "Great Nest of Being" (Wilber, 1998: 8) with an evolutionary impulse to move toward transpersonal realms—evolutionary transcendence (Murphy cited in Wilber, 2000: 51): from prepersonal, personal, and ultimately to transpersonal.

Prepersonal is characterized by the individual existing in a state of undifferentiated connection to the external world. Language and consciousness are largely unformed, and biological/emotional states dominate the organism. The individual wallows in an infant-like state of narcissistic egocentrism, relying heavily on instincts for survival and growth. On the positive side, this level also is the repository and origin of the entity's vital life-force and forms the foundation for the other two levels of consciousness (Pauchant, 2002). One might argue that this state is similar to Freud's notion of the "id."

In the personal, the individual has evolved to a more mature level of cognition, language, reason and morality. A definite split occurs between the "I" and the "world" and the individualized entity now freely develops self-awareness, autonomy, self-determination and a more fully evolved emotional being-state. This level of consciousness corresponds closely to Freud's "ego."

At the transpersonal level the individual develops and comes to appreciate the spirituality of his/her beingness. While less material and mental than the previous two stages, transpersonal consciousness may be achieved only after many years of intense ego-work perhaps through the use of meditation, prayer, therapy, contemplation, or discernment.

In the next sections, we apply this model to the transformation of the extant management paradigm as outlined by Burrell and Morgan's matrix. Our objective is to build upon this analysis and produce some tentative ruminations of a spiritually integral theory of management.

THE BREAKDOWN OF FUNCTIONALIST-DOMINATED MANAGEMENT

Over the last thirty years, many of the non-functionalist quadrants in management theory have been marginalized. It does not seem overstated to suggest that functionalism has become the theoretical default and benchmark by which all other approaches to knowledge making are evaluated. In terms of Figure 2, management has collapsed into a "one-dimensional flatland" (Wilber, 1998: 56) where exterior and objective perspectives on individual and collective behavior have become the prevailing cannon:

> The scientific worldview was of a universe composed entirely of objective processes, all described not in I-language or we-language, but merely in it-language, with no consciousness, no interiors, no values, no meaning, no depth and no Divinity. (56)

Thus, we can see how this imbalance of the "scientific worldview" on management theory and practice has created Koyaanisqatsi (Reggio, 1983)— "life out of balance"—in our global society. Our materialistic bias toward the "IT" nature of the Kosmos generates an organizational landscape devoid of meaning, personal subjectivity, and shared systems of existence. Again, the rationale here is that meaning is not cultivated in the exterior dimensions of the Kosmos, but inside the individual and collective subjectivity of human beings. Warren Bennis identifies the "root cause" of how an "IT" characterized world is not only incomplete, but denigrates the human condition:

> What's missing at work, the root cause of the affluenza syndrome, is meaning, purpose beyond one's self, wholeness, integration. ... The underlying cause of organizational dysfunctions, ineffectiveness, and all manner of human stress is the lack of a spiritual foundation in the work place. (quoted in Preface to Mitroff and Denton, 1999: xi)

The "lack of spiritual foundation" can be traced to two particular inadequacies about the present disintegration of management. First, management is chained, via scientific orthodoxy and unyielding objectivism, to the right hand, exterior quadrants where meaning will never be found. Second, unless management scholars and practitioners accelerate their desire to ascend to the transpersonal realms, even efforts to explore the interior dimensions will collapse into the eye of the mind (empiricism) and eye of the flesh (rationalism). Basically, management needs to not only embrace the left, interior quadrants, but transcend toward the eye of contemplation (mysticism). Otherwise, we are inevitably destined to what Maslow (1968) refers to as a "meta-pathology"—the individual's immutable fixation on self-actualization and corresponding inability to transcend him or herself:

> Maslow is possibly the author who has best described what he calls "meta-pathologies," that can occur if the "personal" development is not integrated and surpassed, if an individual remains too attached to this "need for actualization" and doesn't succeed in transcending it." (Pauchant, 2002: 25)

This stultification of development actually impedes evolutionary transcendence, having manifestations in both the interior worlds of meaning and the exterior world of material progress. This move to transpersonal consciousness would restore both inner meaning and eventually outer prosperity and sustainability in the IT world because of the correlational imperative of the four quadrants. As Wilber (1998: 73) explains:

> Each of these aspects [quadrants]... has correlates with all the others. Each is intimately related to the others, for the simple reason that you cannot have an inside without an outside, or a plural without a singular. The four quadrants, I suggest, might therefore be intrinsic aspects of the Kosmos itself. Erase any one of the quadrants, and the others disappear, because they are so many sides of any given phenomenon.

This correlational imperative stipulates that the quadrants are mutually interdependent and constitutive. Inner lives of managers are co-determined by the physical and behavioral aspects of their lives. Likewise, the collective cultural "worldspace" (Wilber, 2000: 127) influences individual subjectivity that in turn creates particular behavioral outcomes. This cycle strives to be balanced—nature dictates that all phenomenon in the Kosmos are "coevolving" toward a more evolutionarily transcendent state. To impose ideological injunctions, privileging one quadrant over another, is to disturb the delicate integration, co-evolutionary relationality, sacredness, and interconnectedness of life itself. It is little wonder that management, in its disintegrated condition has become responsible for many social and environmental problems. For example, the mentality of "business as usual" with its objective "bottom-line" obsession has generated much alienation and meaninglessness at work (Whyte, 2001) as well as the wholesale destruction of the ecological landscape (Hawken, 1993; Anderson, 1998). Overall, it is arguable that management's myopic, functionalist vision creates neglected shadows of the other quadrants—subjective states of emotion, fulfillment, vision, purpose, passion, and wonder, for example, are absent from management. The negative consequences of this duality and degradation need not continue.

THE EMERGENCE OF AN INTEGRAL THEORY OF MANAGEMENT

This section explores some possibilities for overcoming the breakdown described above by speculating about an integral theory of management. We will describe how an integral management theory overcomes the mutually exclusive paradigm parameters of the current functionalist and even multi-disciplinary approaches to management. In the conclusion, we will foreshadow some transformative possibilities for management practitioners and researchers based on the new model of an integral theory of management.

As we stated above, paradigm plurality is indeed plausible based on Wilber's integral philosophy and an application of its four quadrants (Wilber, 1998: 73). However, Burrell and Morgan's seminal work expressly cautions the ultimate incommensurability of paradigms:

> Before we progress to a review of the four paradigms, one point is worthy of further emphasis. This relates to the fact that the four paradigms are mutually exclusive. They offer alternative views of social reality, and to understand the nature of all four is to understand four different views of society. A synthesis is not possible, since in their pure form they are contradictory, being based on at least one set of opposing meta-theoretical assumptions. They are alternatives, in the sense that one can operate in different paradigms sequentially over time, but mutually exclusive, in the sense that one cannot operate in more than one paradigm at any given point in time, since in accepting the assumptions of one, we defy the assumptions of all the others. (1979: 25)

Thus, we have completely counterpoised views. Burrell and Morgan insist that "synthesis is not possible" while Wilber's entire integral philosophy depends on holonic complementarity—indeed a befuddling paradox! How could these views be so incommensurable? How did Burrell and Morgan overlook the pervasive presence of the Great Chain of Being extant in every major premodern religion (Smith,1991), as well as Huxley's idea of the Perrenial Philosophy (1944)? Is integral philosophy even an appropriate discourse and methodology to apply to management?

While these questions are intriguing, and their solutions may be worth pursuing in some way, they are essentially irrelevant. Kuhn's (1970) analysis of paradigm transformations in science will help us contextualize our present discussion and eliminate these fundamental questions. Kuhn suggests that normal science's regularity of inquiry and truth is disrupted by discrete paradigm shifts. Data empirically derived from the reigning paradigm become somehow irreconcilable with the theory and methodology of the time. Novel theories and methodologies begin to explain the disparate phenomenon. This new paradigm knowledge system incorporates the best ideas and practices of the reigning paradigm. For example, human locomotion develops in three relatively distinct phases: crawling, walking, and running. When the paradigm of crawling becomes obsolete, humans begin to walk. Crawling is not eliminated, just used less frequently and only at appropriate times (e.g., like searching for a contact lens on the floor or escaping from a fire). Running at some point supersedes walking; as useful as it is, we just can't move fast enough for certain activities by walking. And, even when the paradigm of running is firmly encoded into humans' locomotion paradigms, walking and crawling are still useful. As a scientific example, although a quantum mechanical model has come into vogue in physics, classical Newtonian mechanics still explains a great deal of nature's laws[3]. Of course, the old paradigm of Newtonian mechanics does not account for a host of nature's processes revealed in the new paradigm of quantum mechanics.

By analogously employing Kuhn we can revisit our discussion of integrating Burrell's and Morgan's and Wilber's perspectives. Because new paradigms subsume and don't actually eliminate preceding paradigms, we can parsimoniously enfold Burrell and Morgan into Wilber to produce a more evolved and valuable paradigm for management. Wilber describes how higher levels of consciousness "transcend but include" (1998: 67) lower levels. Therefore, Wilber's integral paradigm is not a replacement for Burrell and Morgan, merely a more developed version that includes its insights and utilities into a broader, integral scheme. Thus, while Burrell and Morgan promote a mutually exclusive, 'separate but equal' status for paradigms,

---

[3] See Schmidt-Wilk, 1999; Zohar, 1997; and Youngblood, 1997 for background on the two models.

Wilber maintains an inclusive perspective embodying a 'unity-in-diversity' ethos. For Wilber, paradigms are indeed different, yet mutually constitutive (co-created), interdependently, and interconnected evolutionary holarchy of knowledge. There is not an either/or "paradigm war,"[4] rather a both/and notion of complementarity.

Furthermore, Wilber's encompassing philosophy incorporates a crucial admonition by Burrell and Morgan. They strongly advocate "paradigmatic closure" and "isolationism" (1979: 398) between paradigms that is transcended by Wilber. Burrell and Morgan are concerned that "synthesis and mediation between paradigms will engender "emasculation and incorporation within the functionalist problematic" (398). That is, without "self-preservation by developing on their own account" (398), non-functionalist paradigms will be reduced and repackaged through the functionalist lens—"sucked in" as Burrell and Morgan admonish (28). In Wilber's terminology, all of the "I" and WE" quadrants will be reduced to the "monological flatland"[5] of the "IT" and "ITS"—a formula for co-option, imbalance, and "disaster" (1998: 55–56). Wilber's holonic structure for knowledge allows for a simultaneously paradoxical establishment of differing paradigms (diversity) and one integral paradigm (unity)—unity-in-diversity, a satisfying rejoinder to Burrell and Morgan's strong caveat.

This section outlines the possibilities for a spiritually integral paradigm of management. Figure 3 depicts how such a synthesis might look.

Burrell and Morgan's "Subjectivist-Objectivist" axis corresponds nicely with Wilber's "Interior and Exterior" quadrants. Essentially, both models acknowledge that knowledge and reality can be subjectively understood as a product of individual and collective minds, or objectively determined by empirically examining individual and

---

[4] See Pfeffer, 1993; Van Maanen, 1995: 140; Perrow, 1994; Cannella and Paetzold, 1994; Elsbach, 1994.

[5] Wilber (1998) uses "monological" and "flatland" very specifically. "*Monological* comes from 'monologue,' which means a single person talking by him or herself. Most empirical science is monological, because you can investigate, say, a rock without ever having to talk to it" (36). The "'flatland'" conception of the universe as composed basically of matter (or matter/energy), and this material universe, including material bodies and material brains, could best be studied by science, and science alone" (10).

collective behavior. Because all aspects of reality exist simultaneously via Wilber's correlating quadrants, what were once estranged cousins—subjectivity and objectivity—are now unified in a co-determining and co-evolving relationship. Every observable behavioral phenomenon possesses an interior, subjective dimension—like two sides of a coin, inner and outer are inviolably fused: "Consciousness and the external world are viewed as two sides of the same reality. They are locked in a dialectical relationship in which each defines and influences the other" (Burrell and Morgan, 1979: 280 explicating Hegel).

Similarly, Burrell's and Morgan's "Regulation-Change" axis is easily mapped onto the hybrid framework. This axis is primarily concerned with the degree of flux, transformation, and evolution of management knowledge and systems. Likewise, Wilber's evolutionary transcendence reflects a concern for stasis and dynamism. Thus, a complementary dimension of "Regulation-Change" is added to "Evolutionary Transcendence" in the new diagram. At any point from the center of prepersonal materialistic consciousness to the "farther reaches" (Maslow, 1971) of transpersonal spiritual consciousness, regulation or change can occur. For example, there is much regulation involved in the "eye of the flesh" (Wilber)/"functionalist" (Burrell and Morgan) paradigms. At this level of consciousness, the rigors of the scientific method prevail—replication, not revolution is the mantra. Regulation is necessary for proper functioning within the empirical world. High degrees of change, for example, are appropriately found in the "eye of contemplation" (Wilber)/"radical humanist" (Burrell and Morgan) paradigms. "Radical Humanism" is a knowledge system derived from a transpersonal level of consciousness: "the universe is spiritual rather than material in nature" (Burrell and Morgan, 1979: 279). And, "Radical Humanism" also demonstrates a great degree of change where the individual "creates the world in which he lives" (279). Furthermore, this creation is designed to radically overturn, through critique (critical theory), both one's "mode of existence which he creates" (280) and the "essentially alienated state of man" (279). Change is the norm, an elemental principle of evolutionary transcendence—a strong parallelism between Burrell and Morgan and Wilber.

Perhaps the most striking point about combining Burrell and Morgan and Wilber is in the nature of the sociological paradigms

Figure 3:   A Spiritually Integral Theory of Management (Steingard and Fitzgibbons, 2002)

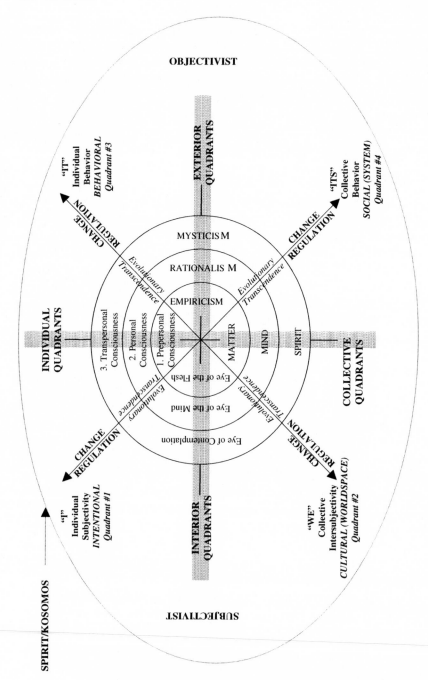

themselves. In Figure 3 there is a conspicuous and deliberate absence of the four paradigms. Where did they go? They have involuted and metamorphosed into their fundamental ontological and epistemological elements. One of the false assumptions underlying these paradigms is their discrete placement on the two continui of subjectivist-objectivist and change-regulation. All methodologies of inquiry and practice are holistically correlated across quadrants; their locations are holographic and mutually constitutive. Functionalism, as we saw with our analysis above, is ultimately not about an exclusively objectivist view of reality. Because it has an interior and collective dimension—co-evolving with individual subjectivity/intentional and collective intersubjectivity/culture, a strictly functionalist outlook is literally impossible. No knowledge system exists in one quadrant, but is integrally comprised across quadrants. Paradigms as we have known them—in the Burrell and Morgan sense—are obsolete, but not forgotten. We can still find the coordinating axes of the Burrell and Morgan schemata in the spiritually integral theory of management, but not rigidly configured with Euclidean coordinates. Subjectivity-objectivity and regulation-change are still vital variables. A sort of quadrangulated validity comes into focus. Now, it is the elemental dimensions of the paradigms that organize inquiry and practice: Wilber's more primordial consciousness and evolutionary transcendence replace the reifying labels of the Burrell and Morgan paradigms. Dissolving the structures of the paradigms creates a methodologically borderless and interconnected field in which truly holistic and interdisciplinary research can unfold. This movement is markedly different from current debates in social science—this revamping (actually restoring) of a spiritually integral theory of management includes but transcends issues like qualitative vs. quantitative, experimenter bias, replicability, generalizability, cross-cultural variables, basic assumptions, and other entrenched issues in research. Because of the "transcend but include" assumption of integral philosophy, the disruption to classical paradigmatic knowledge-making foreshadowed here is paradoxically discontinuous, yet incorporates key aspects of the paradigm it is replacing. The spiritually integral theory of management frees up many possibilities for a profound and impactful re-visioning of management. Now all facets of the beautiful diamond of management can be appreciated.

Table 1: An Integral Evolution of Management Paradigms and Theory

Spirituality in Management Movement as Steward of this Dialectical Process		
THESIS	*ANTITHESIS*	*SYNTHESIS*
Burrell and Morgan's Sociological Paradigms	Wilber's Integral Philosophy	A Spiritually Integral Theory of Management

SPIRITUALITY IN MANAGEMENT AS A VEHICLE TO OPERATIONALIZE A SPIRITUALLY INTEGRAL THEORY OF MANAGEMENT

Thus far, we have established the theoretical potentiality of a spiritually integral theory of management. Every theoretical movement requires a knowledge community to advance praxis. The rising interest in spirituality in management movement is precisely the cultural embodiment of this promising spiritually integral theory of management. Table 1 offers three theses of management theory.

In Hegelian terminology, Burrell and Morgan's paradigms provide the thesis, the starting point to the integral evolution of management paradigms and theory. The catalytic elements of Wilber's integral philosophy serve as the antithesis. A new synthesis of a spirituality integral theory of management is generated. Spirituality in management, as a praxiological intellectual and cultural movement, is the steward for this deep change to management knowledge making and application.

The remainder of this paper examines some of spirituality in management's[6] influence in shaping a spiritually integral theory of management. It also speculates about how the field of spirituality in management might transform in light of a spiritually integral theory of management. Revisiting Figure 2 and building on the integral paradigm conversion discussed above, we gain several new insights. Perhaps the most obvious and exciting is the ability for management research and practice to be genuinely holistic—legitimately integrating the rationally empirical 'outside' of behavior with the subjective (yet no less 'real') 'interior' of phenomenological experience. Meaning,

---

[6] Because there is already a robust plethora of literature established in the field of spirituality in management, we have decided not to review it here.

values, feelings, emotions, and other interior aspects of human beings are now on par and intimately interconnected with exterior behaviorism. The spirituality in management movement is centered upon divinely reinventing work (Fox, 1994) to have more heart (Whyte, 1994) and soul (Bolman & Deal, 1995; DeFoore and Renesch, 1995), be more poetic (Whyte 2001; Windle, 1994), meaningful (Mitroff and Denton, 1999) and even imbued with love (Marcic, 1997).

By coupling this interior dimension with the correlating nature of the quadrants, we create an integrated body-mind-emotion-spirit wholeness (Neal, Forthcoming-a) for managers and management. Management is no longer a disembodied mind trying to operate on the materialistic 'things' of the world—mind, body, emotions, and spirit are always connected in the integral quadrant system. It is an endeavor that involves whole persons—the physical, mental, and spiritual health of human beings. Stress, long working-hours, improper diet, alcohol, tobacco, and other unhealthy behaviors plague a substantial number of Type A managers and researchers. Interestingly enough, yoga, a popular holistic practice that draws on Eastern wisdom traditions, actually means union of mind and body. Mindbody is yoga's integral characterization of how the physiological (exterior) reflects the psychological (interior)—there is no distinction, only different facets of the diamond[7]. Management is already pioneering integral approaches to whole person practice and education (Schmidt-Wilk et al., 2000).

This desire to include subjective dimensions in management research, education, and practice is consonant with the spiritually integral theory of management—a whole new realm of paradigmatically acceptable research is now possible. No longer marginalized, the non-concrete (at least from the exteriorized gaze) is now part of management (although it always was!). Feminist, postmodernist, critical theory, diversity, organizational learning, new science and other innovative, yet peripheral, discourses can now stand alongside traditional approaches as equals. Moreover, since our previous analysis yielded the end to paradigmatic labels for schools of thought, there

---

[7] See Murphy and Donovan (1997) for a good review of "the physical and psychological effects of meditation."

may now be a whole new breed of interdisciplinary work available[8]. Every discipline is now responsible to own its integral foundations: interior/exterior, individual/collective, evolutionary transcendence, and levels of consciousness. It is exciting to imagine the new depth and comprehensiveness available for (formally) marginal paradigms. Likewise, the theoretical elegance and explanatory power of the (formally) mainstream paradigm will flourish as it embraces these new fundamental epistemological and ontological dimensions:

> Ultimately, the dialectical interrelating of the two paradigms [mainstream paradigm and marginal paradigms] will be fruitful for advancing the intellectual profundity and transformative organizational power of both. (Steingard and Schmidt-Wilk, 2001: 311)

The end result of challenging marginal paradigms that champion emancipatory values will be a total transmutation of the modern world of management. Weber's "disenchantment of the world," (cited in Smith, 1989: 105) a deleterious byproduct of the modern bureaucratic state of "scientific management" (Taylor, 1911), is now set to be reenchanted (Moore, 1996; Gablik, 1991; Griffin, 1988; Berman, 1981). The heartless, soulless, alienating, exploitative, environmentally destructive machine of business is now able to resurrect itself from its "monological flatland" (Wilber, 1998) into a humanly inspiring and environmentally sustainable enterprise.

One of the major themes in the spirituality in business literature is the quest for balance and integration (Pierce, 2001; Kremen-Bolton, 2000; Thompson, 2000). Again, we can see the theoretical utility of the spiritually integral theory of management as a framework for understanding the complicated dynamics of work-life integration. From a conventional, dualistic mode of thinking, balancing the competing demands in one's life is basically a suboptimal calculus for dividing a fixed pie—staying home with one's family is detrimental to career advancement, and management success comes at a punishing price of diminished family relations. From an integral, 'both/and' point of view, this "tyrranny of 'either/or'" (Koch, 2001) logic of management

---

[8] For some "new paradigm" interdisciplinary organizational literature see Gustavsson, 2001; Johnson and Macy, 2001; Druhl et al., 2001; Fornaciari and Lund Dean, 2001; Steingard and Schmidt-Wilk, 2001.

(exterior) prosperity vs. life (interior) becomes a non-issue. One's life as a human being is a transcendental unifier of these diverse qualities. Here again we find strong support for the burgeoning spiritually integral theory of management from academics and practitioners of spirituality in management. Management academics are congregating at professional conferences with others interested in integrating their 'whole selves' like the Organizational Behavior Teaching Conference and the Management, Spirituality and Religion interest group of the Academy of Management. They are writing about managers' and entrepreneurs' spiritual processes (Delbecq, 2000), organizations' adventures in becoming more spiritual (Biberman and Whitty, 2000; Barrett, 1998; Guillory, 1997) and their own spiritual adventures as researchers and teachers (Neal, Forthcoming-b; Palmer, 1998; Bolman & Deal, 1995; Neal, 1997; Reason, 1993; and the Special Issue: Spirituality in Management of the *Journal of Management Education*, Volume 24). Entire journals in management education and theory are dedicated to spirituality (*Journal of Organizational Change Management*, Vol. 12, Nos. 3 & 4 plus another forthcoming special issue; a special issue of *Organization*; and Astin and Astin, November, 1999). Overall, the spiritually integral theory of management invites research and scholarship that intrinsically involve the co-constructive subjectivity of the researcher—no longer is the personal dimension of the researcher a contaminant to 'good science'—this evolved form of action research is now essential. Experimenter bias, ironically, after so many years of a "scientistic" (Wolfe, 1982) agenda to sanitize the untoward influence of the researcher, is now the norm for research. Actually, consciousness of this fact produces more ethically aligned research that also brings into being more profound and pragmatic findings.

The concentric circles of consciousness evolution hold a key to the future of management in a spiritually integral paradigm. Radiating from the material world of empiricism outward in a transcendentally evolutionary trajectory, consciousness increases in its ability to incorporate a subtler (spiritual) and encompassing scope of reality. Essentially, as researchers and managers individually and collectively evolve, from the prepersonal to the personal and ultimately to the transpersonal, the more reality is embraced in their research and application. Including more facets of reality will eventually lead to a breakthrough form of management capable of producing viable solutions to world problems. Clearly, management is near mastery in terms of the eye of the flesh/empiricism and the eye of the mind/rationalism. However, without transcending to this more "enlightened"[9] and "Eupsychian" (Maslow, 1998) transpersonal level, management will suffer "metaphysical blindness" (Schumacher, 1993/1973: 38), closing its eye of contemplation/mysticism. Only by looking through this 'third' eye of contemplation toward the spiritual level will new knowledge be cultivated and success be likely—"spiritual intelligence" (Zohar and Marshall, 2000) is a critical faculty in addition to cerebral and emotional intelligence. In this higher dimension of praxis, entire landscapes of fresh ideas become available—opening this third eye makes management's resourcefulness, opportunities, and effectiveness much greater because more of the entire Kosmos is available in decision-making. "Business success" is directly correlated to the degree to which "knowledge of Natural Law [spirit]" is achieved.

> ... [T]he full development of human potential, which is required for business success, depends upon a knowledge of Natural Law [spirit] that goes beyond the accumulation of information, however relevant, and beyond the attainment of technical skills, however sophisticated. (King and Herriot, 1997: 229)

The spirituality of management movement is on the vanguard of helping researchers and managers move along this evolutionary imperative toward higher states of consciousness and a transformative embracing of "Natural Law" (spirit). As Maslow passionately exhorts, this "'higher'" form of psychology underpinning management is the antidote to our getting "sick" when we are firmly rooted in egoistic constructions of ourselves:

> Humanistic Psychology...is now quite solidly established as a viable third alternative to objectivistic, behaviorist psychology and to orthodox Freudianism....There is work to be done here, effective, virtuous, satisfying work which can give rich meaning to one's own life and to others...I should say also that I consider Humanistic, Third Force Psychology to be transitional, a preparation for a still "higher" fourth Psychology, transpersonal, transhuman, centered in the cosmos rather than in human needs and interests, going beyond

---

[9] See Leonard (1994) for a valuable articulation of the difference between Western and Eastern notions of enlightenment.

humanness, identity, self-actualization.... Without the transcendent and the transpersonal, we get sick, violent, and nihilistic, or else hopeless and apathetic. We need something "bigger than we are" to be awed by and to commit ourselves to in a new, naturalistic, empirical, non-churchly sense, perhaps as Thoreau and Whitman, William James and John Dewey did. (Maslow, 1968)

Maslow portends an infinite spiritual realm in which management should be practiced—"centered in the cosmos." This is highly corroborative of the ultimate goal for a spiritually integral theory and practice of management—to simultaneously climb steadily up the quadrants' evolutionary transcendence pathways until one reaches a non-dual state of unity consciousness or, in Vedanta, Brahmin consciousness (Maharishi Mahesh Yogi, 1990/1967) existing "beyond the post-modern mind" (Smith, 1989) and ultimately leading to Self-Realization (Panikkar, 1993; see also Chakraborty, 1997 for a managerial application of an expanded self), or some other conception of ultimate communion with the universe (Capra et al., 1991). One aspires to be a manager of the "Kosmos," functioning at all levels of consciousness, from "dirt to Divinity" (Wilber, 1998).

In the spirituality in business movement, both researchers and managers are actively experimenting with transrational developmental technologies of consciousness like meditation, prayer, yoga, visualization, chanting, spiritually oriented psychotherapy, holistic bodywork, dance, etc[10]. They are moving beyond what Wilber (1999) poignantly distinguishes as "translative" attempts to transcend, and moving into "transformational practices." Spiritually-sourced "transformative practices" are markedly different from "translative" practices which "focus on new ideas or new-paradigms about reality" (Wilber, 1999: 133). These intellectually-sourced practices "simply offer new ways to translate the world, not ways to transform consciousness into subtle, causal, and nondual domains" (133). Essentially, without "genuine contemplative practice—maybe Zen, maybe Shambhala Training, maybe contemplative prayer, or any number of authentic transformative practices"—all intellectual pursuits of Spirit are reduced to "linguistic chitchat and book junk" (Wilber,

---

[10] Teachers are also bringing these technologies into the classroom: Neal, Forthcoming-b; Delbecq, 2000; Palmer, 1998; Nagel, 1994; Neal, 1997; and the *Special Issue: Spirituality in Management* of the *Journal of Management Education*, Volume 24.

1999: 350). While "translation itself is an absolutely necessary and crucial function for the greater part of our lives" (28–29), there is a point where only transformation can provide the boost of evolutionary transcendence necessary to move management into the realm of Spirit and the eye of contemplation:

> But at some point in our maturation process, translation itself, no matter how adequate or confident, simply ceases to console. No new beliefs, no new paradigm, no new myths, no new ideas, will staunch the encroaching anguish. Not a new belief for the self, but the transcendence of the self altogether, is the only path that avails" (29).

Given the burgeoning adoption of non-linear, trans-intellectual, and non-Western ways of knowing, there emerge new possibilities for management development by incorporating Eastern wisdom into management[11]. All types of cross-cultural pollination of ideas and practices are possible because the integral philosophy system purposefully integrates Eastern ways of knowing. Similarly, feminist epistemologies (Alcoff and Potter, 1993) postmodern discourses (Rosenau, 1992), and critical theory (Ingram, 1990) are welcome because all knowledge systems can be located with equal attention and merit somewhere in the unbounded Kosmos of a spiritually integral theory of management.

To note, as we migrate up the evolutionary transcendence continuum, we are not becoming more spiritual and disconnected from the earthly world. Nor if we are slow to progress does it mean we are ignorant and incapable of transcending ordinary states of consciousness. Again, Wilber's "transcend but include" provision suggests that we never lose our feet on the ground. This is due to the entire Kosmos being infused with spirit: "... [A]ll beings and all levels were ultimately enfolded in the all-pervasive and loving embrace of an ever-present Spirit" (Wilber, 1998: 8). Management's entire range of activities—from mundane basic operations to visionary leadership—all originate in Spirit[12]. This means that every act of management and management research is suffused with

---

[11] Efforts in integrating Eastern knowledge into management and its related fields: work (Richmond, 1999), leadership (Heider, 1986), teams (Torres, 1994), career development (Boldt, 1991; Sinetar, 1987), and strategy (Michaelson, 2001).

[12] See Drath (2001) and Owen (1987).

Spirit[13]—there is nothing unholy, disconnected, bounded, alienating, materialistic, or non-evolutionary about management. This insight could spark a renaissance in spirituality in management, helping all people in management find meaning, contribution, and enlightenment in their work.

And this 'Spirit'-ual domain is really the "ground" from which our ontological and epistemological assumptions about management originate. As Harman and Clark (1994) note, in 1924 philosopher of science E. A. Burtt sagaciously illumined these assumptions:

> Burtt pointed out that behind the methodology of science, underpinning all its findings and theories, were a number of assumptions about the nature of the world and the way in which human beings can understand it—ontological and epistemological assumptions—which were neither articulated nor brought into question during the course of normal research. These he called the "metaphysical foundations" (not to be confused with the kind of metaphysics found within the spiritual traditions) because they do not reside within the material world as such, nor can they be proven by empirical experiments, but they form the ground out of which all our conceptual ideas about the physical world arise.

Furthermore, these "metaphysical foundations" offer new possibilities to explore the relationship of consciousness to reality comprehension and construction—almost unheard of in a logical-positivist "IT" world of hard science. A spiritually integral theory of management puts the consciousness of the subject (manager or researcher) as the generating force for reality—"you'll see it when you believe it" (Dyer, 1989). This relocation of the ability to situate reality into the hands of managers and researchers is potentially a huge curative for perceived (and actual) blocks to empowerment. If Spirit as "metaphysical foundations" is used as the basis for managerial thinking and action, then more power is available to combat alienation and technical problems, and for strategizing sustainable, long-term solutions to global exigencies. Spirit's unbounded nature is the always-abundant resource for envisioning new solutions to existing problems or envisioning alternative realities[14].

---

[13] For an excellent immersion of various transpersonal research methods see Braud and Anderson (1998).

[14] For more on how consciousness creates reality see Harman, 1998; Banner and Gagné, 1995; Harman and Clark, 1994; Goswami, 1993; Edelglass et al., 1992; Srivastava and Cooperrider, 1990; Sperry, 1987

It is reasonable to ask at this point, "How does one advance on the evolutionary transcendence continuum of management?" This question is important because, as we have seen, one cannot evolve to transpersonal realms of consciousness and reach her or his full managerial potential without 'getting out of the head'—transcending the tendency to operate in the eye of the flesh and eye of the mind and move to the eye of contemplation.

Perhaps one of the most influential advancements a spiritually integral theory of management can offer is in the area of ethics. Today's management milieu, anesthetized under the spell of instrumental reason, is wallowing in a sea of ethical relativity, moral fecklessness, and aesthetic rigor mortis. That is, because of the collapse of the quadrants into Wilber's functionalist "flatland," managers have not been concerned with conducting management in accord with higher values and principles, only fixated on delivering materialistic, bottom-line, results that can be measured and translated into corporate and personal gain. A spiritually integral theory of management allows these lost domains to be brought into the mainstream processes of management. For example, as meaning matters in a spiritually integral theory of management, exploiting people or the environment as a means to an end is no longer a valid course of action. A manager who transcends the lower stages of prepersonal and personal consciousness will have the acuity and wholeness of vision to make decisions as if she or he were "to take responsibility for the whole" (Harman and Porter, 1997; Harman, 1998) and not just looking out for selfish and materialistic desires associated with these levels of development. It is this personalistic myopia that imperils the healthy functioning and sustainabiltity of person and planet. Transpersonally-conscious managers and researchers will work toward a 'spiritually responsible business'—conducting business affairs as if the well-being of the entire Kosmos were in their hands. Surprisingly, this might appear like self-inflated grandiosity and a serious case of narcissistic delirium. Yet, the purity and efficaciousness of this Kosmic stewardship is possible in these higher states of consciousness where the individual transcends this "skin-encapsulated ego" (Watts in Wilber, 1979) and begins to operate at a much more universal level. Ethically, transpersonally-functioning managers can only make better decisions as more reality is factored into decisions. For example, current enthusiasm for stakeholder management (Carroll and Bucholtz, 2000; Svendsen, 1998; Wheeler and Sillanpaa, 1997) reflects the desire for more omniscient and inclusive decision-making schemes. Stakeholder management and systems theory are precursory steps to managing the Kosmos through transpersonal consciousness. Moreover, as the quadrants open up, other types of bottom-lines will become more commonplace. There are already several non-dualistic conceptions of business operating with an integrated system of profits and principles (e.g., Anderson, 1998; Bollier, 1996; Reder, 1994, 1995; Makower, 1994; Ray and Rinzler, 1993; Chappell, 1993; and Hawken, 1993).

Cultivating the transpersonal consciousness of researchers and managers is a necessary step to producing management knowledge-systems that can transcend the futile duality of either/or constructions of business that, like the unwitting quadrants, implode into the lower, material arena where profits rule at all costs. Wilber suggests that the four quadrants, once expanded from their collapse to the world of "IT" (Wilber, 1998: 76), correspond to the Beautiful (I-intentional-individual subjectivity), the Good (WE-culture-collective intersubjecivity), and the True (IT-behavior-empirical/scientific). Thus, with a spiritually integral theory of management, the pursuit of beauty, goodness, and truth is much more easily facilitated; another bonus of expanding management to the four quadrants and transcending levels of consciousness on an outward trajectory of evolutionary transcendence.

REFERENCE

Alcoff, L. and Potter, E. (Eds.). (1993) *Feminist Epistemologies*. New York: Routledge.

Anderson, R. C. (1998). *Mid-course Correction: Toward a Sustainable Enterprise: The Interface Model*. Atlanta: The Peregrinzilla Press.

Ashmos, D. P. and Duchon, D. (2000). Spirituality at work: A conceptualization and measure. *Journal of Management Inquiry*, 9(2), 134–145.

Astin, A. W. and Astin, H. S. (1999). *Meaning and Spirituality in the Lives of College Faculty: A Study of Values, Authenticity, and Stress*. Los Angeles: Higher Education Research Institute of the University of California, Los Angeles.

Banner, D. K. and Gagné, T. E. (1995). *Designing Effective Organizations: Traditional and Transformational Views*. Thousand Oaks, CA: Sage Publications.

Barrett, W. (1998). *Liberating the Corporate Soul: Building a Visionary Organization*. Woburn, MA: Butterworth-Heinemann.

Berman, M. (1981). *The Re-enchantment of The World*. Ithaca, NY: Cornell University Press.

Biberman, J. and Whitty, M. D. (Eds.). (2000). *Work & Spirit: A Reader of New Spiritual Paradigms for Organizations.* Scranton: University of Scranton Press.

Boldt, L. G. (1991). *Zen and The Art of Making a Living: A Practical Guide to Creative Career Design.* New York: Penguin Books.

Bollier, D. (1996). *Aiming Higher: 25 Stories of How Companies Prosper By Combining Sound Management and Social Vision.* New York: American Management Association/Amacom.

Bolman, L. and Deal, T. (1995). *Leading With Soul: An Uncommon Journey of Spirit.* San Francisco: Jossey-Bass.

Braud, W. and Anderson, R. (1998). *Transpersonal Research Methods for The Social Sciences: Honoring Human Experience.* Thousand Oaks, Calif.: Sage Publications.

Burrell, G. and Morgan, G. (1979). *Sociological Paradigms and Organisational Analysis: Elements of The Sociology of Corporate Life.* London: Heinemann.

Burtt, E. A. (1924). *The Metaphysical Foundations of Modern Physical Science.* London: Routledge and Kegan Paul.

Bygrave, W. (1989). *The Entrepreneurship Paradigm (1): A Philosophic Look at its Research Methodologies, Entrepreneurship Now and Then.* Waco, TX: Baylor University.

Cannella Jr. A. A. and Paetzold, R. L. (1994). Pfeffer's barriers to the advance of organizational science: A rejoinder. *Academy of Management Review,* 19(2), 331–341.

Capra, F., Steindl-Rast, D., and Matus, T. (1991). *Belonging To The Universe: Explorations Of The Frontiers Of Science And Spirituality.* San Francisco, CA: HarperCollins.

Carroll, A. B. and Buchholtz, A. K. (2000). *Business & Society: Ethics and Stakeholder Management.* Cincinnati, OH: South-Western College Publishing.

Chakraborty, S. K. (1997). Wisdom leadership: Leading from the SELF. In W. Harman & M. Porter (Eds.), *The New Business of Business.* San Francisco: Berrett-Koehler.

Chappell, T. (1993). *The Soul Of A Business: Managing For Profit And The Common Good.* New York: Bantam Books.

DeFoore, B. and Renesch, J. (Eds.). (1995). *Rediscovering the Soul Of Business: A Renaissance Of Values.* San Francisco, CA: New Leaders Press.

Delbecq, A. (2000). Spirituality for business leadership: Reporting on a pilot course for MBAs and CEOs. *Journal of Management Inquiry,* 9(2), 117–128.

Drath, W. (2001). *The Deep Blue Sea: Rethinking the Source Of Leadership.* San Francisco: Jossey Bass.

Druhl, K., Langstaff, J., and Monson, N. (2001). Towards a synthesis of the classical and quantum paradigms: Vedic science as a holistic approach to organizational change. *Journal of Organizational Change Management,* 14(4), 379–407.

Dyer, W. W. (1989). *You'll See It When You Believe It: The Way To Your Personal Transformation.* New York: William Morrow and Company.

Edelglass, S., Maier, G., Gebert, H. and Davy, J. (1992). *Matter and Mind: Imaginative Participation in Science.* Edinburgh: Floris Books.

Elsbach, K. D. (1994,). An interview with John Van Maanen. *The Organization and Management Theory Division Newsletter*, 1, 4, 6.

Fornaciari, C. J. and Lund Dean, K. (2001). Making the quantum leap: Lessons form physics on studying spirituality and religion in organizations. *Journal of Organizational Change Management*, 14(4), 335–351.

Gablik, S. (1991). *The Re-enchantment of Art*. London: Thames and Hudson.

Goswami, A. (1993). *The Self-Aware Universe: How Consciousness Creates The Material World*. New York: Jeremy P. Tarcher/Putnam.

Griffin, D. R. (Ed.). (1988). *The Re-Enchantment of Science*. Albany: State University of New York Press.

Guillory, W. A. (1997). *The Living Organization-Spirituality In The Workplace: A Guide For Adapting To The Chaotically Changing Workplace*. Salt Lake City: Innovations International.

Gustavsson, B. (2001). Towards a transcendent epistemology of organizations: New foundations for organizational change. *Journal of Organizational Change Management*, 14(4), 352–378.

Harman, W. (1998). *Global Mind Change: The Promise of The 21st Century*. San Francisco: Berrett-Koehler.

Harman, W. and Clark, J. (Eds.). (1994). *New Metaphysical Foundations of Modern Science*. Sausalito, CA: Institute of Noetic Sciences.

Harman, W. and Hormann, J. (1990). Creative Work: *The Constructive Role Of Business In A Transforming Society*. Indianapolis: Knowledge Systems.

Hawken, P. (1993). *The Ecology of Commerce: A Declaration of Sustainability*. New York: HarperCollins Publishers.

Heider, J. (1986). *The Tao of Leadership: Lao Tsu's Tao Te Ching Adapted For A New Age*. Atlanta: Humanics, Ltd.

Huxley, A. (1944). *The Perennial Philosophy*. New York: Harper and Row.

Ingram, D. (1990). *Critical Theory and Philosophy*. New York: Paragon House.

Johnson, D. B. and Macy, G. (2001). Using environmental paradigms to understand and change an organization's response to stakeholders. *Journal of Organizational Change Management*, 14(4), 314–334.

King, K. and Herriot, S. (1997). Beyond the current paradigm in management thought: Alignment with Natural Law through Maharishi Vedic Management. *Modern Science and Vedic Science*, 7(1), 224–237.

Koch, R. (2001). *The Natural Laws Of Business: How To Harness The Power Of Evolution, Physics, And Economics To Achieve Business Success*. New York: Currency/Doubleday.

Kremen-Bolton, M. (2000). *The Third Shift: Managing Hard Choices in Our Careers, Homes, and Lives As Women*. San Francisco, CA: Jossey-Bass.

Kuhn, T. (1970). *The Structure Of Scientific Revolutions*. Chicago: University of Chicago Press.

Makower, J. (1994). *Beyond The Bottom Line: Putting Social Responsibility To Work For Your Business And The World*. New York: Simon & Schuster.

Marcic, D. (1997). *Managing With The Wisdom of Love: Uncovering Virtue in People and Organizations*. San Francisco, CA: Jossey-Bass.

Maslow, A., Heil, G. and Stephens, D. C. (1998). *Maslow On Management*. New York: John Wiley & Sons.

Maslow, A. H. (1968). *Toward a Psychology of Being* (2nd ed.). New York: Van Nostrand Reinhold.

Maslow, A. H. (1971). *The Farther Reaches of Human Nature*. New York: Penguin/Arkana.

Michaelson, G. (2001). *Sun Tzu: The Art of War For Managers*. New York: Adams Media.

Mitroff, I. A. and Denton, E. A. (1999). *A Spiritual Audit Of Corporate America: A Hard Look At Spirituality, Religion, and Values in the Workplace*. San Francisco: Jossey-Bass.

Moore, T. (1996). *The Re-Enchantment Of Everyday Life*. New York: HarperCollins.

Nagel, G. (1994). *The Tao of Teaching: The Special Meaning of the Tao Te Ching as Related to the Art and Pleasures of Teaching*. New York: Donald I. Fine, Inc.

Neal, J. (Forthcoming-a). Integral learning: Management education for the whole person. In C. Wankel & R. DeFillippi (Eds.), *Rethinking Management Education*.

Neal, J. (Forthcoming-b). Teaching with soul: Support for the management educator. *Journal of Management Systems*.

Neal, J. (1997). Spirituality in management education: A guide to resources. *Journal of Management Education*, 21(1), 121–139.

Owen, H. (1987). *Spirit: Transformation and Development In Organizations*. Potomac, Maryland: Abbott Publishing.

Palmer, P. J. (1998). *The Courage To Teach: Exploring The Inner Landscape Of A Teacher's Life*. San Francisco: Jossey-Bass.

Panikkar, R. (1993). *The Cosmotheandric Experience: Emerging Religious Consciousness*. Maryknoll, NY: Orbis Books.

Pauchant, T. C., & Associates (Eds.). (2002). *Ethics and Spirituality at Work: Hopes and Pitfalls of the Search for Meaning in Organizations*. New York: Quorum Books.

Perrow, C. (1994). Pfeffer slips. *Academy of Management Review*, 19, 191–194.

Pfeffer, J. (1993). Barriers to the advance of organizational science: Paradigm development as a dependent variable. *Academy of Management Review*, 18, 599–620.

Pierce, G. F. A. (2001). *Spirituality@Work: 10 Ways to Balance Your Life On-The-Job*. Chicago, IL: Loyola Press.

Ray, M. and Rinzler, A. (Eds.). (1993). *The New Paradigm In Business: Emerging Strategies For Leadership And Organizational Change*. New York: Jeremy P. Tarcher/Perigree.

Reason, P. (1981). "Patterns of discovery in the social sciences" by Paul Diesing: an appreciation. In P. Reason & J. Rowan (Eds.), *Human Inquiry: A Sourcebook Of New Paradigm Research*. New York: John Wiley & Sons, 183–189.

Reason, P. (1993). Sacred experience and sacred science. *Journal of Management Inquiry*, 2(3), 273–283.

Reder, A. (1994). *In Pursuit of Profit and Principle: Business Success through Social Responsibility.* New York: G. P. Putnam's Sons.

Reder, A. (1995). *Best 75 Business Practices for Socially Responsible Companies.* New York: Jeremy P. Tarcher.

Richmond, L. (1999). *Work as a Spiritual Practice: A Practical Buddhist Approach to Inner Growth and Satisfaction on the Job.* New York: Broadway Books.

Rosenau, P. M. (1992). *Post-Modernism and the Social Sciences: Insights, Inroads, and Intrusions.* Princeton: Princeton University Press.

Schmidt-Wilk, J. and Heaton, D. P. (1999). A quantum metaphor of organizations: Implications for business education. *Business Education Technology Journal,* 1(1), 27–30.

Schmidt-Wilk, J., Heaton, D., and Steingard, D. S. (2000). Higher education for higher consciousness: Maharishi University of Management as a model for spirituality in management education. *Journal of Management Education,* 24(5), 580–612.

Schumacher, E. F. (1993/1973). *Small Is Beautiful: A Study Of Economics As If People Mattered.* London: Vintage.

Sinetar, M. (1987). *Do What You Love, The Money Will Follow: Discovering Your Right Livelihood.* New York: Bantam Doubleday Dell Publishers.

Smith, H. (1989). *Beyond the Post-Modern Mind.* Wheaton, IL: Quest Books.

Smith, H. (1991). *The World's Religions.* San Francisco: Harper Collins Publishers.

Srivastava, S. and Cooperrider, D. (1990). *Appreciative Management and Leadership: The Power of Positive Thought and Action in Organizations.* San Francisco, CA: Jossey-Bass.

Steingard, D. S. and Schmidt-Wilk, J. (2001). Guest editorial: Introduction: New paradigm possibilities for organizational change management. *Journal of Organizational Change Management,* 14(4), 310–313.

Svendsen, A. (1998). *The Stakeholder Strategy: Profiting from Collaborative Business Relationships.* San Francisco: Berrett-Koehler Publishers, Inc.

Taylor, F. (1911). *Principles of Scientific Management.* New York: Harper and Row.

Thompson, C. M. (2000). *The Congruent Life: Following the Inward Path to Fulfilling Work and Leadership.* San Francisco, CA: Jossey-Bass.

Van Maanen, J. (1995). Style as theory. *Organization Science,* 6(1), 133–143.

Wheeler, D. and Sillanpaa, M. (1997). *The Stakeholder Corporation: A Blueprint for Maximizing Stakeholder Value.* London: Pitman Publishing.

Whyte, D. (1994). *The Heart Aroused: Poetry and the Preservation of the Soul in Corporate America.* New York: Currency/Doubleday.

Whyte, D. (2001). *Crossing the Unknown Sea: Work as a Pilgrimage of Identity.* New York: Riverhead Books.

Wilber, K. (1979). *No Boundary: Eastern and Western Approaches to Personal Growth.* Boston: Shambhala.

Wilber, K. (1996). *A Brief History of Everything.* Boston: Shambhala.

Wilber, K. (1998). *The Marriage of Sense and Soul: Integrating Science and Religion.* New York: Random House.

Wilber, K. (1999). *One Taste: The Journals of Ken Wilber.* Boston: Shambhala.

Wilber, K. (2000). *The Collected Works of Ken Wilber: The Revised, Second Edition of Sex, Ecology, Spirituality* (Vol. 6). Boston: Shambhala.

Windle, R. (1994). *The Poetry of Business Life: An Anthology.* San Francisco: Berrett-Koehler.

Wolfe, D. (1982). On the research participant as co-inquirer. Paper presented at the Academy of Management Annual Meetings.

Yogi, M. M. (1990/1967). *Maharishi Mahesh Yogi on the Bhagavad-Gita: A New Translation and Commentary.* New York: Arkana/Penguin Books.

Youngblood, M. D. (1997). *Life at the Edge of Chaos: Creating the Quantum Organization.* Dallas: Perceval Publishing.

Zohar, D. (1997). *Rewiring the Corporate Brain: Using the New Science to Rethink How We Structure and Lead Organizations* (1st ed.). San Francisco: Berrett-Koehler Publishers.

Zohar, D. and Marshall, I. (2000). *Connecting With Our Spiritual Intelligence.* New York: Bloomsburg.

4

.

The Growing Interest in Spirituality in Business: A Long-Term Socio-Economic Explanation

Len Tischler
University of Scranton

INTRODUCTION

There are so many new management ideas and practices occurring in businesses today that it is hard to keep up with them. It seems that almost every year or two there is another "new" way to run a company. Just this decade we have gone from quality to reengineering, to an outward-looking, proactive resource-based view of strategizing for the firm, to information system-based strategies, to EVA, MVA, and share-holder value approaches, to human resource-based strategies. We have moved from the many unrelated diversification mega-mergers of the 1980s to the even larger core-business-centered mergers of the 1990s. There seem to be ever-increasing moves from the real and concrete to the virtual and knowledge-based, and from the independent to the inter-connected in every aspect of running a business. Workers and managers alike are becoming more like independent brokers of their services and knowledge, and are not only looking for money but increasingly for other values such as meaning, personal and professional growth, and even spiritual growth (Drucker, 1993; Renesch & Defoore, 1996; Schmidt & Posner, 1983).

It is this last change that sparked an interest in the topic of this paper. What underlying theory might explain such a movement, especially to spirituality? Why are societies in economically developed countries seeming to move away from a strict focus on money and economic stability and toward also allowing focuses on human growth in a variety of areas? Even more, why are calls for such new focuses being heard and experimented with in businesses? The focus of this paper is to delineate a theory that could explain this trend, especially to spirituality. The theory is based on Maslow's (1943) theory of a hierarchy of needs.

Maslow's (1943) theory of a hierarchy of needs stands the test of time as one of the major theories of motivation in our management and psychology textbooks (Wahba & Bridwell, 1976). Whatever the reasons for its weak empirical showing, the theory seems "obvious" to those who read it, whether school children or sophisticated social scientists. This paper is intended to take Maslow's theory into new territory: the paper will apply the theory to the social level of activity rather than the individual—as a theory of *social* consciousness and motivation. The proposed theory is: as the majority of citizens in any society can be freed from the lower levels of concern, they can, as a society, shift their concern to higher-order needs.

This paper will proceed as follows. First it will review the basics of Maslow's hierarchy of needs theory. Second it will give a brief history of the progress and impacts of the industrial revolution in economically "developed" countries. Third, it will show that there appears to be a relationship between broad economic prosperity and the hierarchy of needs at the social level. Finally it will conclude about implications of this theory.

MASLOW'S HIERARCHY OF NEEDS

There are five basic levels of needs in this theory (Maslow, 1943): physical or survival needs, security needs, social needs, achievement needs, and self-actualization needs. The hierarchical part of the theory is that until an individual is freed from concern about a lower level (order) of need, he cannot be effectively or consistently focused on a higher-order need. Thus, according to the theory, if a worker lives a close-to-subsistence life outside of work, he will work primarily for pay (food, shelter) and will have little motivation or interest in any other kind of human resources benefits or programs. As long as he is intensely concerned for his and his family's daily survival, he cannot have much concern for developing refined social graces, sophisticated language skills, higher-order (and longer-term) achievement skills, or any other higher-order growth. Once freed from such lower-order concerns, however, he can and will begin to explore his higher-order growth needs.

THE HISTORY AND IMPACT OF THE PROGRESS OF THE INDUSTRIAL REVOLUTION

In America and Europe the industrial revolution has evolved over approximately two hundred years. One way to view the quintessential element of this evolution is to focus on its consequent development and spread of economic prosperity: economically "developed" societies have evolved from having most of their population living in almost daily concern about physical survival to having most of their population being free from such concerns. In America and most of Western Europe in the 1990s, even when laid off, most people are not going to starve to death if they are out of work for several months or even for a year or more.

Many elements led to this kind of change: Machines were invented which allowed more goods to be made, transported, and sold at significantly lower costs. Business learned how to plan, organize, lead, and control work and enterprises so that the economy could grow. Social movements grew to try to equalize the power between the wealthy and the masses, leading to unions, anti-trust regulation, the development of corporate and governmental safety nets for workers, and movement toward corporate social and environmental responsibility. We progressed largely with a machine orientation: management reacted to the changing technologies of the time, setting up organizations and practices that matched the technologies (machines), and social movements reacted to management practices that strained people in order to accommodate the technologies or enrich only the few. Additionally, we moved from living in small, self-sufficient communities that changed little, to creating mass societies with rapid change, leading to the need for national-level governmental safety net and responsibility programs to ameliorate the negative impacts of individual economic dislocations and of society-wide and environmental effects (Drucker, 1993; Galbraith, 1967; Reich, 1991).

Recently we have been evolving into a "post-industrial," "information," or "knowledge" age. The hallmarks of this shift appear to be a focus on each individual who is a part of the economy and on the betterment of society. For example, we have increasing empowerment and participation within the company coming from the quality revolution (Deming, 1993; Juran, 1992), from a corporate application of Eighteenth century political theory (Pinchot & Pinchot, 1993), from an insightful understanding of knowledge (as opposed to machines, money, or labor) as the true basis for economic growth (Romer, 1990; Toffler, 1980), from a social conscience (Boje & Dennehy, 1993), and from a hard-nosed understanding of what will make a company more "sustainable" (Magretta, 1997). In addition, we have increasing social voice outside the company with a heavy emphasis on accommodating to customer wants (Deming, 1993; Juran, 1992), increasing private- and public-sector monitoring of safety, quality, and environmental standards (e.g., ISO 9000, ISO 14000, Sierra Club, FDA, OSHA), and a budding social interest in sustainable products and practices (e.g., MADD, SADD). Moreover, we have grown from a recognition that people's perceptions and feelings can affect their work (productivity and quality; Roethlisberger & Dickson, 1966), to a variety of social and technical approaches to try to ameliorate or inspire feelings in ways that will improve productivity and quality (e.g., the human relations and behavioral science approaches). Systems theorists have evolved from a sole focus on quantitative techniques to an equal or primary focus on the human element in business (Deming, 1993; Hammer & Stanton, 1995). We have also moved from "one size fits all" approaches to contingency approaches, which themselves have evolved from only a few macro contingencies to understanding that although there are patterns to be understood, each person and situation is unique (deserves individual attention and respect).

We seem to be moving toward an era of emphasizing that a business does better for its survival and profitability when it creates an environment (culture) that emphasizes "teamwork, customer focus, fair treatment of employees, initiative, and innovation" (*Fortune*, 1998: 218); that emphasizes the betterment of society and the environment

(Gardner, 1990; Greenleaf, 1973; Magretta, 1997; Renesch & Defoore, 1996); and that understands that human motivation is mainly intrinsic (Deming, 1993; Kohn, 1993; Senge, 1990). This last point emphasizes that merely using the old approaches to worker motivation, coercion, or bribery (pay and incentives), will no longer work; it is also becoming necessary for sustainable company growth to offer employees inspiring work and to help employees grow in ways that are best for them. In fact, a growing number of business leaders seem to be wanting to move us toward an era that emphasizes individual self-actualization as both the ultimate human end goal and as the best means to creating even more success and wealth for individuals and companies (Bolman & Deal, 1995; Hendricks & Ludeman, 1996; Herman, 1994; Jaworski, 1998; Renesh & Defoore, 1996).

What we have seen over the past two hundred years, then, is an evolution

- *from* an agrarian society of little change for the majority of people
- *through* an industrial society that through a machine orientation created
- comparatively enormous wealth for most people in developed countries,
- a mass society with attendant changes in social structure, and social consciousness, and
- an unimaginably faster and increasing pace of change
- *to* a post-industrial society that focuses on individual achievement and self-actualization growth for as many people as possible in a socially, economically, and environmentally sustainable and responsible manner.

ECONOMIC PROSPERITY AND THE HIERARCHY OF NEEDS

Another way to view this evolution is through the lens of a hierarchy of human needs. In the agrarian age most people spent their entire lives daily focused on their physical survival and security. Many of the five to ten percent of each society's elite could spend some of their time on higher-order needs (social, esteem, self-actualization), but most people did not have that luxury.

As the industrial revolution created wealth for more people, increasing numbers of people had time and money to spend on more than their survival and security needs. Although most people have not yet gained this extra time, the 1960s generation began to look beyond the "work for money" ethic. They experimented with new types of human relationships (e.g., "free love," communes, co-ops), new ways to build self-esteem (other than business or money achievement), and various approaches to self-actualization (e.g., meditation, yoga, etc.). Their experiments did not directly or quickly infiltrate the business world; rather, they were an early part of the gradual transition from the industrial age to the post-industrial age. The 1960s youth of America and Europe were the first generation in history in which the majority of a society were pretty well assured of physical (economic) survival, stability, and growth. They didn't know hardship, depression, or the ravages of war or major disease. They were free to dream dreams that their parents could not relate to and that horrified their grand-parents. They were being accused of trying to tear down the very fabric of society that led to and underpinned modern prosperity and freedom. Meanwhile, two concurrent forces arose. As workers became increasingly aware that survival was assured even if they lost their jobs, many, especially educated workers, began to want more than just money from their jobs (Drucker, 1993; Galbraith, 1967). They craved more affiliation and esteem values; some even craved self-actualization growth. Moreover, as knowledge has become an increasingly important competitive factor (Davis & Davidson, 1991; Romer, 1990), companies have had to increasingly offer their educated employees many new kinds of opportunities and benefits. Continuous learning, formal and informal, is needed to stay on the cutting edge in each field of knowl-edge. Broader and freer access to in-house and external information is needed. Broader and richer kinds of affiliations are needed: collabora-tion across internal departments and specialty areas, affiliation with external professional and industry groups, teamwork, open, trusting work with suppliers and customers, etc. (Senge, 1990; Wheatley,1992)

More than this, workers who have broken their dependence on an almost exclusive money orientation at work are increasingly intrin-sically motivated (Deming, 1993; Kohn, 1993; Senge, 1990). This has brought about the need for a proliferation of job design elements and their integration (Hackman & Oldham, 1980) and of organizational structures (Galbraith & Lawler, 1993; Levy, 1998), as well as for a new understanding of human behavior (Argyris, 1993; Kohn, 1993; Vaill, 1996). As workers decreasingly look to outer situations, people, and structures to motivate their behavior and impact their feeling and thinking, they look increasingly inward for direction, esteem, and the creation of their own happiness.

Most recently, during the past decade or so, there has been a rising call to include spirituality in our workplaces. In response, for example, the Transcendental Meditation movement of the 1960s and 1970s has developed the "Maharishi Corporate Development Program" for the 1990s (Maharishi Center for Excellence in Management, 1997). The number of conferences about spirituality in business has gone from none to almost a dozen per year in the United States alone in 1998, and several throughout the rest of the world. Books on personal growth and spirituality have continued to proliferate this past decade; the re-markable part of this trend is that many have moved from an exclusive focus on personal, individual growth to bringing this growth into the workplace and to corporate transformation using similar approaches or principles (Bolman & Deal, 1995; Hendricks & Ludeman, 1996; Herman, 1994; Jaworski, 1998; Renesh & Defoore, 1996; Wheatley, 1992).

CONCLUSION AND IMPLICATIONS

In summary, we have seen that as the industrial revolution progressed in societies, it produced widespread prosperity. As a large portion of a society becomes free from the need to focus almost exclusively on physical and security needs for survival, it appears that the society as a whole can move in the direction of focusing on the higher needs: social, esteem, and self-actualization, including spirituality. We have seen this occur so far in the United States and in the economically "developed" countries of Europe. This trend seems to point to a hierarchy of human needs at the social level. Such a theory of social change can offer us new ways to understand many of the social changes of our time, including our rising interest in spirituality in business.

This theory can also shed light on some of the difficulties of the less economically developed societies that are trying to move up the economic ladder. The spread of wealth in a society does not immediately change social outlooks and attitudes; social changes seem to lag behind economic prosperity by a generation or two. Trust must evolve over time that the system will support the population economically even in hard times. In addition, it is not the overall wealth of a society that leads to social change toward higher-order levels of concern, but the spread of wealth to a majority of the society's people over time.

This theory can also help us to predict conditions that would lead to a deterioration of a society from a higher-order focus to a lower-order focus: when economic conditions deteriorate dramatically, or when the economy shifts so that wealth is again hoarded by a few, and the majority are back to worrying about their short-term survival. On the other hand, it could be possible that if a society can spread and sustain its higher-order mentality long enough, a new, higher-order consciousness could develop which locks the society into this mentality and in return supports the continuation of an economy that sustains the majority of the society's people.

REFERENCE

Argyris, C. (1993), *Knowledge for Action: A Guide to Overcoming Barriers to Organizational Change*, Jossey-Bass, San Francisco, CA.

Boje, D. M., & Dennehy, R. E. (1993), *Managing in the Post Modern World: America's Revolution Against Exploitation*, Kendall/Hunt, Dubuque, IA.

Bolman, L. G., & Deal, T. E. (1995), *Leading with Soul: An Uncommon Journey of Spirit.* Jossey-Bass, San Francisco, CA.

Davis, S., & Davidson, B. (1991), *2020 Vision*, Fireside, New York.

Deming, W. E., (1993), *The New Economics for Industry, Government, Education*, MIT Center for Advanced Engineering Study, Cambridge, MA.

Drucker, P. F., (1993), *Post-capitalist Society*, HarperBusiness, New York.

Fortune (1998), "What Makes a Company Great?" October 26, p. 218.

Galbraith, J. R., Lawler, E. E., & Associates (1993), *Organizing for the Future: The New Logic for Managing Complex Organizations*, Jossey-Bass, San Francisco, CA.

Galbraith, J. K. (1967), *The New Industrial State*, Houghton Mifflin, Boston, MA.

Gardner, J. W. (1990), *On Leadership*, The Free Press, New York.

Greenleaf, R. K. (1973), *The Servant as Leader*, Center for Applied Sciences, Peterborough, NH.

Hackman, J. R., & Oldham, G. R. (1980), *Work Redesign*, Addison-Wesley, Reading, MA.

Hammer, M., & Stanton, S. A. (1995), *The Reengineering Revolution: A Handbook*, HarperBusiness, New York.

Hendricks, G., & Ludeman, K. (1997), *The Corporate Mystic: A Guide-book for Visionaries with Their Feet on the Ground*, Bantam Books, New York.

Herman, S. M. (1994), *The Tao at Work: On Leading and Following*, Jossey-Bass, San Francisco, CA.

Jaworski, J. (1998), *Synchronicity: The Inner Path of Leadership*, Berrett-Koehler, San Francisco, CA.

Juran, J. M. (1992), *Juran on Quality by Design: The New Steps for Planning Quality into Goods and Services*, The Free Press, New York.

Kohn, A. (1993), *Punished by Rewards: The Trouble with Gold Stars, Incentive Plans, A's, Praise, and Other Bribes*, Houghton Mifflin, Boston, MA.

Magretta, J. (1997), "Growth Through Global Sustainability," *Harvard Business Review*, Jan–Feb 1997, 75 (1), pp. 78–88.

Maharishi Center for Excellence in Management (1997), "The Maharishi Corporate Development Program," *Web*: www.tm.org/mcdp/index2.html.

Maslow, A. H. (1943), "A Theory of Human Motivation," *Psycho-logical Review*, 50, pp. 370–396.

Pinchot, G., & Pinchot, E. (1993), *The End of Bureaucracy & the Rise of the Intelligent Organization*, Berrett-Koehler, San Francisco, CA.

Reich, R. B. (1991), *The Work of Nations: Preparing Ourselves for 21st Century Capitalism*, Alfred A. Knopf , New York.

Renesch, J., & Defoore, B. (eds.) (1996), *The New Bottom Line: Bringing Heart and Soul to Business*, New Leaders Press, San Francisco, CA.

Roethlisberger, F. I., & Dickson, W. I. (1966), *Management and the Worker*, Harvard University Press, Cambridge, MA.

Romer, P. (1990), "Endogenous Technical Change," *Journal of Political Economy*, 98 (5) Part 2, pp. 71–102.

Schmidt, W. H., & Posner, B. Z. (1983), *Managerial Values in Perspective*, American Management Association, New York.

Senge, P. M. (1990), *The Fifth Discipline: The Art and Practice of the Learning Organization*, Doubleday Currency, New York.

Toffler, A. (1980), *The Third Wave*, William Morrow, New York.

Vaill, P. B. (1996), *Learning as a Way of Being*, Jossey-Bass, San Francisco, CA.

Wahba, M. A., & Bridwell, L. G. (1976), "Maslow Reconsidered: A review of research on the need hierarchy," *Organizational Behavior and Human Performance*, 16, pp. 212–240.

Wheatley, M. (1992), *Leadership and the New Science: Learning About Organization from an Orderly Universe*, Berrett-Koehler, San Francisco, CA.

5

.

Spirituality at Work:
An Overview

** Dan Butts **

Health Psychologist, Columnist on Social Issues

In the past decade there have been a torrent of thoughtful papers, as we have in this journal, dealing with the role of spirituality at work. Three of the many excellent books on different aspects of this enormously rich, complex, and often confusing topic are: *The Soul of a Business: Managing for Profit and the Common Good* by Tom Chappel, President of "Tom's of Maine"; *The Reinvention of Work: A New Vision of Livelihood for Our Time* by Matthew Fox, ex-priest and founder of Creation Spirituality; and *The Fourth Wave: Business in the 21st Century* by consultant Herman Bryant Maynard, Jr., and trend analyst Susan E. Mehrtens.

What then is spirituality? What goes on in church? New age religions? A set of impractical beliefs? A private experience with little value in working? A state of consciousness? Soul work? Contemplative practices like meditation or prayer? Time-honored principles and tools for living and working with more joy and success? A transpersonal state of human development (beyond individual, skin-encapsulated ego) with new values, priorities, and skills, which is also laying a foundation for a new bottom line?

What's needed is sufficient clarity and theoretical understanding of the meaning of spirituality and how it can apply to work, especially in terms of personal satisfaction, peak performance, and overall business success that can also enrich communities, cultures, and the Earth itself.

Business owners, managers, policymakers, and academic researchers all need to remember, as many surveys indicate, that tens of millions of world citizens are hungering for transmaterial, mind-expanding, soul-enriching, and heart-centered (spiritual) values.

Thomas Moore, popular writer of several books on the soul such as *Care of the Soul: A Guide for Cultivating Depth and Sacredness in Everyday Life* (1992), points in the right direction by telling us how to add spirituality and cultivate soul through more depth, meaning, and the restoration of the sacred in our everyday lives.

ULTIMATE VALUES

One useful way of integrating spirituality in the workplace is through *sacred/ultimate/whole-system values* which enable the human spirit to grow and flourish. These time-honored, life-affirming, and unifying values, which can also enhance profit and productivity, include truth and trust (which liberate the soul), freedom and justice (which liberate creative and co-creative genius), creativity (innovation), collective harmony and intelligence (wholeness, synergy), deeper meaning, and higher purpose. Peters and Waterman (1982) reported that employees perform most energetically, creatively, and enthusiastically when they believe they are contributing to a higher purpose.

OPTIMAL HUMAN DEVELOPMENT

Full or optimal human development, or, to use current business terms, maximizing human capital, is another direction for spirituality at work. Social psychologist Abraham Maslow's "hierarchy of human needs" suggests that if work helps to fulfill personal survival and security needs, and social, self-esteem, and ego needs, then employees would tend to become more oriented toward higher self-actualization and being (spiritual) needs. Maslow (1970) also wrote on human values and peak experiences.

Early in the 1990s, Peter Senge (1990, 1993) introduced the model of the learning organizations new workplace paradigm that provides a fertile landscape for the cultivation of soul and spiritual values. Senge, the director of the Center for Organizational Learning at MIT's Sloan School of Management, has a model and popular training program consisting of five disciplines (skills and tools) for creating a highly effective organization: shared vision, personal mastery, new mental models, team learning, and systems thinking.

Social psychologist Daniel Goleman (1995, 1998) has developed the idea of *emotional intelligence,* which integrates a range of skills in three critical areas of soul development and practice at work and in life. This model is also consistent with the emerging team-based organizational paradigm which requires that managers and workers develop a higher level of self-discipline, interpersonal and ethical skills (emotional intelligence): knowing one's emotions (self-awareness); managing emotions (self-control and resilience); self-motivation (creativity); recognizing emotion in others (empathy); handling relationships (social and organizational skills, handling diversity, resolving conflicts, transformational leadership).

TRANSCENDENCE IN THE WORKPLACE

Psychologist Mihaly Csikszentmihalyi (1990), in his 25-year research on optimal *experience (flow),* has identified the characteristics of work (and life) experience that can liberate human spirit and creativity. In his research with surgeons and other groups, he found clear goals, total immersion in the activity, transcendence of ego boundaries and merging with the environment, and high levels of motivation, self-confidence, competence, enjoyment, and other intrinsic rewards.

For the past two decades, enlightened companies have encouraged employees to participate in various human potential programs or what could be called psychospiritual disciplines or technologies. Meditation, prayer, and guided imagery (visioning or "futurizing") are three of the more common practices. Course on Miracles, shamanic journeying, and various yogic paths are also of growing interest in corporate America.

There are six essential elements, all of which are important at work, "that constitute the heart and *art of transcendence*" in all major religions and spiritual growth traditions: "ethical training; development of concentration; emotional transformation; a redirection of motivation from egocentric, deficiency-based needs to higher motives, such as self-transcendence; refinement of awareness; and the cultivation of wisdom" (Walsh & Vaughan, 1993).

Emotional transformation involves releasing destructive emotions such as fear and anger, and cultivating positive emotions such as equanimity, joy, love, and compassion. Ethics is widely regarded as an essential foundation of mental training and transpersonal (spiritual) development. Unethical behavior both stems from and reinforces destructive mental factors such as greed, anger, and hatred. Conversely, ethical behavior dissipates these and cultivates positive mental factors such as calm, kindness, and compassion (ibid., pp. 48–50). Ultimately, after transpersonal maturation occurs, ethical behavior is said to flow spontaneously as a natural expression of identification with all people and all life (universal, cosmic, or Christ consciousness).

SPIRITUAL PSYCHOLOGIES

Transpersonal psychology, which began about 25 years ago as an extension of humanistic or existential psychology, encompasses authentic living and working, realms of consciousness far beyond ordinary waking consciousness, soul-liberating disciplines like meditation, and transpersonal experiences extending beyond (trans) the individual or personal to embrace wider aspects of humankind, life, psyche, and cosmos. Jungian psychology reminds us of the archetypal depths and power of the collective unconscious and the therapeutic potency of images, myths, and symbols.

Asian systems such as Buddhist, yogic, Vedantic, and Taoist psychologies complement Western approaches by describing stages of transpersonal development and providing techniques for realizing them. Taoism, for example, is based on the integration of the yin and the yang, or the female and male energies or principles of consciousness (or leadership). Yoga psychology recognizes seven chakras, or subtle energy systems, that have various correspondences including personality type and levels of consciousness. Buddhist psychology recognizes that all our individual and social (and work-related) pathologies are based on aversions, addictions, delusions, and dualisms.

In future issues of the JOCM, we will explore other critical dimensions of spirituality at work including ethics and community, the essential organizational context for both learning and spiritual growth (see *Community Building: Renewing Spirit & Learning in Business* edited by K. Gozdz, 1995).

REFERENCE

Chappell, T. (1993), *The Soul of a Business: Managing for Profit and the Common Good*, Bantam Books, New York.

Csikszentmihalyi, M. (1990), *Flow: The Psychology of Optimal Experience*, Harper & Row, New York.

Fox, M. (1994), *The Reinvention of Work: A New Vision of Livelihood for Our Time*, HarperCollins, New York.

Goleman, D. (1995), *Emotional Intelligence: Why it can matter more than IQ*, Bantam Books, New York.

Goleman, D. (1998), *Working with Emotional Intelligence*, Bantam Books, New York.

Gozdz, K. (Ed.) (1995), *Community Building: Renewing Spirit & Learning in Business*, New Leaders Press, San Francisco, CA.

Maslow, A. (1970), *Religions, Values, and Peak-Experiences*, Viking Press, New York.

Maynard, H. B., & Mehrtens, S. E. (1993), *The Fourth Wave: Business in the 21st Century*, Berrett-Koehler, San Francisco, CA.

Moore, T. (1992), *Care of the Soul: A Guide for Cultivating Depth and Sacredness in Everyday Life*, HarperCollins, New York.

Peters, T., & Waterman, R. H. (1982), *In Search of Excellence: Lessons from America's Best-Run Companies*, Harper & Row, New York.

Senge, P. (1990), *The Fifth Discipline: The Art & Practice of the Learning Organization*, Currency Doubleday, New York.

Senge, P., et al (1994), *The Fifth Discipline Fieldbook: Strategies and Tools for Building a Learning Organization*, Currency Doubleday, New York.

Walsh, R., & Vaughan, F. (Eds.) (1993), *Paths Beyond Ego: The Transpersonal Vision*, Tarcher/Pedigree, Los Angeles, CA.

6

■

Festivalism at Work: Toward Ahimsa in Production and Consumption

David M. Boje
New Mexico State University

My spiritual teacher, Gurudev Chitrabhanu, is a Jain monk who worked alongside Gandhi and spent twenty years walking about India with a message of non-violence. He now spends half his time in Mumbai and the other leading and inspiring the Jain communities in the United States. In November 1997, I toured India with my wife Grace Ann Rosile and Gurudev Shree Chitrabhanu. As I saw India, I was even more resolved than before, that world capitalism is a tragic coevolutionary play led by the spectacle of inhumanity to all sentient beings. I saw the world's future if we are not able to coevolve in more sensitive ways; it was written all over the streets of Mumbai, in people and animals sleeping in doorways, in the faces of starving children. Gurudev is a former Jain monk, now a spiritual teacher of non-violence. Gurudev says, "the decision is up to us to be violent or non-violent." He vows no harm to any sentient being.

Satish Kumar, also a Jain monk, after walking halfway around the world promoting peace and disarmament, settled in England. Satish founded Schumacher College, named after E. F. Schumacher, the author of *Small Is Beautiful*. Schumacher's (1973) book, *Small Is Beautiful:*

Economics as If People Mattered, challenges the concepts of unlimited growth, predatory competition, and violent forms of production and consumption. In bringing Jain teachings of non-violence to Western countries, both Satish and Gurudev have endured much criticism. Decades ago, it was considered highly inappropriate for Jain monks to use modern transportation systems and travel abroad. Both speak to the discontent people in the West experience with a crisis of identity and meaning, from spectacle lifestyles of over consumption and violent production. Both spend hours each day in meditation to separate from the influences of what I call spectacle. Ahimsa teaching has had a profound impact on major figures.

Reverend Martin Luther King Jr., for example, applied Ahimsa non-violent teachings of social change. His nonviolent Civil Rights marches, open prayers, and other forms of protest captured the imagination of millions who did not realize that there were violent racial relations all around them. Nonviolent action brings about awareness, and it is then up to people to make their own choices. But, spectacle does not reform so easily. It is able to appropriate a reform movement and make it part of spectacle appeal. For example, Cohen and Solomon (1995) comment on how Martin Luther King's life story has become part of the annual media spectacle of his ritualized annual holiday television consumption.

> What TV viewers see is a closed loop of familiar file footage: King battling desegregation in Birmingham (1963); reciting his dream of racial harmony at the rally in Washington (1963); marching for voting rights in Selma, Alabama (1965); and finally, lying dead on the motel balcony in Memphis (1968).

Spectacle is selective in its storytelling. What the ritualized King spectacle leaves out in its annual tributes is how in the last years of his life Reverend King turned his attention to the growing gap between rich and poor. King observed that a majority of Americans below the poverty line, and these were mostly white folks. The year of his assassination, he was calling for radical changes in the distribution of wealth and proposing a poor man's march on Washington, D.C. Ahimsa and Gandhi influenced these three spiritual leaders.

Mahatma Gandhi was also deeply influenced by the Ahimsa philosophy. Ahimsa is part of the three-millennia Jain philosophy of India (Yashovijayji, 1974). To Gandhi "not to hurt any living thing" is an important part of Ahimsa, but not the most important element.[1] The important elements are to avoid hatred, lying, wishing ill, and to realize that millions of microorganisms live in and around us. Ahimsa is not just non-violence; it is unconditional love combined with self-control.

> To hear suggestive stories with the ears, to see suggestive sights with the eyes, to taste stimulating food with the tongue, to touch exciting things with the hands, and then at the same time expect to control the only remaining organ is like putting one's hands in the fire, and expecting to escape being burnt.[2]

Gandhi's choice was to be celibate to sustain his self-control. Gandhi sought alternatives to silk production, a process that kills the silk worms during the manufacturing process. I attended the Gandhi Institute and observed one of his inventions, a cotton spinning machine that any person with a bit of training and patience can operate. He distributed the spinning machines to create an alternative to the then British controlled manufacture of cotton and the nation's dependency on silk garments. My friend Susan Segall brought back this factory in a box machine so that I might also meditate while I spin threads. It takes a lot of patience and higher levels of skill than I now possess. It does allow me to meditate on non-violent options in my own production and consumptive practice. I am eager to find non-violent patterns of living in a world saturated with violence. In what follows I want to apply Ahimsa philosophy to a different understanding of what I study as "spectacle and festival."

Spectacle is above all a legitimating narrative for social engineering and social control masking the violent (non-Ahimsa) acts of production and consumption. By spectacle I mean Debord's (1967) *Society of the Spectacle*, the often violent and oppressive social control that masquerades as a celebration of betterment by recycling pseudo-reforms, false desires, and selective sightings of progressive evolution, never devolution. By violent I mean the willful and careless and often unnecessary disruption or extinction of the life of another, including the life of non-human species. "The spectacle is the moment when the commodity has attained the *total occupation* of social life" (#42). "In particular the ways in which technical development becomes a substitute

[1] Gandhi's Non-Violent Resistance, p. 41.
[2] Ibid, p. 45.

for natural development" (#24, 36). "Last year, Americans, who make up only five percent of the world's population, used nearly a third of its resources and produced almost half of its hazardous waste" (Affluenza, 1997). The Situationaliste answer to the ideological social control of spectacle is festival, by which we self-manage and self-produce our own production and consumption practices. In this way we redefine our needs and desires.

Festival is the "very keynote of the life" I see beyond a critique of spectacle . . . *Play* is the ultimate principle of this festival, and the only rules it can recognize are to live without dead time and to enjoy without restraint (Situationist International, 1966: 14). Many cities and nations still conduct annual festivals, a tradition that goes back centuries in many parts of the world. Yet, the festivals have taken on thick outer spectacle shells, becoming gaudy consumption rituals, without much referentiality to what makes a festival festive in the first place. Most organizing attempts of festival find they are mutating due to their organizing situations into bizarre affairs. The Pittsburgh Irish Festival, for example, features a Bingo Tent, Dog Tents, and a Gaelic Mass. Is this a strange or suitable organization? Perhaps it is a collage of spectacles more than a festival. Or, perhaps it is the bizarre juxtaposition that keeps it festive. Festival was once about narratives and theatrics that reversed or otherwise parodied the portrait of power. On Fool's Day, the peasants became magistrates, clergy, and nobles, while all these elites took on lesser positions. In the Tomato Festival, people tossed tomatoes at everyone and on the next day life went back to its normal spectacle routines.

The pre-capitalism festival ways of life were appropriated and transformed by spectacle capitalism. Festival has been replaced by spectacles of theatrical consumption (the mall and the stores in the mall) as well as by spectacular organizations (producers of spectacles and themselves spectacles). The peasant is everywhere, composing as much as two-fifths of the world's population, many working at slave wages to provide the spectacle to the advantaged. The peasants sit on the margins of spectacle, ready to reclaim cyclical time and local spaces, and perhaps replace spectacle with festival.

The festival had something to do with one's conscious awareness, and with a focusing of that awareness. Festival is defined as expressing inner happiness in a context of social activity. Spectacle is defined as material displays of happiness in a context of over consumption. When festival is more about materialism than play, self-reflection, and social commentary, it becomes disempowered, just another spectacle. When the message of festival is in the externalities, the inner spirituality of the event is suspect.

Consider the similarities. Both spectacle and festival combine theatrics, storytelling, crafts, and other arts into a community of performance. Both festival and spectacle incorporate food, story, theatrics, music, art, and other entertainment. I want to open up the question of what is festival for more rigorous exploration. They are oftentimes found together, occupying the same time and place. The same work organization has both festive and spectacle garniture. Two people can be in the same organization, doing the same job, for the same boss. One sees festive situations; another sees spectacles of misery, self-indulgence, and addictions to overproduction and conspicuous, even eco-destructive consumption. One will experience a sense of joy; the other will find only frustration. Many events with the label "festival" do not appear to be festivals at all to all of the participants. I want to show the basis of festive and spectacle processes in modern organizations.

Shakespearean Festivals, Renaissance Festivals, Craft Festivals, Harvest Festivals (dates, chili, wine, apple, etc.), Film Festivals, and Music Festivals are all the rage. They define the community, but so do spectacles. Disneyland, a modern organization spectacle, defines Los Angeles County, though it is really located in Orange County. Renaissance Festivals, oftentimes, reenact fifteenth and sixteenth century Europe as a celebration of cyclical time and a local reverence for place, even though they are reenacted outside of Europe, in places like Kansas and Idaho. Yet most of festival is not separate from spectacle. It seems every state in the Union and most countries have their festivals and their spectacles, without much differentiation between what is one and the other.

What is a Festival Organization?—Be it simple or complex, behind the festival stalls, booths, theater, exhibitions, and merchandising, there is the festival organization, and perhaps a spectacular one masquerading as festive. Some festival organizations construct fictive fantasies of the good olds days of King Arthur Knights of the Round Table or Elizabethan splendor in a Renaissance Festival. Spectators are invited to come dressed as princesses, wenches, noblemen, and barbarians, as they enjoy the jousting and feasting. Others go to great length to make the historical period become "living history." They re-create the architecture, dress, and customs of a particular epoch. Yet, in many cases, they are no more authentic than the Pirates of the Caribbean or the Haunted Mansion at Disneyland are. The sense of "authenticity" of a festival, be it a Renaissance Faire, Shakespearean Theater, or Bluegrass Music Festival, varies from one situation to the next. The name "festival" in the title of the event is not a way to tell its pedigree.

There is much contemporary spectacle mixed into the festival. For example, the Colorado Renaissance Festival advertises that for a price you and fifty guests can be part of a Royal Wedding. For just $2,500 you can have the fairy tale wedding managed by expert wedding coordinators, complete with the melodious murmur of the King's bagpiper, escorting you to the newly refurbished Canterbury Chapel where you will be a player in an Elizabethan Wedding Ceremony. A King and Queen wedding feast follow this wedding. Costuming and wet bar are extra. Is there something in Jain philosophy that can help us sort this out?

> In Jain teachings there is a story about a prince who is about to marry. Just before the wedding feast, he observes the preparations. He sees a courtyard full of cages of all the various animals about to be slaughtered for his wedding feast. The moment is transformative. He decides to become a monk, and seeing his example, his bride elects to become a nun. They each lived lives of renunciation. To me, the meaning of the story is that the couple developed conscious awareness of the difference between a festival and a spectacle. They developed conscious awareness of a spectacle of material celebration and saw that this path would not lead them to attain higher spiritual values. Instead, they chose to renounce material possession and material violence in favor of non-violence and simplicity.

Ahimsa is a modification and reform of spectacle, a way to live spectacles that are non-violent. Festival can be antispectacle; it can lie beyond spectacle, in ways that I envision being non-violent. Festival is not an escape from spectacle. The practical concern of Ahimsa is with worker and community health and safety; alternatives to child labor and prison labor; living wages; enlightened work conditions; freedom of worker association; ecological sustainability; globally equitable pro- duction and consumption practices; future generations. Festival is doing something proactive about inequality. Two hundred twenty-five

Table 1: Spectacle and Festival

Spectacle	Festival
1. Work	1. Play
2. Work or play time	2. Work and play
3. Imposed patterns of behavior	3. Freely constructed behavior
4. Dead time	4. Live time
5. Religions of consumption	5. Self
6. Pseudo-desires	6. Transparent desires
7. Pseudo-needs	7. Transparent needs
8. Loss of self	8. Self-management
9. Colonized spaces	9. Free spaces
10. Spectator	10. Participant/co-designer
11. Functionary	11. Self-managed
12. Survival of the fittest/richest	12. Coevolution and co-survival

billionaires now have more annual income than half the planet's 6.1 billion population. The festival is an attempt to make leisure more important than work.

We do not see the spectacles we grow up in, we do not see who makes our products, and we do not even glimpse how violent the production process has become. All we see are the glitzy lights at the mall, the sexy displays of TV ads, and the corporate claims to excellence on all web sites.

On the Relations of Violence to Spectacle—the Society of the Spectacle desensitizes its participants to violence, in what Whitmer (1997) calls the "Violence Mythos." The myth here is a self-sealed logic of violence legitimation. Violence is everywhere, in the streets, in schools, in the workplace, and in the home. Our children scream if we deny them a Nintendo kill-game of "realistic" violence. Beneath the spectacle illusion of progress through technology and gadget accumulation-equals-happiness lies the brutality and cruelty to animals, humans, and mother earth to sustain our lifestyles. I seek to enter the festive world, to walk and breathe real life "situations" as an active yet non-violent participant, not a passive spectator in everyday life space. I was socialized to accept and tolerate violence and to consume violence willingly as leisure.

It is often assumed that the most technologically advanced economies are the least violent. The United States is the most violent of all industrialized nations on the planet with the least safe places to live and work. According to a 1994 Justice Department report, nearly one million violent crimes occur in the workplace each year. There were more than 6,200 deaths on the job due to traumatic injuries in the United States in 1997. The death toll from work-related disease is nearly 10 times higher (Weissman, 1999). There were more than 6 million work-place-related injuries and illnesses recorded in 1997, with more than 1.8 million of them causing time lost from the job. The United States has the highest rates of childhood homicide, suicide, and firearms-related death among all of the industrialized countries. In 1995 alone, 35,957 Americans were killed with firearms, in homicides, suicides, and accidents (National Center for Health Statistics, 1997). Every day in 1994, 16 children aged 19 and under were killed with guns (National Center for Health Statistics, 1994). Firearms kill more people between the ages of 15 and 24 than all natural causes combined (National Center for Health Statistics, 1994).

Empirical research is consistent in its findings. According to the American Psychological Association's 1993 report, "Violence and Youth: Psychology's Response," there are not just one but four long-term effects of viewing violence:

1. Increased aggressiveness and anti-social behavior
2. Increased fear of being or becoming a victim
3. Increased desensitization to violence and victims of violence
4. Increased appetite for more and more violence in entertainment and real life

The long-term impact of children growing up watching thousands of hours of violence is that they role model what they see in the spectacle of violence. The Center for Media and Public Affairs reports that the total number of violent scenes in entertainment programming increased by 74% in three years—from 1,002 in 1992 to 1,417 in 1994, to 1,738 in 1995—reaching an average of nearly 10 incidents of violence per channel per hour during the most recent season, even after excluding commercials and all non-fiction programming.[3]

---

[3] Center for Media and Public Affairs. "Study Finds Rise in TV Guns and Violence Cable Movies and Cartoons Are Culprits, Not the Networks." September 11, 1996 http://www.cmpa.com/archive/viol95.htm

Violence is also increasing among spectators. After the Vancouver Canucks lost the Stanley Cup, 70,000 mad fans took their violence to the streets, amid clouds of tear gas. Some 200 people were injured including two with critical head injuries.[4]After the Detroit Tigers won the 1984 World Series, United States fans in Detroit and Chicago took their violence to the street, again destroying property and one another. Seventy-three University of Wisconsin students were crushed against a fence after a 13–10 win over Big Ten rival Michigan.

Violence is not only increasing in frequency in TV and movies, it is also increasing as a way of advertising. Violence in commercials also rose 30% since 1992. The 948 violent scenes tabulated during commercials in 1995 nearly equaled the 1,002 violent scenes recorded during all entertainment programming in 1992. Ads have a few moments to show something interesting enough to attract the viewer. The easy way out is to show something violent.

"Land Ethic" and Non-Violence. There is a close parallel between Leopold's "Land Ethic" and Ahimsa. Both see ignorant interference in the evolution of other species as a form of violence. Leopold's "biotic pyramid" defines ecology as an interdependent web of life, which includes the land.

| Larger Carnivores |
| Omnivores—bears, racoons, man |
| Herbivorous mammals |
| Insect-eating birds and rodents |
| Plant-eating insects |
| Plants |
| Soil |

Leopold contended that undisciplined human technology (e.g., guns, strip mining tractors, and laws allowing for mass extermination of wolves and other species) resulted in violence to the biotic web of life. Leopold's (1949) "Land Ethic" can be stated very simply: "A thing

---

[4] Robert Lee "Fan sports violence also common in United States" July 7, 1994
http://beaconwww.asa.utk.edu/issues/v66/archives/www/v66/n11/violence.11l.html

is right when it tends to preserve the integrity, stability, and beauty of the biotic community. It is wrong when it tends otherwise." The contemporary result of land ethics is the bioethics movement (Koch, 1992):

> Through technology, we are rapidly changing the earth. These changes have accelerated as man moved from a hunter/food gatherer to a member of an agricultural society and finally into the industrial age. Many of the present technological changes are irreversible, damaging to the land and clashing with our increasing scientific knowledge of how biotic communities function. Individuals are faced with a moral environmental responsibility.

Ahimsa is not about blame, it is about finding alternatives to violence, and letting people find their own way. Ahimsa, for me, recognizes that you just do not wake up one morning and turn off the television, turn vegetarian, and the next morning awaken in a non-violent world. Rather, it is a matter of cultivating a taste for non-violence in a spectacle that encourages just the opposite. It is the path of non-violent resistance, not blame and judgment.

The Web of Life. In sum, the Ahimsa worldview encompasses the nonviolence philosophy of Gandhi, Chitrabhanu, Kumar, King Jr., and Leopold. It applies to issues such as gun violence, domestic violence, TV violence, animal violence, and other aspects of a world nurtured in the spectacle of production and consumption.

People do resist spectacle—there is hope for spectacle transformation. There are eco-teams forming in Europe and North America to look at ways to cut back on our over consumption patterns. Consumer groups are forming that resist shopping addictions, credit-card addiction, workaholism, and television/Nintendo/Web cyber dependency. Turning Point, for example, runs full-page ads to raise questions about the impact of technology and transnational corporate strategies on the environment and the ability of nations to sustain growing populations with a quality of life for their people (Murphy, 1999: 1).

Table 2 contrasts spectacle and more Ahimsa Festival assumptions. In particular, there are differences in how progress, happiness, and spiritual value are defined.

Table 2 is focused on simplicity. Simplicity is a movement to cut out unneeded consumption and production in the hopes that others on the planet will have the means to live. Jain teachings apply to simplicity.

Table 2: Assumptions of Spectacle and Ahimsa Business Practices

Spectacle Assumptions	Ahimsa Festival Assumptions
✓ Progress defined as material accumulation	✓ Progress defined as spiritual accumulation
✓ Material accumulation = happiness	✓ Self-awareness = happiness
✓ Spectacles of production and consumption grow by resource use	✓ Planet has finite and dwindling resources to be preserved
✓ Economic productivity	✓ Eco-sustainable productivity
✓ Material values	✓ Spiritual values and awareness
✓ Work that is drudgery	✓ Work that is ennobling/ actualizing
✓ Business that pollutes	✓ Business is non-polluting
✓ Technology advances to sustain competitive progress	✓ Technology used sparingly to sustain natural splendor
✓ Survival of the fittest = richest	✓ Survival of the cooperative
✓ Consume for immediate gratification; live for today	✓ Consume in ways healthy for our offspring; live for their future
✓ Conspicuous consumption = good	Frugal consumption = good

The monk does not store possessions, has no roof over his head, and some do not wear clothes or own anything at all. He seeks simplicity in his daily life and equality with his fellow human beings. Merchants are encouraged not to stock products of animal sacrifice and consumers are galvanized not to consume such products.

> Let no one run away with the idea that this type of merchant exists only in my imagination. Fortunately for the world, it does exist in the West as well as in the East. It is true, such merchants may be counted on one's fingers' ends, but the type ceases to be imaginary, as soon as even one living specimen can be found to answer to it (Gandhi, *Non-Violent Resistance*, p. 49).

To the Jain businessperson, we are in the initial stages of transforming the old Spectacle assumptions into the new Ahimsa assumptions of what makes for an enlightened business organization. I think it takes daily meditation and critical awareness of the violence of the production and consumption spectacles, as well as the opportunities to make Ahimsa choices. The New Testament says, "to be as harmless as doves and wise as serpents in our actions." Harman (1994: 48) argues "we are moving from a culture dominated by materialistic values to one that recognizes the role of deep intuitive wisdom in guiding our collective future." The Ahimsa business paradigm would transform spectacles of production and consumption:

1. Engage in business practices that are non-violent to other species.
2. Limit economic growth to what is ecologically sustainable.
3. Develop ecological awareness through reduce, recycle, and reuse practices.
4. Cultivate personal self-development through servant leadership, introspection time, and community service.

Festival means cutting back on an over consumptive and conspicuous production lifestyle. Materiality does not bring happiness. It also means overcoming societal addictions to violent entertainment. Festival is taking a critical look at commodity and production needs that are inherently artificial prescriptions for the happy person in the happy society. Part of Ahimsa philosophy is to treat all living beings as equal to one's own self. This means not interrupting or degrading the evolution of plants, animals, and humans. While not everyone can make such a commitment or make it all at once, the challenge is to encourage more people to behave with less violence. This would necessitate a critical look at animal rights, the living planet, and ways in which we are tampering with all species in the Biotech Century. It means looking at the coevolution of humans, their technology, animals, and planets.

I would like to look at Ahimsa as a non-violent way of doing business, an alternative philosophy to late modern capitalism and state socialism. Both seem to me to enact manic consumption habits. Spiritualism and Marxism are opposed, as are capitalism and post-modernism. Marxism seeks to reform and transcend the violence of capitalism and capitalism sees itself as a competitor and successor to (state) Marxism. The festival is, for me, a middle ground, at the center of capitalism, Marxism, spiritualism, and postmodernism. It is my attempt to open the flow of non-violent practices of production and consumption that can coexist with other capitalisms, post-Marxists, spiritualities, and postmodernisms. The critical postmodern and Marxist approaches allow a critique of capitalist spectacle and Pollyanna or capitalist spiritualism in order to find where festival is sustainable. A critique of techno-determinism, linear progress, and evolutionism in capitalism is necessary. As is a critique of the technocratic and teleology of Marxism. I seek the "life capitalism" of festival. Without the critique the festival quickly reverts to spectacle.

In affluent pockets of economies, we the affluent can design a story for our lives in which we design ourselves as the main character using a variety of scattered and disconnected elements and fragments. We can design our body, our career, our environment, and live a life of simulation, playing virtual and theatric games, and never touch real at all. What is "authentic" in a world in which every aspect of spectacle is by designer choice?

Spectacle is ubiquitous to both market capitalism and state socialism. Beyond the extreme, an often-violent (to humans and ecology) spectacle of "free market" capitalism and "state bureaucratic" communism, there is a third path I call festivalism. Festivalism is both post-capitalism and post-communism because there is a resituation of both these violent extremes in favor of non-violence.

Is it possible to transition capitalism and state socialism to a higher stage of development? Whereas free capitalism adheres to free market to distribute resources, the mechanism of state socialism is one of central planning to equitably distribute resources. Each views the other as an exploitative apparatus. The "affluent monster" in both systems continues to outstrip the earth resource base and widens the gap between rich and poor (Marcuse, 1969: 7). I view Ahimsa and festival as a different moral aesthetic and transcendent value system that will change work and consumption practices.

Festivalism makes five assumptions. First, festival assumes we can create companies that earn a capitalist profit and maintain non-violent ecological and social practices. Second, festival assumes local stakeholder groups of workers, citizens, and managers can balance the burgeoning power of global corporate monopolies by expressing their non-violent preferences through their market behavior. Third, festival assumes the myopic corporate focus on short-term accumulation could be abandoned when there is an understanding of the living whole. Fourth, when festival citizens recognize the difference between living to work versus working to live, then they will be able to tame their shopaholic and addictive consumption appetites, thereby letting others live. Fifth, non-violent work, fun, and leisure are possible. In sum, *Festival is defined as the pragmatics of long-term sustainability in a non-violent culture, in balance with the whole planet.*

The spectacle employee. It takes many employees to produce spectacles for others to consume. The employees are separated one from the other, and do not always see how their respective tasks make up the spectacles being produced for consumption. Each task may appear totally and completely non-violent. The spectacle employee is sometimes, maybe often, the distracted workaholic, the sacrificing breadwinner, never seeing how little leisure is left, or their children growing up without them.

The spectacle consumer. We are taught to be spectators, to look, but not to see, to be a spectator but not to be an active participant when we consume. Firat and Dholakia (1998), in marketing, are also writing about "theaters consumption"—that is, becoming more interactive, blurring the line between producer and consumer, by allowing consumers to self-design their experience. They argue the separation between production and consumptive activities is changing, but corporate control remains. The Jain monk leaves spectacle altogether, in some cases forsaking even clothing, along with all worldly possessions. Jain lay people, in particular businesspeople, do not forsake all spectacles. They only seek involvement with the least violent forms of spectacle and the most minimal forms of accumulation.

I am learning that each of my possessions—my car, my books, my computer, my house, my furniture, my tools, etc.—is an attachment, a weight on my life. With each possession comes the attachment of caring for it. At work, each project, each conference, each dissertation committee, each class, each student, each e-mail is also an attachment. I live in a whole web of material and social attachments. I am learning slowly to choose my attachments, to decide how I spend my time and energy, caring for relationships or caring for material possessions.

"The celebrity" says Debord (#60) is "the spectacular representation of a living human being, embodies this banality by embodying the image of a possible role." Corporations such as Disney, Nike, IBM, Toyota, Intel, and Microsoft also become celebrities. In the Jain philosophy, each person must find their own uniqueness instead of emulating their fantasy about being the copy of another. Spectacles provide a mirage, a phantasm, and an illusion that allows us to safely avoid looking beneath the fabricated images, product stars, and corporate icons.

There are also those who see a future of spectacles that will be as nightmarish as Metropolis, Bladerunner, and the many sour predictions of the Biotech Century (Rifkin, 1998). To read spectacles of production and consumption requires a theory of spectacle. We are taught to not read and to ignore the "technical apparatus of contemporary" spectacles, "the means and methods power employs, outside of direct force, which subject individuals to societal manipulation, while obscuring the nature and effects of capitalism's power and deprivations" (Best & Kellner, 1997: 84).

Spectacle, says Debord, is an opium that allows us to sleep-walk, as if drugged, stumbling blindfolded through a devolving landscape of ecological and human horror, while cocooned in artificiality and illusion, mind-numbed by cyber media into passive stupefied spectators. This is why it is not easy for people socialized in spectacles and consumption images of the good life through consumption to step outside of its mechanisms of persuasion and see its impact on nature, social systems, and the manipulation of our own desires. Our life is just too "saturated with spectacles" and we are too pacified in their "permanent opium war" (Debord, 1967: #44).

In the postmodern condition, spectacle and festival intermingle and we are left to live in their nexus. For example, on July 23, 1964, the first Meadow Brook Music Festival was held, featuring the Detroit Symphony Orchestra. The Meadow Brook Music Festival staged its first ballet in 1968. The first laser show was Starship Encounters in 1978. The festival features choral company, ballet, and symphony music. In 1980, the types of music expanded to include Jazz. In 1982, there were Fourth of July fireworks. In 1984, there were performances of the Marine Band and bluegrass groups. In 1990, the festival included the nights of laser shows to attract a more family audience. In 1992, Dolly Parton and the Mormon Tabernacle Choir launched the Music Festival. In 1993, there was a more diverse or fragmented schedule including "Bugs Bunny on Broadway," James Brown, Dwight Yoakum, 10,000 Maniacs, Peter Paul and Mary.

Some of the postmodern festivals have an activist agenda. For example, the Amnesty International Film Festival takes on a more activist role than most other film festivals. They actively deconstruct the rhetoric and propaganda of governments violating human rights by putting their reports side by side with the oppressor claims that there are no such violations. Another type of activism is represented in the International CRÈCHE Festival. They present an interesting purpose:

Organizations in many nations are addressing the issue of the loss of biological diversity on this planet. Our organization attempts to speak to the loss of cultural diversity. We are attempting, in one small way, to help the folk artists of the world gain recognition of their arts and crafts and help them find a global market for their work at a fair price. If the folk artist cannot survive neither can the folk arts.[5]

This particular festival advocates that the artist receives a fair price for their labor. Other festivals and craft associations are not so equalitarian.

CONCLUSIONS

Guy Debord (1967) sought to abolish (modern) spectacle, to smash the spectacle in avant-garde revelation, *not* to transform or reform it. Yet modern spectacle is everywhere. A group of students (SI, 1966) had the vision of festive play, as a dream beyond the spectacle. Yet spectacle is everywhere. Debord called himself a Situationist (#191) because he wanted to replace the spectacle of official illusion with a deep awareness of the situation of violence, and how spectacle inverts reality.[6] If we are to dissociate festival from spectacle, we must begin with awareness.

In the postmodern, any line between festival and spectacle gets quite blurred. The 1998s Edinburgh Festival Fringe was a cyber-festival, filled with "frivolities and finito," including festive chat rooms with comedy stars.[7] The cybertech world affords us new art, new virtual forms of interaction, and new ways to live out our fantasies.

REFERENCE

Affluenza (1997), "Running Out of Time." Affluenza is a production of KCTS/Seattle and Oregon Public Broadcasting: A PBS Special http://www.pbs.org/kcts/affluenza/show/about.html.

American Psychological Association Report on Violence and Youth (1993). "*Is Youth Violence Just Another Fact of Live?*" From the American Psychological Association,

---

[5] Source, http://www.creche.org

[6] Numbers refer to paragraph numbers in Guy Debord's *Society of the Spectacle* (1967). La Société du Spectacle was first published in 1967 by Editions, Buchet-Chastel (Paris); it was reprinted in 1971 by Champ Libre (Paris). The full text is available in English at http://www.nothingness.org/SI/debord/index.html

[7] Source, http://www.comedyzone.beeb.com/edinburgh98/

Commission on Violence and Youth. Violence & Youth: Psychology's response (Vol 1). Washington, D.C.

Best, Steven, and Kellner, Douglas (1997), *The Postmodern Turn*. New York/London: The Guilford Press.

Boje, David M. (1999), *Spectacle and Festival of Organization: Managing Ahimsa Production and Consumption*. Book being published at Hampton Press (CA), expected release is 2001.

Center for Media and Public Affairs. "Study Finds Rise in TV Guns and Violence Cable Movies and Cartoons Are Culprits, Not the Networks." September 11, 1996.

Chitrabhanu, Gurudev Shree (1977), *The Philosophy of Soul and Matter*. Clare Rosenfield (ed.). New York: Jain Meditation International Center.

——. (1980), *Twelve Facets of Reality: The Jain Path to Freedom*. Clare Rosenfield (ed.). NewYork: Dodd, Mead & Company.

Debord Guy (1967), *Society of the Spectacle*. La Société du Spectacle was first published in 1967 by Editions, Buchet-Chastel (Paris); it was reprinted in 1971 by Champ Libre (Paris). The full text is available in English at http://www.nothingness.org/SI/debord/index.html.

Firat, Fuat A., and Nikhilesh Dholakia (1998), *Consuming People: From Political Economy to Theaters of Consumption*. London/New York: Routledge.

Gandhi, Mohandas K. (1957), *Gandhi, An Autobiography: The Story of My Experiments with Truth*. Boston, MA: Beacon Press.

——. (1951), *Non-Violent Resistance (Satyagraha)*. New York/London: Schocken Books.

Harman, Willis (1994), "The New business of business: work as if the earth and people mattered." Interview edited by Ronald S. Miller, *Science of Mind 67(9)*, 38–49.

Ismat, Abdal-Haqq (1989), "Violence in Sports," http://ericps.crc.uiuc.edu/npin/respar/texts/ teens/violence.html.

Koch, Carl (1992), "In Search of a Land Ethic." Woodrow Wilson Biology Institute. http://www.gene.com/ae/AE/AEPC/WWC/1992 /land_ethics.html.

Lee, Robert (1994), "Fan Sports Violence Also Common in United States," July 7, 1994, http://beacon-www.asa.utk.edu/issues/v66/archives/www/v66/n11/violence.111.html.

Leopold, Aldo (1949), *A Sand County Almanac and Sketches Here and There*. New York, Oxford University Press.

Marcuse, Herbert (1969), "*One Dimensional Man: Studies in the Ideology of Advanced Industrial Society.*" Boston, MA: Beason Press.

Murphy, Pat (1999), "Campaign to Change the World." Environmental News Network, November 1, Retrieved September 7, 2000, from the World Wide Web: http://www.enn.com/enn-features-archive/1999/11/110199/turning_6583.asp.

Nakhre, Amrut W. (1982), *Social Psychology of Nonviolent Action: A Study of Three Satyagrahas*. Delhi, India: Chanakya Publications.

National Center for Health Statistics (1994) Summary: Firearm-Related Deaths and Hospitalizations Wisconsin. 1994, Firearm-Related Deaths and Hospitalizations Continued Firearm-related injuries. Report retrieved September 7, 2000, from the

World Wide Web: http://www.cdc.gov/mmwr/PDF/wk/mm4535.pdf.

National Center for Health Statistics (1997) "Report on Nation's Health Documents Toll of Injuries in U.S. Firearm Mortality Down 11%, Traffic Fatality Rates up 2%, 1993–1995" News Release dated July 24, 1997. Retrieved September 7, 2000, from the World Wide Web: http://www.cdc.gov/nchs/releases/97news/hus96rel.html.

Rifkin, Jeremy (1998), *The Biotech Century: Harnessing the Gene and Remaking the World*. New York: Tarcher/Putnam.

Rosenfield, Clare, & Segall, Linda (undated) *Ahimsa Is Not a Religion, It Is a Way of Life*. New York: Jain Meditation International.

Situationalist International Strasbourg Pamphlet (1966), "On the Poverty of the Student Life." This pamphlet was a prelude to the May 1968 revolt in France and has been translated into more than a dozen languages and reprinted in over half a million copies. Ken Knabb's English translation is at http://www.slip.net/~knabb/SI/poverty.html.

Weissman, Robert (1999), "Want to kill somebody and get away with a slap on the wrist?" *Corporate Focus Newsletter* (April 27, 1999, e-mail newsletter) - Focus on the Corporation columns available at rob@essential.org.

Whitmer, Barbara (1997), "*The Violence Mythos*." New York: State University of New York Press.

THE INDIVIDUAL WITHIN ORGANIZATIONS

Embers

■

by Tom Brown

That very first day
On that very first job:
The call, the work, the quest —
How you did aspire!

You stormed all tasks,
You donned no masks,
You seldom felt much higher.

The secret to that heady time?
Oh, to be driven by the fire.

No "boss" could make you feel
Like that —
No, not then, not even now.
The pay for you was more than cash:
Striving hard, showing strong,
And pining to achieve.

The advances sought,
The problems caught,
Each improvement wrought —
It was what *you*
Created,
Crafted,
Sired.

The magic of those moments when?
Oh, to be driven by the fire.

How different now,
How sadly less,
It seems your work berates.
The job's all task;
Your smile's a mask;
False starts, you fluctuate.

It doesn't feel so warm inside,
When you're an ember dying.
When wonder's gone,

Is your memory strong?
Oh, to be driven by the fire.

What would it take,
Whom would you need,
To spark that flame again?
Is it leading,
Or being led,
That lacquers a life with glee?

That first day
On that first job:
You knew the answer then.

The future begs; will you recall?
Oh, to be driven by the fire!

— from *The Anatomy of Fire: Sparking a New Spirit of Enterprise*
by Tom Brown © 2000 by MANAGEMENT GENERAL
http://www.mgeneral.com

7

■

Religion in the Workplace: Correlates and Consequences of Individual Behavior

Nancy E. Day
University of Missouri, Kansas City

Religion is an increasingly important aspect of diversity management. However, while much scholarly work exists regarding spirituality, little addresses relationships between religiosity and individual outcomes that may affect organizational functioning. Reviewing past research from psychology and management literatures, this paper describes correlates of religiosity that may affect individual behavior in the workplace, such as physical and mental health, coping, concern for others, creativity, commitment, ethical behavior, prejudice, intelligence and personality. Recommendations for future research call for theory-based conceptualizations with well-articulated measures conducted in organizational samples.

Key Words: *Religion, Workplace, Individual Behaviour*

It is news to no one in American business or academe that the workforce will continue to become less white and less male (Fullerton and Toossi, 2001). However, religious diversity is also

An early version of this manuscript was presented at 2004 Academy of Management meetings.

on the rise. While most of the 1500 religious organizations in the US are Christian (about 900), there are over 75 denominations that are Buddhist and over 100 that are Hindu (Atkinson, 2000). By 2010, Islam will constitute the second largest religion in the United States (Digh, 1998). The Civil Rights Act of 1964 requires employers to make reasonable accommodations to provide for employees' participation in religious services and other observances such as religious dress and prayer time, unless they would cause an undue hardship to the business (Cash and Gray, 2000; Lindsay and Bach, 1999; Wolf, Friedman and Sutherland, 1998). However, complaints about religious discrimination made to the EEOC are rising faster than are other types of discrimination claims (Atkinson, 2004; Geller, 2003), by 40% between 1992 and 2000, with settlement amounts increasing as well by almost 300% (SHRM and Tannebaum Center, 2001). HR managers seem to believe that religious discrimination or conflict is not a workplace issue, but a majority of employees, particularly those from non-traditional American faiths, experience religious bias at their workplaces (SHRM and Tannenbaum Center, 2001) (albeit often without reporting these incidents to their human resource departments).

Not only are there more religions, but also workers want to more openly and frequently express their religious practices or beliefs (Atkinson, 2000). Indeed, employers may need to expand the criteria by which they grant reasonable accommodation for religious observance to include those individuals in non-traditional religions as well as those with a serious spiritual orientation outside organized religion (Cash and Gray, 2000).

Complicating the issue is a trend for some executives to promote religion, particularly Christianity, as part of their organizational cultures. At-work religious activities such as lunchtime Bible reading and prayer groups are encouraged (Hicks, 2003). Some organizations even include Christian evangelism as part of their mission statement (Shimron, 2003). A similar trend is seen in the movement of some organizations to become more "spiritual," presumably in an attempt to allow employees to more fully integrate personal dimensions into their work experiences (Cash and Gray, 2000; HRMagazine, 1996; McKibbin, 1995; Mitroff and Denton, 1999a). Indeed, work organizations have been hypothesized to serve as "secular religions" through normative controls that "impart an encompassing cosmology that connects the individual to a wider system of meaning and purpose . . ." (Ashforth and Vaidyanath, 2002, page 368).

Thus, a diverse and more active religious workforce makes the current business environment dynamic and potentially unstable, especially given that new management approaches to incorporating spirituality into the workplace may make religious affiliation markedly salient. Religious differences in the workplace may create legal challenges and accelerate interpersonal conflicts. While these potential negative consequences are obvious, little is known about how religious workers differ from or are similar to their nonreligious counterparts. For managers and executives to effectively lead their organizations, more knowledge of how religiousness affects workplace attitudes, relationships and outcomes is needed.

Plan and Purpose of the Paper

The purpose of this paper is to address and explore the role that religion may have in the workplace in its potential effects on important outcomes. To do this, I will first briefly discuss the extent of existing management literature related to the study of religion, and distinguish between spirituality and religion, two concepts that are related but quite distinct. The next section discusses theoretical perspectives of religion that may be particularly useful in studying religious experience in the workplace. The paper will then review the psychological research that investigates relationships between religiosity and outcomes that may affect attitudes and behavior in work settings: physical and mental health, concern for others, creativity and problem solving, commitment to the organization, ethical behavior, prejudice and tolerance, intelligence, and personality. Finally, I conclude with recommendations for future research on religion in a business setting.

This paper is limited to a discussion of the impact that religiosity may have on individual workplace behavior and attitudes. While management's acceptance or rejection of spirituality or religion in the workplace may have significant consequences on organizational issues such as culture and firm performance, these issues are beyond the scope of this paper, whose main purpose is to illustrate the potential relevance of psychology of religion research to employment relationships.

MANAGEMENT RESEARCH ON RELIGION

Definitions: Spirituality and Religion

Before discussing current management research, it is worthwhile to distinguish between "spirituality" and "religion." Scholars seem to unanimously agree that they are decidedly different constructs (Giacalone and Jurkiewicz, 2003a and 2003b; Mitroff and Denton, 1999b), although no generally accepted definition of spirituality exists (Brown, 2003). In 1905, William James (2003) proposed a personal and an institutional religious perspective, defining these similarly to how the contemporary terms "spirituality" and "religion" are used (Morgan, 2004). Similarly, designations of "personal and "workplace" spirituality can be found in contemporary scholarship (Brown, 2003; Giacolone and Jurkiewicz, 2003b).

Most of the scholarly writing that exists addressing spirituality in organizations is quite optimistic about the benefits that promoting spirituality may bring (Brown 2003; see Hicks, 2003, for cautionary discussions regarding leadership support of spirituality into the workplace). Generally speaking, management scholars define spirituality as a search for meaning and purpose (Buchholz and Rosenthal, 2003; Dehler and Welsh, 2003; Milliman, Czaplewski, and Ferguson, 2003; Tepper, 2003), self-knowledge and self-development (Ashforth and Pratt, 2003; Dehler and Welsh, 2003) seeking a "higher power," the "sacred," or a larger purpose (Dehler and Welsh, 2003; Mitroff and Denton, 1999b; Paloutzian, Emmons and Keortge, 2003; Zellars and Perrewe, 2003), an interconnectedness (Mitroff and Denton, 1999b), the ability to experience transcendent states (Hill and Smith, 2003; Paloutzian, Emmons and Keortge, 2003), and holistic, personal and individualized experience (Ashforth and Pratt, 2003; Mitroff and Denton, 1999a; Mitroff and Denton, 1999b; Rhodes, 2003). While some definitions include moral beliefs, such as knowledge of right and wrong (Buchholz and Rosenthal, 2003), most definitions of spirituality eschew dogma and belief systems, leaving them instead for the domain of religion. Indeed, while seeing spirituality as generally, if not revolutionarily, beneficial (Brown, 2003), some scholars associate religion with negative connotations (Lips-Wiersma, 2003) such as authoritarianism (Hill and Smith, 2003), closed-mindedness, restrictiveness (Mitroff and Denton, 1999b), divisiveness, and intolerance (Mitroff, 2003).

Religion, on the other hand, is usually seen as possessing a spiritual component, but is concerned with dogma, institutional organization, structure and formalization (Brown, 2003; Hill and Smith, 2003). One can be spiritual and religious, spiritual and not religious, not spiritual but religious, and neither spiritual nor religious (Marler and Hadaway, 2002; Zinnbauer, et al., 1997).

Religion: An Ignored Step-Sister?

While much management literature deals with spirituality, significantly less addresses religion. Several journals have had specially focused issues on spirituality in organizations (e.g. *Journal of Organizational Change Management*, the *Journal of Business Ethics*, *Journal of Management Inquiry*, and the *Journal of Management Education* (Brown, 2003; Lund-Dean, Fornaciari, and McGee, 2003), but generally religion has not been studied except as an ancillary to spirituality. A significant exception to this is a body of work relating religiosity to ethical behavior. For example, the March 1997 issue of *Business Ethics Quarterly* focused specifically on religion, discussing the topic from the perspective of individual religions such as Judaism and Christianity and their relationships to ethical intentions and behavior. In response to inconsistent results found in this research, Weaver and Agle (2002) developed a model of how religion might affect business ethics in their application of a symbolic interactionist perspective to religion's role in ethical behavior.

A substantial amount of research that is potentially relevant to the workplace does exist in fields of psychology of religion and health psychology. This work is relevant because it deals with variables related to states and behaviors that could affect organizational outcomes, such as health, concern for others, prejudice, ethical behavior, and more. After discussing religious conceptions and measures, I will review these findings.

RELIGION: CONCEPTUALIZATIONS AND MEASURES

Like many human constructs, "religion" seems simple until we try to precisely define and measure it. Defining what we mean by "religion" and "religiosity" is critical, particularly since research outcomes tend to depend on how the concept is defined and measured (Pargament, 2002a; Weaver and Agle, 2002). Many scholars have pointed out that religion is not a unified concept. Religious commitment has been conceptualized as serving several needs: An experiential dimension that provides some sort of religious experience; a belief dimension in which belief systems are adopted along with adherence to a particular faith; a ritual dimension, which provides the adherent with ritualistic experiences; a devotional dimension that provides for private, individual experiences; an intellectual dimension that requires that an adherent know and understand the religion's teachings (Glock, 1959; Glock and Stark, 1965).

Religiosity has been measured in many ways. Indeed, Hill and Hood (1999) describe 125 measures of religion and spirituality. There is growing disagreement about how religion should be measured, including concerns about construct validity and issues surrounding self-report measurement (Slater, Hall and Edwards, 2001).

Religion has been frequently studied by comparing reactions of individuals from various faiths or denominations, or comparing the religious with the nonreligious, as in contrasting residents of religious Israeli kibbutzim with residents of non-religious kibbutzim (e.g. Kark, Carmel, Sinnreich, Goldberger, and Friedlander, 1996; Kark, Shemi, Friedlander, Martin, Manor, and Blondheim, 1996). Common self-report behavioral measures include frequency of church or worship attendance, frequency of prayer, doctrinal orthodoxy or denomination (Pargament, 2002a). However, given that religious workplace diversity involves a variety of faiths, some of which may not fit a simple measure (for example, faiths that do not require attendance at services), as well as those individuals who consider themselves religious or "spiritual" outside an organized faith, measures that investigate religiosity as a psychological construct, rather than behaviors, are preferable in the study of workplace diversity. Additionally, religiosity is probably more accurately seen as a continuum (Miller and Thoresen, 2003), therefore, may be more precisely measured by a scaled instrument.

Intrinsic, Extrinsic and Quest Dimensions

Early conceptualizations of religion for psychological study (notably Allport and Ross, 1967) postulated that religious beliefs could be either intrinsic or extrinsic. Intrinsic religious motivations are based in the belief system itself; to be intrinsically religious means that religion and its expression are not means to an end, but the end in themselves. Extrinsic religion motivations are based on external gains that religious affiliation or expression may provide for the individual. Examples may be self-justification of behavior or career advancement through attending a church with influential people (Pargament, 2002a).

In an effort to more completely capture Allport's original formulation of religiosity, Batson, Schoenrade and Ventis (1993) expanded the intrinsic and extrinsic dimensions to include a third dimension of "quest." A quest dimension, they propose, better captures Allport's concept of "mature" religion. A religiously mature person does not need to reduce the complexity of ultimate problems such as ethics and evil to simple solutions. Additionally, such a person would acknowledge that doubt and self-criticism are constructive parts of belief. Finally, such a person would perceive his or her faith as incomplete and tentative, requiring constant search in order to effectively respond to the ultimate questions of life.

Based on these three dimensions and utilizing previous measures of intrinsic and extrinsic religiosity, Batson et al. created a scale through factor analyses procedures and validation that includes three dimensions: "Religion as Means," "Religion as Ends," and "Religion as Quest." These dimensions should be conceptualized as independent of each other; for example, an individual could be highly intrinsically as well as extrinsically motivated. The "means" or intrinsic scale contains nine Likert-type items; the "ends" or extrinsic scale contains six, and the "quest" scale contains twelve (Batson et al., 1993). Researchers also use Allport's original measures of intrinsic and extrinsic dimension (Allport and Ross, 1967) and the Revised I/E Scale (Gorsuch and McPherson, 1987).

Some religion researchers have argued that the "quest" dimension is merely a measure of agnosticism, and not truly one of religiosity (Donahue, 1985; Kojetin, McIntosh, Bridges and Spilka, 1987; Weaver and Agle, 2002). However Batson and his colleagues have countered these arguments with several studies showing that individuals who would otherwise be considered religious showed predictable quest scores, given their religious life roles (Batson and Schoenrade, 1991; Batson, et al., 1993; Ferriani and Batson, 1990).

Religious Integration

Whether or not religion is effectual for an individual may be determined by evaluating whether or not religion is "integrated" into the person's life (Cacioppo and Brandon, 2002; Pargament, 1997 and 2002a). Integration can occur socially, such as in a religious communal living arrangement. Integration can also be viewed as the degree to which the person's religious means and ends match, or, in other words, the degree to which his or her life's activities are chosen in direct response to religious beliefs. Integration also refers to the degree to which the individual's religious problem-solving is congruent with the problem at hand (Pargament, 2002a). Praying for good grades rather than studying is an example of a non-integrated solution. Finally, religion may be integrated to the degree to which a person's relationships, beliefs and practices are integrated with each other (Pargament, 2002a). Pargament, Tyler, and Steele (1979) found that highly non-integrated individuals who attended frequent religious services but showed low religious commitment had lower mental health than well-integrated religious people.

Because of its multidimensionality, religious integration is generally measured using descriptive assessments, such as comparing stated religious attitudes and behavior (e.g. level of commitment to one's religion compared with frequency of church attendance, Pargament, 2002a). Since this concept has been frequently used in investigations of religious coping effectiveness, Pargament and his colleagues have also developed RCOPE, a scale that measures religious coping patterns (Pargament, Koenig, and Perez, 2000).

Religious Identification: Internalization versus Introjection

Religiosity can be viewed also as either internalized or introjected (Ryan, Rigby, and King, 1993). Internalized religious people have personally chosen and value their religion. "Introjected" religious people are those whose faith is adopted out of fear or through external pressure. Research shows that people with higher internalization tend to have lower anxiety, depression and social dysfunction, and higher self-esteem. More highly introjected people tend to have higher anxiety, depression, lower self-esteem and more negative physical symptoms (Pargament, 2002a).

Since identification is based on specific religious beliefs, its measurement is specific to the religion being investigated. For example, the Christian Religious Internalization Scale (Ryan, et al., 1993) was used to assess internalization or introjection in a study of undergraduate students who had self-identified as Christian.

Religion, Social Roles and Identities

Weaver and Agle (2002) use a symbolic interactionist perspective to propose a framework for the study of religion's role in ethical business behavior, speculating that such a framework would generalize to other aspects of work-related behavior. Religion will affect behavior when role expectations, self-identity and identity salience are aligned with a religious identity. Different religious affiliations would specify varying role expectations of their adherents; for example, some religions encourage loyalty to parents and family over that to the self, and thus an expected role would be that of "responsible child." When a person identifies him- or herself with a religious identity, he or she would be likely to accept the roles the religion dictates. Further, when the identity is salient, such as when many reminders of the religion are present at work, the individual would be more likely to act in consort with those role expectations.

Similarly, religious affiliation may be seen as a method by which individuals establish social identities, or categorize themselves as members of desirable social groups, thereby reducing uncertainty and more clearly defining expectations as well as desired behaviors (Ashforth and Mael, 1989; Hogg, and Terry, 2000). Self-categories become more important in terms of their impact on behavior if they are more highly valued, frequently used, or salient due to the situation in which the individual finds him or herself (Hogg and Terry, 2000). Therefore, religion may drive behavior at work to the extent that employees have categorized themselves into a particular religious group, the value of that group membership to the individual is high, and the religious group membership is salient in the work context.

PAST PSYCHOLOGICAL RESEARCH RELATED TO WORK ISSUES

Understanding the ways in which religion and religiosity have been formulated are important to understanding implications of past research on religion and human behavior. Given that the experience and expression of religion can be described in these multiple conceptualizations, it is reasonable to assume that behavior and attitudes differ based on religious affiliations, orientations, or motivations. How religiosity might affect life aspects that could in turn impact work-related behavior and attitudes is the focus of this section. Specifically, I will address past relationships found between religion and physical and mental health and coping, concern for others, creativity and problem-solving, commitment to the organization, ethical behavior, prejudice, intelligence and personality. All of these correlates of religion can be surmised to have potential relationships with desired work outcomes, such as morale, performance, or cost effectiveness.

Physical Health

The climbing cost of benefits and the criticality of encouraging a healthy workforce is well known. Physically healthy workers cost the organization less in terms of health care benefits, as well as in lower absenteeism and perhaps even enhanced performance (Ivancevich and Matteson, 1980). Employees with health or addiction problems not only pose performance problems themselves, but sometimes inhibit effective performance in those around them (De Groot and Kiker, 2003).

A bulk of information exists that supports a positive link between religion and health (Koenig, McCullough and Larson, 2001; Miller and Thoresen, 2003). While there are some exceptional examples that show religiosity as negatively related to physical health (faiths that deny modern medical care in favor of prayer, or condone extreme physical child discipline), the bulk of the research shows a positive relationship between many measures of religiosity and many forms of health (Koenig et al., 2001). Included in the list of health issues upon which religion has been shown to have desirable effects are alcoholism and drug abuse, hypertension, stroke (although results are weak), immune system function and cancer recovery (Koenig et al, 2001; Seeman, Dubin and Seeman, 2003).

Not all researchers are unequivocal about a positive religion-health relationship, however. A recent review of relevant literature determined that, while there is persuasive evidence that service attendance protects against death, and some evidence that religiosity protects against cardiovascular disease, findings in other relationships are either based on low quality research or fail to consistently find a positive religion-health relationship (Powell, Shahabi, and Thoresen, 2003). In fact, the same review cites some evidence that religiosity could actually inhibit recovery from illness, particularly if the individual believed that he or she was looked on with disfavor by God (Powell, et al., 2003).

Part of the skepticism about a religion-health link can be construed as due not to religiosity but to factors associated with religious activity, such as increased social support, healthier lifestyles (not smoking or drinking and less sedentary life styles, for example) and decreased risky behavior (such as wearing seatbelts and limiting sexual partners) (George, Ellison and Larson, 2002; Koenig et al., 2001). However, some research that controls for healthier life practices finds that religiosity still accounts for significant independent variance (Cacioppo and Brandon, 2002).

Thus, while results are not conclusive, there seems to be positive support that, whatever the dynamics of the relationship, religiosity is positively related to health. This understanding may lead us to the conclusion that religious people, since overall they may be healthier, may be more productive and cost-effective workers.

Mental Health

Emotionally stable, happy workers are good for organizations. Common sense would tell us that mentally healthy workers will be more dependable, more energetic, easier to get along with, and perhaps more productive than mentally unhealthy workers. They may also be less expensive, since they are less likely to suffer from severe mental illnesses that are economically costly in terms of insurance premiums, derailed productivity, absenteeism and accidents (Cooper and Cartwright, 1994; Paul, 2003). Mentally healthy workers experience a greater sense of control, more autonomy and enhanced participation than their less healthy coworkers (Mackie, Holahan, and Gottlieb, 2001).

Research shows that, in general, religious people are happier. Indeed, in a review of 100 empirical studies investigating religious activity and feelings of well-being, 80 reported positive relationships. Religiosity is negatively related to depression (Fehring, Miller and Shaw, 1997) and positively related to recovery from it (Braam, Beekman, Deeg, Smit, and van Tilburg, 1997). Religiously active people tend to be lower in hostility and higher in optimism and hope (Koenig, et al., 2001).

Even after healthy lifestyle habits were controlled for, religious involvement continued to predict self-esteem, life satisfaction, and hopefulness (Cacioppo and Brandon, 2002). Religious practices may encourage positive emotions by broadening an individual's repertoire of thinking and action as well as building long-term personal resources (Fredrickson, 2002). Similarly, religious organizations may promote "emotionally intelligent" people. In other words, these faiths teach their members emotionally adept skills through providing opportunities for catharsis, encouraging practices that elicit well-being such as meditation or prayer, or providing access to confessors such as priests, rabbis and ministers who can assist members in monitoring and controlling emotions (Pizarro and Salovey, 2002).

Positive well-being is predicted by the source of the motivation (intrinsic or extrinsic; intrinsic is related to well-being), the type of "attachment figure" in which God is experienced (secure or insecure; secure is better), the level of commitment to religious beliefs (higher is better) and the amount of coherence and meaning about ultimate, "life and death," questions that the believer experiences (more is better) (Simpson, 2002).

Coping and Responses to Stress. Part of mental health is the ability to cope with stressful and unpleasant circumstances. Workplaces today present ambiguous landscapes that require the need for facile coping mechanisms and the ability to deal with constant stressors. Rapid technological changes, economic downturns that result in environmental and organizational uncertainty, reduced workforces and increased competition create minefields of pressure and stress in contemporary organizations (Cooper, 1984; Cooper and Cartwright, 1994). Thus, workers who have the ability to handle stress and cope with difficult and ambiguous situations will undoubtedly fare better in the work world (Ivancevich and Matteson, 1980).

Religious individuals often assert that religion provides them with one of their most effective coping mechanisms, both for extreme situations and daily stressors (Koenig, et al., 2001). Religious belief may facilitate coping through the schema or "mental picture" (Kreitner and Kinicki, 2004) of effective coping it provides the individual; in times of stress, the person has an established cognitive structure to explain negative events or circumstances (McIntosh, 1997). Indeed, past research has found that specific religious coping methods (e.g. congregational support and the belief that "God is on my side") may account for favorable outcomes in negative events over and above non-religious coping methods (Pargament 1997; Pargament and Park, 1997).

Of three types of religious coping (deferring, which gives God the problem-solving responsibility; self-directed coping, in which the individual believes that God gives him or her the ability to solve problems; collaborative coping, which utilizes the belief that both God and the individual work hand-in-hand to solve problems), collaborative coping seems to be associated with the most favorable outcomes (Pargament and Park, 1997).

However, negative religious coping strategies result in negative outcomes. These strategies are based on a tense, anxious, and shaky relationship with God, an ominous worldview and an experience of religious struggle. Characteristics of negative strategies include questioning God and his powers, anger towards God, discontentment with the church (its members and leaders), punitive evaluations of negative situations and evaluations of religious situations that include demonic components (Pargament, 2002a).

These relationships between religiosity and enhanced coping may mean that religious people with positive coping skills are advantaged in stressful workplaces, since they may be able to deal better with daily stressors and long-term ambiguities.

Health and religiosity: A summary. In a recent review of the literature of religion and psychology, Pargament (2002a) asserts that five conclusions can be reached in understanding the relationships between religion and mental and physical health. First, different types of religion have differential effects on well-being. Religion that is intrinsically motivated, internalized, and based on a secure relationship with God is positively related to well-being, and religion that is imposed, unexamined and represents an insecure relationship with God is negatively related to well-being. Second, all types of religions and denominations have advantages and disadvantages in terms of their effects on well-being. Third, religion is more likely to be beneficial to marginalized groups, such as minority group members and women, as well as to those whose lives are more intricately intertwined with their religion (Cacioppo and Brandon, 2002). Fourth, situations of stress are particularly assisted by religious beliefs. Fifth, religion is efficacious to the degree that it is integrated into the lives of the religious.

Concern for Others

The contemporary emphasis on teamwork and cooperation in organizations (Kreitner and Kinicki, 2004) calls for workers who share a genuine concern for each other. Managers who have better interpersonal skills (Van Velsor and Leslie, 1995) and those able to build social capital (Baron and Markman, 2000) will fare better in their careers and contribute more to their organizations than will other workers.

While there is a general assumption that religious people will be more socially active and more concerned for others, there is little research that supports this assertion. In fact, there is evidence that only people with certain types of religious orientation show genuine concern. Batson and his colleagues (1993) found that individuals with higher intrinsic religiosity report higher concern for others but their actions may not be tailored to the target person's needs. While those higher in quest religiosity were not likely to report higher concern, their helping behaviors were more matched to the person's needs. Batson et al. conclude that intrinsic orientation may be more accurately related to "looking good" rather than "being good." Those high in the quest dimension may be more closely attuned to others' needs and respond in more appropriate ways (Batson et al., 1993).

These results do not encourage us to think that religious people will be genuinely concerned for others in the workplace. While intrinsically religious people may want to "look good" at work by being helpful to others, unless they also have a strong quest orientation, they may not help others in meaningful ways. However, given that helping activities in the workplace are usually task-focused rather than emotion-focused, individuals who are motivated to only "look good" may still provide sufficient helpfulness for the job at hand.

Creativity and Problem Solving

Many organizations need employees who can creatively respond to problems, contributing useful and effective solutions to a myriad of business issues, and there is a general consensus that creativity and innovation are essential to organizational health and survival (Oldham and Cummings, 1996; Scott and Bruce, 1994; Sternberg, 2003; Taggar, 2002; Thompson, 2003; Unsworth, 2001). Little research exists that links creativity and religion. However, proposing that individuals who undergo religious experiences may be prone to do so because they are higher in creativity, Batson et al. (1993) present empirical work showing that religious experiences include a sequence that is similar to that used in creative activities. Creative experiences change the cognitive structure to accommodate new ways of looking at things, similar to cognitive restructuring that occurs in existential or religious experiences.

Further, religious belief can be conceptualized as "schemas" (McIntosh, 1997), mental representations of an event or object, which may serve to organize data and determine solutions. Like all schemas, religious schemas enable the person to fill in lost details about events and situations, which increases the repertoire of data available for problem solving. Lechner (1990) found that people who had clearly defined God concepts better integrated faith in their lives, indicating that higher religiosity may lead to more complex schemas that affect nonreligious aspects of life (McIntosh, 1997). A more complex schema would provide the individual with access to richer, more precise representations, thus enhancing problem-solving options. Similarly, some research shows that higher intrinsic religious motivation is associated with possessing internal loci of control (Koenig et al., 2001), which have been found to be related to higher motivation and superior problem solving (Norris and Niebuhr, 1984).

Thus, religiosity and creativity and problem solving may be positively associated. Carrying this idea into the workplace may mean that religious workers may be able to solve problems more effectively and creatively.

Organizational Commitment

Organizationally committed workers plan on staying longer with the organization (Hackette, Lapierre and Hausdorf, 2001), tend to be more satisfied with their jobs (Tett and Meyer, 1993) and perhaps perform better (Riketta, 2002). Thus, from the organization's perspective, commitment is a desirable attitude.

Most conceptualizations of organizational commitment include a congruence of the values of the individual with those of the organizations (Mathieu and Zajac, 1990; Mowday, Porter and Steers, 1982), and thus organizationally committed workers would be more likely to see their work as a vocation or calling (enjoyable and socially instrumental) (Wrzesniewski, McCauley, Rozin and Schwartz, 1997). Indeed, Davidson and Caddell (1994) found that religious people were more likely to see their work as a calling, particularly if they are well-rewarded for it. Similarly, research in family psychology and the psychology of religion shows that when individuals sanctify an aspect of their lives, they are more likely to treat it differently from aspects they consider profane. For example, couples who view their marital relationships as sacred are more likely to be satisfied, committed, collaborative, and to show less aggression than others (Mahoney, Pargament, Jewell, Swank, Scott, Emery, and Rye, 1999). Given that workers, particularly in Western countries, experience a vocational work ethic that includes self-fulfillment and social obligation (Giorgi and Marsh, 1991), it is reasonable to expect that to the extent the individual sees his or her work as aligned with religious values and aspirations, a higher level of commitment may be experienced.

If these dynamics can be extrapolated to the work world, then workers who see their employment as part of a divine vocation may experience a feeling of sanctification of work, which may be related to enhanced commitment to the organization. This reasoning provides some support to those organizations, discussed briefly above (Mitroff and Denton, 1999a) that seek to create a spiritual environment at work.

Ethical Behavior

Recent corporate scandals and reports of cheating and plagiarism among students have underscored the importance of ethical behavior in business. Indeed, in adhering to the AACSB's standards, most business schools include ethics courses or components in their curricula. Because of the nature of religion, one would predict that individuals higher in religiosity would also be higher in ethical behavior. For instance, since some religious affiliations encourage limiting sexual partners and avoiding substance abuse (George, Ellison and Larson, 2002; Koenig et al, 2001), we might assume higher ethical behavior from their adherents. However, while research is ample, it is far from conclusive, particularly that done on US subjects (Worden, 2003). Indeed, we might question whether it is appropriate to "presume that religion is inherently ethical" (Worden, 2003, page 150).

Much of the business-related research is based on reactions to ethical situations rather than on actual behavior. Findings in these studies generally show a positive relationship between religiosity and ethical attitude or intention (see, for example, Angelidis and Ibrahim, 2002 and 2004; Barnett, Bass, and Brown 1996; Conroy and Emerson, 2004; Hoge, and De Zulueta, 1985). McDevitt and Van Hise (2002) found that of six spheres affecting decision-making (the workplace, family, religion, legal system, community, and profession), religion was among the lowest in predicting response to an ethical breach, but 60 percent of the respondents said that religion was an important consideration.

Findings researching actual ethical behavior rather than attitude or intention are mixed (Weaver and Agle, 2002), with some finding negative relationships between ethical decisions and religion (Clark and Dawson, 1996) and some finding positive relationships (Kennedy and Lawton, 1998). Using a symbolic interactionist perspective, as suggested by Weaver and Agle (2002), it could be predicted that religion would affect ethical behavior when identity and role variables are aligned. We would expect religiosity to positively influence ethical behavior when an employee adopts a specific religious identity that requires ethical behavior and the religious identity is salient to the individual in the work environment (Weaver and Agle, 2002).

The need for ethical behavior in business is undisputed nowadays. An understanding of how religious orientations may be encouraged to elicit such behavior would be extremely valuable, as long as such encouragement does not violate norms of diversity management or legal constraints.

Prejudice and Intolerance

We have seen that current literature substantiates relationships between religion and some positive outcomes. It is reasonable to conclude that such positive outcomes may transfer to the workplace. However, there are potential downsides to religiosity, such as interpersonal strains through disagreements about religious beliefs and prejudice toward other religious groups (Exline, 2002). Further, religious belief systems may have excluded some groups, notably women, from full participation in the workforce until relatively recently (Hicks, 2003).

While past research has found positive relationships between extrinsic religiosity and prejudice, a meta-analysis across several studies found no significant mean correlation between an intrinsic orientation and prejudice (Donahue, 1985). Batson et al. (1993) more closely examined and expanded this research, concluding that extrinsically motivated religious people tended to be less accepting of other groups. They also concluded that intrinsically motivated religious people expressed acceptance of groups that they were "supposed" to tolerate, but they were not more likely to act acceptingly. They were also less likely to accept groups for which their faith did not expect toleration. People high in quest religious motivation, however, tended to be less prejudiced toward all groups.

Thus, there may be a propensity for certain types of religiosity to be associated with prejudice, although the relationships are not simple. Given the diversity of the workplace, attitudes of prejudice and discriminatory acts can be toxic. Thus, certain types of religiousness may be undesirable in demographically diverse workgroups.

Intelligence

There is a tremendous amount of research showing that one of the most consistent predictors of job performance across nearly all job types is intelligence, making this attribute critical to organizations in terms of selection and performance (e.g. Hunter, 1986; Gottfredson, 1986; Landy and Shankster, 1994) as well as trainability (Ree and Earles, 1991).

Early research seems to show that, in general, religious people are less intelligent than non-religious people, and religious conservatives are less intelligent than religious liberals. An initial assumption could be made that higher intelligence "protects" people from religious beliefs (Scobie,

1975). However moderators, such as the type of religious orientation (e.g. intrinsic, extrinsic or quest), may influence this relationship. Thus, while some evidence negatively links religion and intelligence, this relationship is not clear.

Personality

Much research has recently illustrated the power of the Five Factor Model (FFM, including traits of conscientiousness, agreeableness, extraversion, emotional stability and openness to experience) in predicting job-relevant behavior (e.g. Barrick and Mount, 1991; Vinchur, Schippmann, Switzer and Roth, 1998; Salgado, 1997). While the FFM could be helpful to our understanding of religion (Piedmont, 1999), little empirical research regarding how religious beliefs and attitudes are related to FFM currently exists.

Conscientiousness is a highly consistent predictor of performance across jobs and organizations (Heneman and Judge, 2003). Extraversion has been associated with better sales performance (Heneman and Judge, 2003). While little evidence exists that agreeableness is a good predictor across jobs (Heneman and Judge, 2003), it is reasonable to assume that it may be associated with superior team performance. Some research shows that religiosity is positively related to all three of these personality factors (Saroglou, 2002), and that in particularly, intrinsically religious people seem to be higher in agreeableness and conscientiousness (Taylor and MacDonald, 1998). Thus, these findings suggest that religious (or perhaps intrinsically religious) individuals might be better performers across a wide range of job types.

Emotional stability predicts performance over many jobs, particularly sales, teaching, and management, but openness to experience has not been consistently associated with performance. However, it may be associated with performance in creative jobs (Heneman and Judge, 2003). Research shows that extrinsic religious orientation may be related to lower emotional stability and lower openness to experience (Taylor and MacDonald, 1998). Those high in "open-mature" religiosity (similar to the quest orientation), tended to be more open to experience (Saroglou, 2002). Thus, extrinsically religious people may not be suited for some occupations, and an "open-mature" religious orientation may be associated with higher creative performance.

Earlier work on religiosity and personality outside the FFM has been impressive in its volume, but inconsistent in findings. Some evidence indicates that religious people may score higher on neuroticism scales (Scobie, 1975) although this relationship disappeared after gender was controlled for in a later study (Francis, 1985); neither was an association between neuroticism and religiosity found among students of religious studies (Fearn, Lewis and Francis, 2003). Some evidence has also been found that sudden converts (Scobie, 1975) and those with high religiosity (Francis, 1985) tend to be more introverted, but that the conservatively religious tend to be more extroverted (Scobie, 1975). However, another study found no relationship between extraversion and religiosity (Fearn, Lewis and Francis, 2003). Fundamentalist Christians have been seen to be less open to experience than non-fundamentalists (Saroglou, 2002; Streyffeler and McNally, 1998), and both fundamentalists and non-fundamentalists were lower than the general population in neuroticism and higher in extraversion (Streyffeler and McNally, 1998).

Thus, while it is possible that dimensions or types of religiosity are related to personality traits that may affect workplace attitudes and behaviors, not enough is known about these relationships to make conclusions about what the impact would be. More research, particularly incorporating personality traits of the FFM, is needed.

CONCLUSIONS AND SUMMARY

Several conclusions can be drawn from this review. First, while spirituality has been a topic of much management interest over the past few years, religion, a distinctly different concept, has not. Given the increasing religious diversity of the American workplace, we need to know much more.

Second, we have seen that religion in the workplace could be conceptualized in several ways: as behaviors (worship attendance or prayer frequency); as integrated (or not integrated) into various facets of life; as internalized or introjected; as a means (extrinsic), ends (intrinsic), or a search for meaning (quest); as driven by the degree to which the individual takes on a religious social identity. How we conceive religiosity in the workplace will in part determine any outcomes we may find.

Third, this review has shown that religion is relevant to the workplace in its relationships with employee attributes that, in turn, may affect attitudes and performance. In particular, religious workers may be more cost-effective (they may be healthier), more satisfied and better performers (they may be both physically and mentally healthier, more committed to the organization), able to deal with stress more effectively, more creative, more effective problem solvers and better team players (if stated concern for others translates into appropriate helping behaviors). However, they may also be prone to conflict due to religious differences, more prejudiced against their coworkers, and less intelligent. Little can be said about whether or not they will behave more ethically, or whether they have personality traits that help or hinder work performance.

In summary, then, we know very little about how religious workers will differ from their nonreligious or less religious counterparts. Given the increased religious diversity in the US and the growing importance of their religious beliefs to many Americans, further research is in order.

FUTURE DIRECTIONS

The dynamics of religion and religiosity in the workplace should be investigated through careful consideration and design based on three fundamental pieces of the research puzzle: theory, measures, and samples.

Theory

To understand workplace religiosity, the conceptualizations discussed in this paper should be applied using theoretical frameworks. For example, Weaver and Agle (2002) present a viable framework that could provide testable hypotheses about how dimensions of religion and conceptualizations of religiosity could impact work attitudes and behaviors. The previous discussion generates some thought-provoking questions: How do role expectations differ based on religious affiliation or on the type of religious motivation (i.e. intrinsic, extrinsic, or quest)? In what ways would salience of the religious role be affected by these three types of religious motivations? What organizational practices could be used to make religious role expectations either more or less salient? How could organizations use the religious orientations of their employees, through increasing salience or encouraging religious identities, to maximize desirable organizational outcomes, while maintaining legal defensibility against religious discrimination charges?

Additionally, other motivational aspects of religion have not been applied to research in the workplace, notably the intrinsic-extrinsic-quest construct. Applying this conceptualization to work-related outcomes would also pose some interesting questions. For example, since individuals high in the quest dimension seem to respond more appropriately to others' needs and are less prejudiced, would they be better team members? Would those high in intrinsic motivation be more likely to be committed to the organization since they may be more likely to define their work role as a calling?

Within this investigation, appropriate mediators and moderators should be considered (Cacioppo and Brandon, 2002; Pargament, 2002b). For example, positive relationships between religion and mental health have been hypothesized to be attributable to the effects of key mediators, such as social support (Joiner, Perez and Walker, 2002), or many religions' emphasis on hope (Snyder, Sigmon and Feldman, 2002). In fact, religion itself may serve to moderate or mediate between independent and dependent variables (Pearlin, 2002). Development and utilization of sound theoretical models would effectively incorporate relevant mediators and moderators.

Further research that incorporates these and other theoretical frameworks would create a much stronger foundation for future research in the field of religion in the workplace.

Measures

A major difficulty in drawing conclusions about past research is that religiosity is not defined or measured consistently (Hill and Hood, 1999; Hill and Pargament, 2003; Powell, Shahabi and Thoresen, 2003; Seeman, Dubin, and Seeman, 2003; Slater, Hall, and Edwards, 2001). As discussed above, measures range from single-items about church attendance to scales measuring different psychological constructs.

Religious workplace diversity involves a variety of faiths, some of which may not fit a simple single-item measure (for example, faiths that do not require attendance at services). Also, some people may consider themselves religious or "spiritual," but do not belong to an organized faith. Thus, a measure of religiosity as a psychological construct will be more generalizable across diverse individuals and are preferable in the study of workplace diversity. Religiosity is probably more accurately seen as a continuum (Miller and Thoresen, 2003), and therefore will be more precisely measured by a scaled instrument. Future research should abandon single-item measures of religious affiliation or frequency of attendance in favor of psychological constructs that are useful across faith traditions. Incorporating a theoretical framework, as suggested above, would provide the basis from which an appropriate measure could be devised.

Samples

Research on religion in the workplace should be done in organizational contexts. By itself, this would increase the diversity of samples found in the previous psychological research (Weaver and Agle, 2002), thus enhancing the generalizability of the results across faiths and providing avenues by which we can generalize more appropriately to the workforce.

Not surprisingly, much research from the US has centered on the effects of Christian faiths, notably Protestants, limiting the generalizability of results to non-Christians (Batson, et al., 1993; Pargament, 2002b; Snibbe and Markus, 2002). There may be key differences between Christian and non-Christian beliefs, such as whether or not God offers a personal relationship, or whether religious beliefs and concepts of the self are free from or constrained by social forces (Snibbe and Markus, 2002). Indeed, while well-being and religion have been associated in many small samples, in one study of large samples that were culturally and demographically diverse the relationship weakened (Diener and Clifton, 2002).

Research should also consider non-cross-sectional designs. For example, an individual's religiosity "score" undoubtedly changes over time for nearly all people (Pargament, 2002a). People coping with a terminal illness, a job loss, or dysfunctional children may be more religious than at other times in their lives. Since nearly all past research has been cross-sectional, how religiosity changes over time, and its relationships to key variables is not known.

This review has shown that understanding religiosity is probably relevant to the workplace in that differing religious orientations or motivations may have differential impacts on work attitudes and behaviors. Although organizations are prohibited by legal (and one would hope, ethical) limits in restricting the hiring of workers based on religious affiliation, understanding how differing religious approaches interact and affect individual behavior in the work environment will significantly enhance management's ability to effectively manage diversity.

REFERENCE

Allport, G.W. and Ross, J.M. (1967) Personal religious orientation and prejudice, *Journal of Personality and Social Psychology*, 5, 432–433.

Angelidis, J.P. and Ibrahim, N.A. (2002) Practical Implications of Educational Background on Future Corporate Executives' Social Responsibility Orientation, *Teaching Business Ethics*, 6, 117–126.

Angelidis, J.P. and Ibrahim, N.A. (2004) An Exploratory Study of the Impact of Degree of Religiousness Upon an Individual's Corporate Social Responsiveness Orientation, *Journal of Business Ethics*, 51, 119–128.

Ashforth, B.E. and Mael, F. (1989) Social identity theory and the organization, *Academy of Management Review*, 14, 20–39.

Ashforth, B.E. and Pratt, M.G. (2003) Institutionalized spirituality: an oxymoron? in R. A. Giacalone, and C. L. Jurkiewicz, eds., *Handbook of Workplace Spirituality and Organizational Performance*, 93–107, Armonk, NY: M.E. Sharpe.

Ashforth, B. and Vaidyanath, D. (2002) Work organizations as secular religions, *Journal of Management Inquiry*, 11, 359–370.

Atkinson, W. (2000) Divine accommodations: religion in the workplace, *Risk Management*, 47, 12–17.

Atkinson, W. (2004) Religion in the Workplace: Faith Versus Liability, *Risk Management*, 15(12), 18–23.

Barnett, T., Bass, K. and Brown, G. (1996) Religiosity, ethical ideology, and intentions to report a peer's wrongdoing, *Journal of Business Ethics*, 15, 1161–1174.

Barrick, M.R., and Mount, M.K. (1991) The big five personality dimensions and job performance: a meta-analysis, *Personnel Psychology*, 44, 1–26.

Baron, R.A. and Markman, G.D. (2000) Beyond social capital: how social skills can enhance entrepreneurs' success, *Academy of Management Executive*, 4, 106–116.

Batson, C.D., and Schoenrade, P. (1991) Measuring religion as quest: validity concerns, *Journal for the Scientific Study of Religion*, 30, 416–429.

Batson, C.D., Schoenrade, P. and Ventis, W.L. (1993) *Religion and the Individual*, New York, NY: Oxford University Press.

Braam, A.W., Beekman, A.T., Deeg, D.J., Smit, J.H., and van Tilburg, W. (1997) Religiosity as a protective or prognostic factor of depression in later life: results from a community survey in The Netherlands, *Acta Pscyhiatrica Scandinavia*, 96, 199–205.

Brown, R.B. (2003) Organizational spirituality: the skeptic's version, *Organization*, 10(2), 393–400.

Buchholz, R.A. and Rosenthal, S.B. (2003) Spirituality, consumption, and business, in R. A. Giacalone and C. L. Jurkiewicz, (eds.), *Handbook of Workplace Spirituality and Organizational Performance*, 152–180, Armonk, NY: M.E. Sharpe.

Cacioppo, J.T. and Brandon, M.E. (2002) Religious involvement and health: complex determinism, *Psychological Inquiry*, 13, 204–206.

Cash, K.C. and Gray, G.R. (2000) A framework for accommodating religion and spirituality in the workplace, *Academy of Management Executive*, 143, 124–134.

Clark, J.W., and Dawson, L.E. (1996) Personal religiousness and ethical judgements: an empirical analysis, *Journal of Business Ethics*, 15, 359–372.

Conroy, S.J. and Emerson, T.L. N. (2004) Business ethics and religion: religiosity as a predictor of ethical awareness among students, *Journal of Business Ethics*, 50, 383–396.

Cooper, C.L. (1984) Executive stress: A ten-country comparison, *Human Resource Management*, 23, 395–407.

Cooper, C.L., Cartwright, S. (1994) Healthy mind, healthy organization - a proactive approach to occupational stress, *Human Relations*, 47, 455–471.

Davidson, J.C. and Caddell, D.P. (1994) Religion and the meaning of work, *Journal for the Scientific Study of Religion*, 33, 135–147.

Degroot, T. and Kiker, D.S. (2003) A meta-analysis of the non-monetary effects of employee health management programs, *Human Resource Management*, 42, 53–69.

Dehler, G.E. and Welsh, M.A. (2003) The experience of work: Spirituality and the new workplace in R.A. Giacalone and C.L. Jurkiewicz, (eds.), *Handbook of Workplace Spirituality and Organizational Performance*, 108–122, Armonk, NY: M.E. Sharpe.

Diener, E., and Clifton, D. (2002) Life satisfaction and religiosity in broad probability samples, *Psychological Inquiry*, 13, 206–208.

Digh, P. (1998) Religion in the workplace: make a good-faith effort to accommodate, *HRMagazine*, 43, Dec., 84–92.

Donahue, M.J. (1985) Intrinsic and extrinsic religiousness: review and meta-analysis, *Journal of Personality and Social Psychology*, 48, 400–419.

Exline, J.J. (2002) Stumbling blocks on the religious road: fractured relationships, nagging vices, and the inner struggle to believe, *Psychological Inquiry*, 13, 182–189.

Fearn, M., Lewis, C.A., and Francis, L.J. (2003) Religion and personality among religious studies students: a replication, *Psychological Reports*, 93, 819–822.

Fehring, R.J., Miller, J.F. and Shaw, C. (1997) Spiritual well-being, religiosity, hope, depression and other mood states in elderly people coping with cancer, *Oncology Nursing Forum*, 24, 663–671.

Ferriani, N.A. and Batson, C.D. (1990) Religious orientation and traditional versus charismatic Bible study: a validation study, Unpublished manuscript, University of Kansas.

Francis, L.J. (1985) Personality and religion: theory and measurement in the psychology of religion, in L.B. Brown, (ed.) *Advances in Experimental Social Psychology*, 171–184, New York: Pergamon Press.

Fredrickson, B.L. (2002) How does religion benefit health and well-being? Are positive emotions active ingredients? *Psychological Inquiry*, 13, 209–213.

Fullterton, H.N. and Toossi, M. (2001) Labor force projections to 2010: steady growth and changing composition, *Monthly Labor Review*, 124(11), 21–38.

Geller, A. (2003) Religion can create tension in the workplace, *St. Joseph News-Press*, January 25, C-1–C-2.

George, L.K., Ellison, C.G. and Larson, D.B. (2002) Explaining the relationship between religious involvement and health, *Psychological Inquiry*, 13, 190–200.

Giacalone, R.A. and Jurkiewicz, C.L. (2003a) Toward a science of workplace spirituality, in R.A. Giacalone and C.L. Jurkiewicz, (eds.), *Handbook of Workplace Spirituality and Organizational Performance*, 3–28, Armonk, NY: M.E. Sharpe.

Giacalone, R.A. and Jurkiewicz, C.L. (2003b) Right from wrong: the influence of spirituality on perceptions of unethical business activities, *Journal of Business Ethics*, 46, 85–97.

Giorgi, L. and Marsh, C. (1991) The Protestant work ethic as a cultural phenomenon, *European Journal of Social Psychology*, 20, 499–517.

Glock, C.Y. (1959) The sociology of religion, in R. Merton, L. Bloom, and L. Cotrell, (eds.), *Sociology Today: Problems and Prospects*, 153–177, New York: Basic Books.

Glock, C.Y. and Stark, R. (1965) *Religion and Society in Tension*, Chicago: Rand McNally.

Gorsuch, R.L. and Mcpherson, S.E. (1987) Intrinsic/extrinsic measurement: I/E-revised and single-item scales, *Journal for the Scientific Study of Religion*, 28, 348–354.

Gottfredson, L.L. (1986) Societal consequences of the g factor in employment, *Journal of Vocational Behavior*, 29, 379–410.

Hackett, R.D., Lapierre, L.M. and Hausdorf, P.A. (2001) Understanding the links between work commitment constructs, *Journal of Vocational Behavior*, 58, 392–413.

Heneman, H.G. and Judge, T.A. (2003) *Staffing Organizations*, Middleton, WI: McGraw-Hill/Irwin.

Hicks, D.A. (2003) *Religion and The Workplace: Pluralism, Spirituality, Leadership*, Cambridge: Cambridge University Press.

Hill, P.C. and Hood, R.W. (eds.) (1999) *Measures of Religiosity*, Birmingham, AL: Religious Education Press.

Hill, P.C. and Smith, G.S. (2003) Coming to terms with spirituality and religion in the workplace, in R.A. Giacalone and C.L. Jurkiewicz, (eds.), *Handbook of Workplace Spirituality and Organizational Performance*, 231–243, Armonk, NY: M.E. Sharpe.

Hill, P.C. and Pargament, K.I. (2003) Advances in the conceptualization and measurement of religion and spirituality: implications for physical and mental health research, *American Psychologist*, 58, 64–74.

Hoge, D.R. and De Zulueta, E. (1985) Salience as a condition for various social consequences of religious commitment, *Journal for the Scientific Study of Religion*, 24, 1–118.

Hogg, M.A. and Terry, D.J. (2000) Social identity and self-categorization processes in organizational contexts, *Academy of Management Review*, 25, 121–140.

HRMagazine (1996) Eleven steps to a more spiritual company, April: 86.

Hunter, J.E. (1986) Cognitive ability, cognitive aptitudes, job knowledge, and job performance, *Journal of Vocational Behavior*, 29, 340–362.

Ivancevich, J.M. and Matteson, M.T. (1980) Optimizing human resources: a case for preventive health and stress management, *Organizational Dynamics*, 9, 4–10.

James, W. (2003) *The Varieties of Religious Experience*, New York: New American Library.

Joiner, T.E., Jr., Perez, M. and Walker, R.L. (2002) Playing devil's advocate: why not conclude that the relation of religiosity to mental health reduces to mundane mediators? *Psychological Inquiry*, 13, 214–216.

Kark, J.D., Carmel, S., Sinnreich, R., Goldberger, N. and Friedlander, Y. (1996) Psychosocial factors among members of religious and secular kibbutzim, *Israel Journal of Medical Science*, 32, 185–194.

Kark, J.D., Shemi, G., Friedlander, Y., Martin, O., Manor, O. and Blondheim, S.H. (1996) Does religious observance promote health? Mortality in secular vs. religious kibbutzim in Israel, *American Journal of Public Health*, 86, 341–346.

Kennedy, E.J. and Lawton, L. (1998) Religiousness and business ethics, *Journal of Business Ethics*, 17, 163–175.

Koenig, H.G., McCullough, M.E. and Larson, D.B. (2001) *Handbook of Religion and Health*, New York: Oxford University Press.

Kojetin, B.A., McIntosh, D.N., Bridges, R.A. and Spilka, B. (1987) Quest: constructive search or religious conflict? *Journal for the Scientific Study of Religion*, 16, 111–115.

Kreitner, R. and Kinicki, A. (2004) *Organizational Behavior* (6th ed.), New York: McGraw-Hill/Irwin.

Landy, F.J., and Shankster, L.J. (1994) Personnel selection and placement, *Annual Review of Psychology*, 45, 261–296.

Lechner, P.I. (1990) Application of theory and research on cognitive schemata to the concept of God, *Dissertation Abstracts International*, 50(10), 5298–5299.

Lindsay, R.A. and Bach, E.H. (1999) SHRM white paper: prohibiting discrimination based on religion: an employer's obligation, *Religion in the Workplace Survey*, Alexandria, VA: Society for Human Resource Management.

Lips-Wiersma, M. (2003) Making conscious choices in doing research on workplace spirituality: utilizing the holistic development model to articulate values, assumptions and dogmas of the knower, *Journal of Organizational Change Management*, 16, 406–425.

Lund-Dean, K., Fornaciari, C.J. and Mcgee, J. (2003) Research in spirituality, religion, and work: walking the line between relevance and legitimacy, *Journal of Organizational Change Management*, 16, 378–395.

Mackie, K.S., Holahan, C.K. and Gottlieb, N.H. (2001) Employee involvement management practices, work stress, and depression in employees of a human services residential care facility, *Human Relations*, 54, 1065–1092.

Mahoney, A., Pargament, K.I., Jewell, T., Swank, A., Scott, E., Emery, E. and Rye, M. (1999) Marriage and the spiritual realm: the role of proximal and distal religious constructs in marital functioning, *Journal of Family Psychology*, 13, 321–338.

Marler, P.L. and Hadaway, C.K. (2002) Being religious or being spiritual in America: a zero-sum proposition? *Journal for the Scientific Study of Religion*, 41, 289–300.

Mathieu, J.E., and Zajac, D.M. (1990) A review and meta-analysis of the antecedents, correlates and consequences of organizational commitment, *Psychological Bulletin*, 108, 171–194.

McDevitt, R. and Van Hise, J. (2002) Influences in ethical dilemmas of increasing intensity, *Journal of Business Ethics*, 40, 261–274.

McIntosh, D.N. (1997) Religion-as-schema, with implications for the relation between religion and coping, in B. Spilka and D.N. McIntosh, (eds.), *The Psychology of Religion*, 171–183, Boulder, Colorado: Westview Press.

McKibbin, S. (1995) The soul of a corporation, *Hospitals and Health Networks*, 69, 20–26.

Miller, W.R., and Thoresen, C.E. (2003) Spirituality, religion and health, *American Psychologist*, 58, 24–35.

Milliman, J., Czaplewski, A.J. and Ferguson, J. (2003) Workplace spirituality and employee work attitudes, *Journal of Organizational Change Management*, 16, 426–447.

Mitroff, I.I. (2003) Do not promote religion under the guise of spirituality, *Organization*, 10, 375–382.

Mitroff, I.I., and Denton, E.A. (1999a) *A Spiritual Audit of Corporate America: A Hard Look at Spirituality, Religion, and Values in The Workplace*, San Francisco, CA: Jossey-Bass.

Mitroff, I.I. and Denton, E.A. (1999b) A study of spirituality in the workplace, *Sloan Management Review*, 40(4), 83–92.

Morgan, J.F. (2004) How should business respond to a more religious workplace? *S.A.M. Advanced Management Journal*, 69(4), 11–19.

Mowday, R.T., Porter, L.W. and Steers, R.M. (1982) *Employee Organization Linkages: The Psychology of Commitment, Absenteeism, and Turnover*, New York: Academic Press.

Norris, D.R. and Niebuhr, R.E. (1984) Attributional influences on the job performance-satisfaction relationship, *Academy of Management Journal*, 27, 424–431.

Oldham, G.R. and Cummings, A. (1996) Employee creativity: personal and contextual factors at work, *Academy of Management Journal*, 39, 607–634.

Paloutzian, R.F., Emmons, R.A. and Keortge, S.G. (2003) Spiritual well-being, spiritual intelligence, and health workplace policy, in R.A. Giacalone and C.L. Jurkiewicz, (eds.), *Handbook of Workplace Spirituality and Organizational Performance*, 123–136, Armonk, NY: M.E. Sharpe.

Pargament, K.I. (1997) *The Psychology of Religion and Coping: Theory, Research and Practice*, New York: Guilford.

Pargament, K.I. (2002a) The bitter and the sweet: an evaluation of the costs and benefits of religiousness, *Psychological Inquiry*, 13, 168–181.

Pargament, K.I. (2002b) Is religion nothing but . . . ? Explaining religion versus explaining religion away, *Psychological Inquiry*, 13, 239–244.

Pargament, K.I., Koenig, H.G. and Perez, L.M. (2000) The many methods of religious coping: development and initial validation of the RCOPE, *Journal of Clinical Psychology*, 56, 519–543.

Pargament, K.I., and Park, C.L. (1997) In times of stress: the religion-coping connection, in B. Spilka, and D.N. McIntosh, (eds.), *The Psychology of Religion*, 43–53, Boulder, Colorado: Westview Press.

Pargament, K.I., Tyler, F.B., and Steele, R.E. (1979) Is fit it? the relationship between church/synagogue member fit and the psychosocial competence of the member, *Journal of Community Psychology*, 7, 243–252.

Paul, R.J. (2003) Managing employee depression in the workplace, *Review of Business Jamaica*, 24, 31–37.

Pearlin, L. (2002) Some institutional and stress process perspectives on religion and health, *Psychological Inquiry*, 13, 217–220.

Piedmont, R.L. (1999) Strategies for using the five-factor model of personality in religious research, *Journal of Psychology and Theology*, 27, 338–350.

Pizarro, D. and Salovey, P. (2002) Religious systems as emotionally intelligent organizations, *Psychological Inquiry*, 13, 220–222.

Powell, L.H, Shahabi, L. and Thoresen, C.E. (2003) Religion and spirituality, *American Psychologist*, 58, 36–52.

Ree, M.J. and Earles, J.A. (1991) Predicting training success: Not much more than g, *Personnel Psychology*, 44, 321–332.

Rhodes, T.L. (2003) When the spirit moves you: Administration, law, and spirituality in the workplace, in R.A. Giacalone and C.L. Jurkiewicz, (eds.), *Handbook of Workplace Spirituality and Organizational Performance*, 378–389, Armonk, NY: M.E. Sharpe.

Riketta, M. (2002) Attitudinal organizational commitment and job performance, *Journal of Organizational Behavior*, 23, 257–266.

Ryan, R.M., Rigby, S. and King, K. (1993) Two types of religious internalization and their relations to religious orientations and mental health, *Journal of Personality and Social Psychology*, 65, 586–596.

Salgado, J.F. (1997) The five-factor model of personality and job performance in the European community, *Journal of Applied Psychology*, 82, 30–43.

Saroglou, V. (2002) Religion and the five factors of personality, *Personality and Individual Differences*, 32, 15–25.

Scobie, G.E.W. (1975) *Psychology of Religion*, London: Batsford.

Scott, S.G. and Bruce, R.A. (1994) Determinants of innovative behavior: A path model of individual innovation in the workplace, *Academy of Management Journal*, 37, 580–607.

Seeman, T.E., Dubin, L.F. and Seeman, M. (2003) Religiosity/spirituality and health: a critical review of the evidence for biological pathways, *American Psychologist*, 58, 53–63.

Shimron, Y. (2003) In the company with God, *Kansas City Star*, March 15, G-1, G-4.

Simpson, J.A. (2002) The ultimate elixir? *Psychological Inquiry*, 13, 226–229.

Slater, W., Hall, T.W. and Edwards, K.J. (2001) Measuring religion and spirituality: where are we and were are we going? *Journal of Psychology and Theology*, 29, 4–21.

Snibbe, A.C., and Markus, H.R. (2002) The psychology of religion and the religion of psychology, *Psychological Inquiry*, 13, 229–234.

Snyder, C.R., Sigmon, D.R. and Feldman, D.B. (2002) Hope for the sacred and vice versa: positive goal-directed thinking and religion, *Psychological Inquiry*, 13, 234–238.

Society for Human Resource Management and Tannenbaum Center (2001) *Religion in the Workplace Survey*, Alexandria, VA: Society for Human Resource Management.

Sternberg, R.J. (2003) WICS: a model of leadership in organizations, *Academy of Management Learning and Education*, 2, 386–401.

Streyffeler, L.L. and McNally, R.J. (1998) Fundamentalists and liberals: personality characteristics of protestant Christians, *Personality and Individual Differences*, 24, 579–580.

Taggar, S. (2002) Individual creativity and group ability to utilize individual creative resources: a multilevel approach, *Academy of Management Journal*, 45, 315–330.

Taylor, A. and MacDonald, D.A. (1998) Religion and the five factor model of personality: a exploratory investigation using a Canadian university sample, *Personality and Individual Differences*, 27, 1243–1259.

Tepper, B.J. (2003) Organizational citizenship behavior and the spiritual employee, in R.A. Giacalone and C.L. Jurkiewicz, (eds.), *Handbook of Workplace Spirituality and Organizational Performance*, 181–190, Armonk, NY: M.E. Sharpe.

Tett, R.P. and Meyer, J.P. (1993) Job satisfaction, organizational commitment, turnover intention and turnover: path analysis based on meta-analytic findings, *Personnel Psychology*, 46, 259–293.

Thompson, L. (2003) Improving the creativity of organizational work groups, *Academy of Management Executive*, 17, 96–111.

Unsworth, K. (2001) Unpacking creativity, *Academy of Management Review*, 26, 289–297.

Van Velsor, E. and Leslie, J.B. (1995) Why executives derail: perspectives across time and cultures, *Academy of Management Executive*, 9, 62–72.

Vinchur, A.J., Schippmann, J.S., Switzer, F.A. and Roth, P.L. (1998) A meta-analysis of the predictors of job performance for salespeople, *Journal of Applied Psychology*, 83, 586–597.

Weaver, G.R. and Agle, B.R. (2002) Religiosity and ethical behavior in organizations: a symbolic interactionist perspective, *Academy of Management Review*, 27, 77–87.

Wolf, M., Friedman, B. and Sutherland, D. (1998) *Religion in the Workplace: A Comprehensive Guide to Legal Rights and Responsibilities*, Chicago, IL: American Bar Association.

Worden, S. (2003) The role of religious and nationalist ethics in strategic leadership: the case of J.N. Tata, *Journal of Business Ethics*, 47, 147–164.

Wrzesneiwski, A., McCauley, C., Rozin, P. and Schwartz, B. (1997) Jobs, careers, and callings: people's relations to their work, *Journal of Research in Personality*, 31, 21–33.

Zellars, K.L. and Perrewe, P.L. (2003) The role of spirituality in occupational stress and well-being, in R.A. Giacalone and C.L. Jurkiewicz, (eds.), *Handbook of Workplace Spirituality and Organizational Performance*, 300–313, Armonk, NY: M.E. Sharpe.

Zinnbauer, B.J., Pargament, K.I., Cole, B.R., Mark S., Butter, E.M., Belavich, T.G., Hipp, K.M., Scott, A.B. and Kadar, J.L. (1997) Religion and spirituality: unfuzzying the fuzzy, *Journal for the Scientific Study of Religion*, 36, 549–564.

8

■

Spirituality For Managers:
Context and Critique

Gerald F. Cavanagh, S.J.
University of Detroit Mercy

There has been a dramatic upsurge in interest in spirituality among those who study, teach, and write about business management. This new interest is also apparent among practicing managers. Spirituality in the workplace helps many. However, the trend is disturbing to others. Among proponents, the need for spirituality is stated simply: "The modern focus on objectivity and the separation of science and spirituality, taken to fullness, leaves people separate from one another, separate from nature, and separate from the divine" (Whitney, 1997). Those who find it disturbing fear that spirituality in the workplace will lead to coercion and favoritism in the workplace. This potential for divisiveness will be addressed later.

NEED FOR SPIRITUALITY IN BUSINESS

The needs that businesspeople often feel are a separation from other people, alienation from their work, and a lack of meaning in their lives. They often experience their work, family life, and faith to be in separate compartments—50 to 70 hours per week at work, an hour on weekends for worship, and the time left over for family. This separation leaves one feeling dry, unfulfilled, and unhappy, and is often experienced as a profound absence or vacuum in one's life.

Parker Palmer finds a basic unconscious fault with many leaders. He calls it "functional atheism—the belief that ultimate responsibility for everything rests with *me*." According to this view, if anything useful is going to happen, I cannot expect God's help. I alone am the one who must make it happen (Palmer, 1994). He goes on to point out that functional atheism leads to dysfunctional behavior on every level of our lives: workaholism, burnout, lack of attention to people in our lives, broken families, and even violence. Note how functional atheism and the resulting narrow view of life and work trap one into a lifestyle and behaviors that are not only not spiritual, but are not even human.

This new movement is triggered by several occurrences that affect people in business, according to Judith Neal, a pioneer participant and scholar in the spirituality in business movement. She sees three major causes for this new interest:

1. The baby boomers, who came of age during the idealistic 1960s, are now reaching middle age. The mid-life journey, which is sometimes a mid-life crisis, occurs at this age. As she puts it, "Many look at their lives and calculate the time they have left. They ask . . . 'What do I want to do with the rest of my life?' 'What is my purpose?' 'Have I accomplished what I set out to do?'"

2. Downsizing and employers' demand for additional hours in the workplace have also triggered reflection. Today people no longer have secure jobs, and that is unsettling and encourages self-examination.

3. Finally, the year 2000, like the New Year, birthdays, religious holidays, and other landmark events, encourages reflection and new commitments for the future (Neal, 1997).

While this new interest is clear, let us nevertheless obtain a more accurate measure of the extent of this concern for soul and spirituality.

MEASURE OF INCREASED INTEREST

There are several indications of a dramatic increase in interest in spirituality among both practicing managers and academics. Some of these indicators are: (1) The increased number of sessions at the Academy of Management annual meetings that discuss spirituality and religion; (2) New books and articles on religion and spirituality in business; and (3) The new courses on religion, spirituality, and contemplation that are being offered in business schools.

ACADEMY OF MANAGEMENT

The 1998 annual Academy of Management meetings in San Diego attracted 5,000 management teachers, scholars, and managers from around the world. The overall theme of the 1998 meeting was "What Matters Most?" At least seven sessions explicitly discussed spirituality and/or religion and its relation to leadership and work. Six of the seven sessions were jointly presented by two or more of the 22 separate divisions of the Academy of Management. These six sessions thus merited special notice in the program as "Showcase Sessions," and were listed prominently in the program and were repeated in the individual section portions of the program.

It should be noted that this number is out of a total of about 900 sessions, and so is a very small percentage of the total. However, if we include the sessions explicitly devoted to business ethics, corporate social responsibility, ecology, and service learning, it would constitute perhaps 10 percent of the total. Significant here is the fact that the number of sessions on spirituality and/or religion has grown from zero in the last five years.

BOOKS, ARTICLES, JOURNALS, AND CONFERENCES

A bibliography distributed at a session on spirituality in the organization at the 1998 Academy of Management meeting lists no fewer than 72 books on the subject of spirituality and business. Showing the rapid rise in interest in this subject, 54 of these books have been published since 1992.

Many articles also have been published in recent years on spirituality and work, both in professional and in popular journals. Professional journals, such as *Personnel Journal* and *Training*, have carried articles, as have *Business Week* and *Fortune*. Even the *Wall Street Journal* (1998) carried a front-page article on spiritual direction.

There are at least two journals on spirituality: *Spirit at Work*,[1] edited by Judith Neal, professor of management, New Haven University, and *Business Spirit*.[2]

Conferences on spirituality at work abound, with 1998 conferences in Washington, D.C., Santa Fe, NM, Minneapolis, MN, Indianapolis, IN, Loveland, CO, British Colombia, Canada, and Puerto Vallarta, Mexico. The Puerto Vallarta conference attracted more than 500 attendees. Not suprisingly, some of the same people appear as presenters at these conferences. Some are also consultants, who are trying to sell their services.

COURSES ON SPIRITUALITY AND CONTEMPLATION

Several courses were offered in schools of business on spirituality at work and on contemplation in Fall, 1998. The courses were held at University of Scranton, University of Detroit Mercy, and Chapman. One of the more notable was at Santa Clara University and is designed by Andre L. Delbecq, McCarthy University Professor, Leavey School of Business and Administration. Delbecq was awarded a year-long fellowship by the American Council of Learned Societies to develop this course. He offered it to eight active chief executive officers (one commuting from Boston) and eight graduate business students. This course discusses substantive and very important issues of: business leadership as a calling; listening to the inner voice in the midst of turbulent business environments; the need for self-integration; discernment and senior business leadership; approaches to prayer and meditation; challenges of leadership power; the spiritual challenges of wealth vs. poverty of spirit; contemplative practices; and the mystery of suffering. Toward the end of the course the group will do a weekend retreat together.

Delbecq has superb credentials to initiate this course. He has done extensive consulting with CEOs, is past dean of the Santa Clara School of Business, is the author of many dozens of professional books and

---

[1]*Spirit at Work*, P. O. Box 420, Manalapan, NJ 07726. Journal is 6 issues per year for $35. The journal contains articles, lists of resources, book reviews, and commentary.

[2]*Business Spirit* is published 6 times per year by The Message Company, 4 Camino Azul, Santa Fe, NM 87505. Subscriptions are $29 per year.

articles, and is a Dean of Fellows of the Academy of Management. Initial reports on the course reveal that it is very successful.

This interest in spirituality embraces diverse traditions. The influence of the Koran on his business decisions and activities is cited by Farooq Kathwarai, CEO of Ethan Allen Interiors. Ranwal Rekhi, CEO of CyerMedia, speaks of how Sikhism affects his management style. *Forbes,* in July 1998, quoted these executives and many others on how their religion and spirituality affects them and their businesses.

Mark Belton, Vice President of General Mills, led a seminar at the National Black MBA Convention in Detroit entitled "Jesus in Blue Jeans." Belton cites the instability that the global economy and downsizings have brought as being one cause of the current interest in religion and spirituality in business. Work and jobs are no longer a source of security. As Belton puts it, "People are beginning to ask, Upon what rock will I build my future? Most are smart enough not to bet on their jobs" (*Detroit Free Press*, 1998).

CONTENT OF NEW SPIRITUALITY

This new spirituality in business means many things to different people. On the one hand, to many people spirituality means a search for personal meaning and a relation to the Supreme Being that many of us call God. For some religious executives and entrepreneurs, it means an affirmation of God and the Gospels in the workplace. On the other hand, to others it contains much that is "New Age" religious movement fad. For them, it is little more than acknowledgment of the importance of feelings and a "new consciousness."

DEFINITIONS

Proponents and those who practice spirituality in the workplace are not always clear in defining their efforts. However, in a 1998 "All Academy Symposium" that was addressed to the entire Academy of Management, Ian Mitroff, Professor of Management at the University of Southern California, defined spirituality as "the desire to find ultimate purpose in life, and to live accordingly."

Others define spirituality loosely as energy, meaning, knowing, etc. Some authors rely heavily on Taoist, Buddist, Hindu, Zen, and Native

American spiritualities. These authors correctly claim that these non-Western societies are better in integrating personal life, work, leisure, prayer, religion, and other aspects of one's life.

Another aspect of this movement is the growing number of "Christian capitalists," that is, believing Christians who are entrepreneurs. These entrepreneurs and managers make their faith known explicitly to their employees, customers, and others with whom they deal. They often encourage prayer groups among employees—often meeting an hour or so before work. This movement is made up largely of "born-again" Christians, and they tend to be conservative in their views and the causes they support (*U.S. News & World Report*, 1995).

These entrepreneurs are often Christian evangelicals, and they are committed to particular religious, social, and political beliefs. Their blending of religion and the workplace is made possible because they are the owners of the firm. This is difficult or impossible for a manager in a large publicly held firm.

The older religious traditions also have significant influence. For example, currently there is an upsurge in interest in spiritual direction. The *Wall Street Journal* (1998) ran an article about business and professional people seeking out a regular spiritual director. Cited in the article were national programs to train spiritual directors in Los Angeles at Loyola Marymount and in Omaha at Creighton University. The author cited the importance of the director listening and discerning, and she acknowledged that this was in the best tradition of Catholic spiritual direction.

Mitroff, at the above symposium, cited sobering data about people's attitude toward spirituality and religion. He estimates that 60% of people, at least in the United States, are positive toward spirituality but negative toward organized religion. He says that 30% of people are positive toward spirituality and religion, while only 10% are negative toward both. While these figures may merely reflect Mitroff's perception, this suspicion of organized religion has had an impact on how interest in spirituality has developed. In addition, for those who live in a pluralist society, where there is no one dominant religion, there is thus no single religious tradition that is able to lay claim to spirituality. Hence, spirituality in the workplace generally is not tied to a specific religious tradition.

SPIRITUALITY AND RELIGION

Spirituality historically has been rooted in religion. However, its current use in business and in the workplace is most often not associated with any specific religious tradition. There are several reasons for this separation: (1) Most Western societies are pluralistic; that is, there is no one dominant religious tradition that can be used as a foundation; (2) If used as a basis for a firm's vision and mission, depending on a specific religious tradition is not energy giving, but divisive, since people do not share that religious tradition; (3) Use of religion in the public forum can encourage distrust, dislike of outsiders, and suspicion, and that, in turn, can lead to the breakdown of democracy, and sometimes even to revolutions and war; (4) The nineteenth century European Enlightenment has made Westerners distrustful of religious values. Religion is judged to be opposed to rationality and science and the source of superstition and the irrational.

The above attitudes have been criticized, most notably by Stephen Carter, Professor of Law at Yale, in his best-selling book-length analysis, *The Culture of Disbelief* (1993). Carter points out how Western peoples seldom have an outright hostility to religion. Nevertheless, they do tend to trivialize religion, to treat it as a hobby or an unproductive emotional outlet. For most, it is acceptable to make reference to God as a formality; but, and especially for Americans, it is not acceptable to allow religious beliefs to enter into national public policy discussions. Then Carter goes on to make an excellent case of how religion is an essential part of most people's lives, and how they depend upon religious values and beliefs in both personal and public actions.

In spite of the fact that it is difficult to develop depth in any spirituality without a religious foundation, nevertheless spirit, spirituality, and even "the corporate mystic" have received considerable attention in recent years. And most of this emphasis has been severed from religious roots. Moreover, the basic issues are not new. O. H. Ohman in his classic, "Skyhooks," first published in the *Harvard Business Review* but often reprinted, makes a strong case for spirituality (Ohman, 1955).

Most of the books, articles, talks, and consultants who speak of "spirit at work," or "spirituality in the workplace" do not depend upon or make reference to any specific religious tradition. The objective of these efforts, in the words of an ad for a set of six taped talks that would help one to become a "corporate mystic," is to form "a higher level of consciousness . . . a spiritual perspective—which gives greater insight, creativity, and productivity—awakening new levels of joy, energy, opportunity, and personal satisfaction." Forty dollars will bring you six lectures that will enable you to become a "corporate mystic"![3] In the next section of this paper, we will examine the spirituality in business movement from the standpoint of Christian traditions.

SPIRITUALITY AND JUDEO-CHRISTIAN TRADITIONS

The spirituality in business movement is to some extent a descendent of the New Age Movement. It is difficult to critique either, because both are complex and diverse. The older and more widespread New Age Movement is criticized as egocentric, fringe, and somewhat unorthodox by the mainline Christian churches (Saliba, 1993). The cited article is from the spirituality journal, *The Way* (1993), which devoted an issue to the New Age spirituality. The spirituality in business movement is more focused, and thus does not merit the same criticism.

The spirit in business movement is becoming more popular, so it is fulfilling a need. Many of those who embrace spirit in business have felt that the mainline religions have not responded to their needs. In addition, many of these people are simply not aware of the wide variety of profound and time-tested spirituality traditions within Christianity.

GOD, PRAYER, PEOPLE, AND SUSTAINABILITY

There are many positive features of the spirituality in business movement. The following aspects of the movement are of help to men and women and also congruent with traditional Judeo-Christian traditions:

- People in the movement generally have a belief in God.
- Emphasis on quiet, prayer, and contemplation in one's life.
- Emphasis on the centrality of people and listening to others. This generally results in better relations with family and col-leagues.
- A commitment to better relations among peoples, and to help bring greater peace and harmony in the world.

---

[3] Ad mailing from Nightengale Conant in Niles, IL.

- The movement is also optimistic about the perfectibility of human nature and business culture; they are convinced that people and the world can become better.
- Commitment to a sustainable environment, to pass on a better world to future generations. This aspect of the movement is sometimes called eco-spirituality and has its own literature.

Two major figures in eco-spirituality are Catholic priests. The pioneer and prime inspiration for the theological reflection on God and the environment is the Jesuit Pierre Teilhard de Chardin (1959). Thomas Berry (1988) is a Passionist who has devoted himself to theology and ecology.

LIMITATIONS OF BUSINESS SPIRITUALITY

While most of the spirit in business movement is beneficial, there are some elements with which Christian theologians find fault. Spirit in business advocates are often pantheistic, that is, they see the Supreme Being as existing in all things. Such a God is not transcendent and is not a personal God. Thus, they are less likely to have faith in a loving God whose grace is essential for our salvation.

The New Age Movement has received vehement criticism from fundamentalist and evangelical Christians, sometimes even calling it Satanic and a product of the Antichrist. Yet both New Age and evangelical Christians share many common attitudes. Both find society in crisis. Both have a new enthusiasm for God and prayer. And both find traditional churches deficient. One critic comments:

> Evangelical Christianity (and other contemporary religious fundamentalism) and the New Age Movement are in fact sibling rivals sharing at least similar (if slightly eccentric) presuppositions about history and salvation. (Woods, 1993)

Another element that both evangelical Christianity and the spirituality in business movements share is a person-centered individualism. In the old American tradition dating back to the observations of Alexis de Tocqueville (1946), both groups find that it is *my* fulfillment and *my* relationship to God that is essential. There is little conviction of the important role of organizations of any kind, and less realization of the importance of the common good.

Another limitation of spirituality in business can occur when a particular religious tradition is espoused by a chief executive officer (CEO). Some CEOs are so enthusiastic about their own spiritual beliefs that they seem to demand that others embrace the same religious faith. There is then a danger of coercion for some and, for others, favoritism to those with similar beliefs. If handled well, common religious and spiritual beliefs in an organization can be fruitful. But if not handled well, they can lead to divisiveness and even lawsuits.

BUSINESS ETHICS, SPIRITUALITY, AND RELIGION

Business ethics has become a major concern of most business-people over the last few decades. Yet the spirituality in business movement has developed largely independent of this related movement. This lack of connection is not suprising in our fractured culture; but it is ironic, since the two movements could support one another, and there are many parallels in goals and inspiration. For example, both movements are: (1) focused on personal integrity and moral growth; (2) concerned with making the work and business environment more humane; (3) led by more visionary business executives; (4) Concerned with the physical environment and a sustainable future for all; and (5) growing in popularity with new books, articles, conferences in both the popular and academic circles. One reason for this may be that religion, which is a stimulus and source for traditional spirituality, has historically not been a significant resource for business ethics. A recent attempt to demonstrate the contribution of religious thinkers to business ethics is a special issue of *Business Ethics Quarterly* (1997). The editor of this special edition, Stewart Herman, sought contributions from representatives of Judaism, Roman Catholicism, and Protestant Christianity. He limited contributions to these religious traditions in order to "keep the project manageable in scope." The articles in this issue are widely read, very well received, and widely cited. The editor-in-chief of the journal, Dr. Patricia Werhane of the University of Virginia, says that she has had more requests for this issue than any other issue of the journal. Many have asked for another special issue, perhaps examining other traditions, such as Orthodox Christianity, Islam, Buddhism, Confucianism, and Hinduism. Another attempt to bridge the gap is the compilation of 150 articles on the influence of Christianity on economics and business, *On Moral Business: Classical and Contemporary Resources for Ethics in Economic Life* (Stackhouse et al., 1995).

In conclusion, the spirituality in business movement helps the businessperson to become more centered on the important things in life: God, people, family, and a physical world that can be passed on to our children. It enables the business person to gain a better sense of the role of God and other people in our world. Let us now examine in greater detail the meaning of this movement for businesspeople.

IMPLICATIONS FOR BUSINESS AND PRACTICING MANAGERS

Rich experiences need not be relegated to experiences outside of work and the firm. Many people would be much happier if their broader aspirations and desire for service wouldn't have to be left out of their business life. Many current leadership books, both scholarly and popular, cite the fact that our world is fragmented and that there is a "new search for purpose and meaning." Real leaders are most often proud of "their own feelings of inspiration, passion, elation, intensity, challenge, caring, and kindness—and yes, even love" (Kouzes and Posner, 1995).

FORD MOTOR AND SERVICE

Ford Motor Co. began a new three-day training program in 1998 for all upper and middle managers called the Business Leadership Institute. Most of the program is focused on "increasing shareholder value," but on the last day of the program Ford managers are asked to do a half-day of service work in the city. This work involves helping at a soup kitchen, homeless shelter, or building homes with Habitat for Humanity. The rationale for this half-day of activity, in which the managers, time is fully paid by Ford, is articulated by a Ford executive, in a written response to a participant:

1. It is the company's fundamental responsibility to the community in which it exists. This community is the source of our sales and we have a responsibility to give back to the world in which we live. This is not about selling cars. It is about being good corporate citizens.

2. We can learn from people in these agencies who have tremendous drive, teamwork, leadership, and organizational values. Most of these agencies accomplish great results on a shoestring. They know how to get things done with limited resources. As a company we need to emulate these traits. We can learn from them.

Ford has a comprehensive program for trying to bring spirit to its managers. But Ford is not alone.

SPIRIT BRINGS VISION AND INNOVATION

Executives, workers, and often the companies they are with, attempt to bring quiet, wholeness, spirit, and even contemplation and prayer into their lives. Boeing has enlisted poet David Whyte (1994) to read poems and stories to executives in order to encourage their creativity. Lotus Development has a "soul committee" that tries to build a strong culture and to aid teamwork. AT&T sends middle managers off for a three-day training that is aimed at helping managers better understand themselves and be able to listen to their employees (*Business Week*, 1995).

> In addition, . . . corporations like Chase Manhattan Bank, DuPont, AT&T, Apple Computer and others have tackled the subject of contribution by including a new question in their search for vision, "What is our higher purpose?" (Channon, 1992: 58)

DuPont agricultural products division created a vision topped by a banner headline: "A New Partnership with Nature." Such vision can create energy, enthusiasm, and creativity within the firm.

In searching for a source for such a new vision, some have turned to explicit spirituality. The source of much of that spirituality comes from "the great founders of the world's religions: Jesus, Moses, Buddha, Zoroaster, Mohammed, Krishna. . . . Their core values are always there: inner peace, truth, right-conduct, nonviolence, and above all, love" (Miller, 1997). Love of others is certainly the core of the teachings of Jesus Christ. A book that provides wisdom and a model for managers examines the life of Jesus, and how he as a leader dealt with his followers and others (Jones, 1995). Laurie Beth Jones takes passages from the Gospels and finds remarkably up-to-date messages for contemporary managers among the sayings and actions of Jesus. The book was so popular that it reached the national best-seller lists.

The spirit in business movement can bring vision and enthusiasm to a work environment. An executive who takes spirit seriously will be able to more readily lead and articulate vision for the firm. Tom Chappell, founder and CEO of Tom's of Maine, is an excellent example of such an executive. In his popular book, *The Soul of the Corporation*, he describes how his firm grew from a small natural soap and toothpaste firm to one that marketed nationally in supermarkets. But in the process, he found that he and others in the firm had lost a sense of personal mission and common purpose.

Looking for new insights, Chappell enrolled at Harvard Divinity School, and while there resolved to use his role as CEO to bring soul back to the firm. Chappell realized that "common values, a shared sense of purpose, can turn a company into a community where daily work takes on a deeper meaning and satisfaction" (Chappell, 1993).

Robert Greenleaf is an early pioneer of this movement. Decades ago he founded the now widespread "Servant-Leader Movement." Greenleaf's career was at AT&T, and after doing much management development work there, he reflected on the task (Greenleaf, 1973). Greenleaf's inspiration came from Jesus in the Gospels. His description of the effective leader is one who is a servant of those he leads. Greenleaf and the Greenleaf Center[4] have had an immense impact on business executives and other leaders over the past decades.

Several top managers of firms have articulated the overtly Christian vision that guided them as chief executive officers of their respective firms. Max DePree was chairman and CEO of Herman Miller. The firm was regularly listed on Fortune's list of "best managed" and "most innovative" companies during DePree's tenure. Max DePree spelled out his humane and religiously based philosophy of management (DePree, 1989). James Autry, who had been CEO of Meredith Communications, does much the same (Autry, 1991).

AGENDA FOR BUSINESS SCHOOLS

Schools of business are now challenged to bring some of the rich dimensions of vision and spirituality into business education. This

---

[4]Robert K. Greenleaf Center, 1100 W. 42nd St., Suite 321, Indianapolis, IN 46208.

challenge should be more fully and easily met by universities with religious roots, since religion and spirituality is generally contained in the university and the business school mission.

ACCREDITATION DEMANDS MISSION

The current accrediting criteria of both university-wide regional accrediting agencies and the American Assembly of Collegiate Schools of Business (AACSB) are heavily dependent upon each school's unique statement of their mission. The AACSB accrediting standards require that each school demonstrate that it is fulfilling its own self-declared mission. This statement of mission, plus the evidence that it is being fulfilled, is absolutely essential if a business school is to be accredited.

In their mission or vision statements, religiously rooted universities speak in terms of, for example: "service of faith and the promotion of justice," "compassionate service of persons in need," "concern for the dignity of the person and for the common good of the world community," "integration of the intellectual, spiritual, moral, and social development of students," "promotion of the understanding of religious, spiritual, and ethical dimensions of life," "educating to competence, conscience, and compassion," and "stewardship of resources." Such mission statements generally speak about religious and moral development of students, faith and justice, community, and helping those most in need.

Each business school then is required to demonstrate that it is accomplishing those goals. Over the coming decades, this focusing of efforts will have a profound effect on policies, practices, and hiring at religiously oriented business schools.

SERVICE LEARNING

It is becoming common for business schools to offer courses that require undergraduate and graduate students to do service for those people who are less advantaged in the community. Faculty have described the results of such service learning at professional meetings for a decade. Volunteer work in the local community is done at more than two dozen graduate programs in the United States, including, for example,

Stanford, Wharton, the University of Wisconsin, and the University of Maryland.

Service learning often has a profound influence on the student. Most MBA students have not done volunteer work among the very needy before. Such work generally has a positive impact on: their attitude toward the poor, recognition of the need to jump-start young people who come from broken families, poor schools, and disruptive neighborhoods, their view of the justice of the social and economic systems, and their own willingness to help the needy again in the future.

A critical factor in the success of service or volunteer work is reflection on the experience. Students can be asked to keep a journal and to reflect on such questions as: (1) What was the experience that you had? (2) What about the experience was most troubling? (3) What about the experience was most inspiring or empowering? and (4) How were you effected or changed by the experience? What did you learn? Such reflection is done in a group so that the experience of one can be heard by others, thus reinforcing each person's learning. Finally, students are asked to write a short paper with the above questions as a guide.

FAITH THAT DOES JUSTICE IN JESUIT UNIVERSITIES

The Society of Jesus (Jesuits) in 1975 asked that all Jesuit works focus on the call of Jesus and the special needs of the poor. In 1999 each of the Jesuit universities of the United States did an audit of the progress they made in their activities and policies on "the faith that does justice." The purpose was to examine the results of each individual university's work for social justice, stemming from the Gospels. For example, how have these efforts affected attitudes of students, faculty, staff, hiring, and other policies of each university? The individual university audit also included successes, failures, and the work that is yet to be accomplished.

Each university then sent representatives to regional meetings in 1999 and to an international meeting in 2000. These meetings will enable participants to gain further insight on how faith and the Gospels provide a foundation for an effective university vision and mission. In addition, the meetings will enable each university to see the results of a wide variety of programs for helping those in our society who are most in need, and to learn from the successes and failures of each university.

SPIRITUALITY IN THE CLASSROOM

Bringing spirituality or soul into the classroom and the curriculum should be easier for religiously oriented business schools. Beginning class with a short prayer brings a sense of perspective. This prayer can be largely silence and/or can be said in a fashion that includes men and women of various religious traditions.

Business schools can also find opportunities for students to obtain a clearer sense of their own personal values and goals. Students can be asked to write out their own life goals and to prioritize their own personal values. One method is to ask students to specify their major goals in the areas of: career, personal relationships, leisure satisfactions, learning and education, and religion and spiritual growth. A student then writes a brief paper comparing her or his major life goals in each of the above areas with their top personal values (Cavanagh, 1998, pp. 33–36). In doing so, the student is often able to obtain new insights into their own values and goals. The process enables each person to highlight their own major goals, and to then take steps to better achieve those goals. This also enables a person to make changes in one's life, such as changing jobs, spending more time with family, or reestablishing friendships.

Business schools, like other professional schools, have been accused of teaching techniques of the profession and neglecting the larger historical, social, and ethical issues that undergird the profession. A university typically adds this dimension, and thus provides a broader and ultimately more useful education than do many secular or stand-alone professional schools. Encouraging students to examine the social and moral impact of, for example, global markets, mergers, speculation, downsizings, advertising, and the media, broadens a student's perspective. Larger issues, such as the historical roots of business values, how the values of a firm affect personal values, ethical behavior in business, and maturity and moral development of the person—all give a student a much wider lens with which to view and understand their own work and lives. This knowledge also enables the individual student to more easily establish their own personal goals and moral values, and to more easily cope with the difficult ethical choices with which that student will be confronted in their professional life.[5]

CONCLUSIONS

Spirituality enables a businessperson to gain a better perspective on one's firm, family, neighbors, community, and one's self. Furthermore, acknowledging dependence on God gives the individual manager a more stable and helpful vision. The manager then knows that her success also depends on someone beyond herself, so such a view also lessens stress. Such a vision also enables the manager to integrate one's life so that it is less segmented or compartmentalized.

There is much evidence of this new interest in spirituality in business. Business managers and firms now depend more on vision and spirituality in the workplace. This new movement is manifested in a wide variety of ways, and much of it is compatible with and supports Christian spirituality.

Religiously oriented universities are thus challenged to take a leadership role in helping all universities to integrate spirituality, religion, and religious values into their education. Business schools in religiously oriented universities have an important role to play, both in fulfilling the mission of their university, and also because spirituality provides a unique opportunity to make some of the most valuable elements of our heritage available to others.

REFERENCE

Autry, J. (1991), *Love and Profit: The Art of Caring Leadership*, Avon, New York, New York.

Berry, T. (1988), *The Dream of the Earth*, Sierra Club Books, San Francisco, CA.

Bolman, L., & Deal. T. (1995), *Leading with Soul: An Uncommon Journey of the Spirit*, Jossey-Bass, San Francisco, CA.

Business Ethics Quarterly (1997), Vol. 7, March.

Business Week (1995), "Companies Hit the Road Less Traveled," June 5, pp. 82–86.

---

[5]The substantive issues listed here, along with an evaluation of their influence on personal and organizational values, are the substance of *American Business Values with International Perspectives* (Cavanagh, 1998). The service learning project, along with the journal, group reflection, and paper, are described on pp. 104–105.

Carter, S. (1993), *The Culture of Disbelief*, Basic Books, New York.

Cavanagh, G. (1998), *American Business Values with International Perspectives*, 4th ed., Prentice Hall, Upper Saddle River, NJ.

Channon, J. (1992), "Creating Esprit de Corps." in Renish, J. (ed.), *New Traditions in Business: Spirit and Leadership in the 21st Century*, Berrett-Koehler, San Francisco, p. 58.

Chappell, T. (1993), *The Soul of Business: Managing for Profit and the Public Good*, Bantam, New York.

Chardin, P. T. de (1959), *Phenomenon of Man*, Harper, New York.

Congar, J. (1994), *Spirit at Work: Discovering the Spirituality in Leadership*, Jossey-Bass, San Francisco, CA.

Detroit Free Press (1998), "Taking God to Work: Some Business Leaders Let Religion Influence Vision, Employee Policy," Oct. 2, pp. 1A and 9A.

DePree, M. (1989), *Leadership Is an Art*, Dell, New York.

Greenleaf, R. (1973), *The Servant Leader*, Greenleaf Center, Newton Center, MA.

Harman, W., and Porter, M. (1997), *The New Business of Business*, Barrett-Koehler, San Francisco, CA.

Hexham, I. (1992), "The Evangelical Response to the New Age," in Lewis, J., and Melton, G. (Eds.), *Perspectives on the New Age*, Albany, State University of New York Press.

Jones, L. B. (1995), *Jesus, CEO: Using Ancient Wisdom for Visionary Leadership*, Hyperion, New York.

Kouzes, J., and Posner, B. (1995), *The Leadership Challenge: How to Keep Getting Extraordinary Things Done in Organizations*, Jossey-Bass, San Francisco, CA.

Laabs, J. (1995), "Balancing Spirituality and Work," *Personnel Journal*, Vol. 74, No. 9, pp. 60–64.

Lee, C., and Zemke, R. (1993), "The Search for Spirit in the Work-place," *Training*, June, pp. 21–28.

Miller, W. (1997), "How Do We Put Our Spiritual Values to Work?" in Harman (Ed.), *New Traditions in Business*, op. cit.

Moore, T. (1992), *Care of the Soul: A Guide for Cultivating Depth and Sacredness in Everyday Life*, HarperCollins, New York.

Neal, J. (1997), "Spirituality in Management Education: A Guide to Resources," *Journal of Management Education 21(1)*, February, pp. 121–139.

Ohman, O. H. (1955), "Skyhooks," *Harvard Business Review*, May–June.

Palmer, P. (1994), "Leading from Within: Out of the Shadow, into the Light" in *Spirit at Work*, Congar, J. (Ed.), Jossey-Bass, San Francisco, CA.

Renesch, J. (Ed.) (1992), *New Traditions in Business: Spirit and Leadership in the 21st Century*, Berrett-Koehler, San Francisco, CA.

Saliba, J. (1993), "A Christian Response to the New Age," *The Way*, July, pp. 222–232.

Smith, H. (1958), *The Religions of Man*, Harper & Row, New York.

Stackhouse, M., McCann, D., and Roels, S., with Williams, P. (Eds.) (1995), *On Moral Business: Classical and Contemporary Resources for Ethics in Economic Life*, William Eerdmans, Grand Rapids, MI.

Tocqueville, A. de (1946), *Democracy in America*, Knopf, New York.

Thich Nhat Hanh (1995), *Living Buddha, Living Christ*, Riverhead Books, New York.

U.S. News & World Report (1995), "The Christian Capitalists," March 13, pp. 52–63.

Wall Street Journal (1998), "After Their Checkup for the Body, Some Get One for the Soul," July 20.

Whitney, D. (1997), "Spirituality as an Organizing Principle," in Harman, W., and Porter, M. (Eds), *The New Business of Business*, Barrett-Koehler, San Francisco, CA.

Whyte, D. (1994), *The Heart Aroused: Poetry and Preservation of the Soul in Corporate America*, Currency Doubleday, New York.

Woods, R. (1993), "What Is New Age Spirituality," *The Way*, July.

9

■

What Does Spirituality Mean to Me?

Abbass F. Alkhafaji
Slippery Rock University

ABSTRACT

Spirituality in the workplace is a new concern for management in modern businesses. Many people believe that religion, or God, should be left outside the workplace. Today, there seems to be a changing attitude toward spirituality by some business leaders. How would management or any employee in the organization react if they see or hear someone praying or meditating next to them? This is starting to become common practice in some corporations. John D. Beckett, the president of R.W. Beckett Corporation, believes that spirituality and business should be brought together.[1] This paper will review the benefits of spirituality in the workplace. It will discuss this important issue from the point of view of a Muslim.

INTRODUCTION

Spirituality isn't merely practicing your religion; it's about the search for something bigger that connects you to a higher power that can energize you to perform your job better. You can't go to work every day without

---

[1]Braham, J. (1999, February 1). "The Spiritual Side." *Industry Week,* Vol. 248, Issue 3, pp. 48–56.

believing there's a good reason to do it. People set career goals to attain fulfillment from their job. Today people use their spirituality to help to get them through problems, to gain new perspectives, and to deal with ethical situations. Many people think that spirituality should not be part of the workplace, but for others "business as usual" is changing. The infusion of spirituality is catching on worldwide. These people are moving toward a new set of social values and a strong sense of inner peace.

Socrates taught the goodness of humanity. Because of his beliefs, he was forced to drink poison by the Greeks. He died for telling the truth and what he believed. Socrates, Buddha, and Confucius taught good morality. They taught ethical orientation, the importance of spiritual belief, and the belief in God and the hereafter. Some of the people who wrote about those individuals claim that they must have a divine message like messengers of God before them and after them (Abraham, Moses, Jesus, and Mohammed). All of those messengers stressed the coordination of spiritual aspects of life.

On the contrary, the two major groups of people, the rationalists and traditionalists, have ignored their call for this balance. For example, those who call for the mind embodied (rationalists) have ignored the spiritual dimensions of life—so much so, that they deny that there is such a thing as a soul. However, they make the best use of their mind in satisfying the craving of their bodies, the demands of sex and other necessities. The second group is called the soul embodied (traditionalists). They play down the demands of their bodies and are almost totally preoccupied with the concern of their spirit. In this regard, they go to such extremes that they do not utilize their brains fully.

These two groups in various societies have often been in conflict throughout history. This conflict has only been to the extent of debates, unless some rationalist has infiltrated into the other groups to master their support to hoodwink the masses. Even without any obvious or subtle infiltration, the traditionalists have by their uncaring attitude toward material well-being often allowed the rationalists to usurp the worldly rights of the traditionalists and their blind followers.

There, however, has been an exception to this rule in the form of divine prophets, smaller in number than the other groups. The message of this group has been consistent and persistent throughout the ages and challenging to cultures for both intellectual and spiritual myopia. This influential and consistent message is one for the life of the submission

Mind Embodied	Traditionalists
- Materialism: Do not believe in Soul. - Rationalists: Explain their behavior and use their mind. - Take advice of religious people. - Mostly are corporate people. They are knowledgeable and they run the show. - Less socially responsible.	- Mostly religious people. - Often do not use their brain and allow the rational people to run the country. - They dont care about worldly demands.—They are overspiritualists. - Pre-equipped with their spiritual aspects. - Often do not use technology or politics of the world. - They do not have a good idea of what is happening in the world.

to the providence culminating in the advent of the prophet Mohammed (peace be upon him).

SPIRITUALITY: DEFINITION AND MEANING

Spirituality is any effort that helps to lift individuals up and make them feel connected with a Supreme Being (the creator) in the sense of righteousness and accountability, at the same time remaining down to earth. One should not be overspiritualistic in the workplace. To serve people's needs properly is part of spirituality. It does not mean that we are neglectful of our worldly responsibilities for the absolute purpose of seeking the pleasure of God. (our family, our friends, and our communities).

- It is the needed relationship with the unseen dimension of divinity.
- It is the awareness of the inner and direct relation with God Almighty.
- There is a feeling that we are here to worship and to please God, the Creator and Sustainer of the universe, because we will be facing him again in the hereafter.

- It is how to affiliate your life devotion with God that makes life easier.

In order to please God, it is important to control the material desire, greed, and injustice to others. Some people see spirituality different from religion, while others see them connected. A third group of individuals use religion and spirituality interchangeably to mean the same thing.

We can say that religion is usually associated with an organized structure—i.e., the pope, bishops, pastors or priest, etc. Some of these religions do not have a hierarchy structure—such as the religion of Islam. Islam allows individuals direct relationships with the creator. Religion people usually perform certain rituals collectively. Spirituality is a kind of attitude or an orientation toward satisfying the demand of the metaphysical dimension of life.—i.e., non-material, the demand of your spirit and not the body. Therefore, individuals can enhance their level of spirituality by constantly reminding themselves of the commandments of God through reflection on philosophical issues, and reminding themselves of their origin and duties and responsibilities toward fellow human beings, other forms of life, and the environment.

Recently, some people started taking comfort in religion and talking about soul, mind, spirit, and God. They came to realize the importance of a relationship with God. This is especially the case with those who experienced crises in their life or witnessed their friend's crises. They started being open about their religious practices at home and in the office. For example, after the incident in Jonesboro, Arkansas, people attended Sunday service in record numbers.

Spiritual practices were private and usually conducted in a silent tone. Nowadays, people are more open about their spiritual interests and practices. Spirituality also has an important role in the workplace. Many people at work are attempting to discover their true selves and find a higher purpose and meaning to their lives.

The writer remembers a debate that he had 15 years ago with a corporate officer, who told the author that he will not expand his business to the Middle East or any Muslim country because the workers take time to pray five times a day. He, like many others, did not understand why Muslims pray together. The reason is the quest for unity and direction. The perception that Muslims take time off for prayers during working hours is itself wrong. In reality, no time during the work is utilized for prayers. Prayers are carried out either at home or during the lunch break. The morning prayer is done at home before sunrise, the noon prayer is done during lunch break, and the other three prayers are carried out at home in the evening and night. Friday in the Muslim country is a holiday and people work on Saturday and Sunday. On Friday they gather for a mass prayer in the mosque.

MANAGEMENT'S ROLE

In today's organizations, management is faced with the challenge of understanding and respecting the employee's spiritual right. They need to know how relevant the spirituality of the worker is to their effective performance in the company. The company must encourage these spiritual practices while not compromising the organization's objectives and work requirements. Management should first recognize that this is an important issue and then realize that some people like to practice spirituality privately. Management must make it clear that employees have the right to be spiritual as long as it will not interfere with their job. Make sure that the organizational environment is a tolerant one so that co-workers will understand and respect each other. Management concern should be with doing the job right the first time. Encourage people to work in a team environment, which requires the full understanding and appreciation of every member's capability and involvement.

In today's organizations, there seems to be a changing attitude toward spirituality by top-level management. For example, Jon Huntsman is the CEO of a privately held chemical company that emphasizes family values and spirituality but not a specific religion. He was also a leader in the Church of Jesus Christ of Latter-Day Saints. Huntsman feels that employees are entitled to their spirituality. He preaches that being a good mother or father is more important than the workplace. Apparently his ideas work. His privately held chemical company is the largest in the United States.

Another example is David L. Steward, the CEO of World Wide Technology Inc. This company was founded in St. Louis by Steward and has grown to an estimated $210 million. Steward promotes spirituality in his company. He keeps a Bible in his desk drawer and reads it daily. Steward has built a good relationship with his employees based on trust and integrity. A third example is Jeffrey H. Coors, president of ACX Technologies Inc. Although this is a public company, Jeff Coors still brings spirituality into the business. He regularly talks to his employees about his faith. He encourages people to be spiritual and to do their best in their job. He also believes a company might grow better if God is the focal point.

SPIRITUALITY ON AN INDIVIDUAL LEVEL

- Spirituality is unique to every individual and therefore it is hard to measure.
- It is a level of awareness and sensitivity that surpasses the physical condition.
- It is the awareness of the existence of the source and the oneness of this universe and the oneness of God. Everything in this universe is interconnected.
- It is how to discover comfort to make your life more meaningful.

Spirituality and religion are connected, but you can have one without the other. For example you belong to an organized religion, but you do not practice or attend services regularly. Or, you meditate or do yoga, but do not belong to a particular religion. The usual case, however, is that you have a religion and are spiritually motivated. Religion, however, is a more recognized part of a person's life. How people feel and think has a lot to do with their spirituality and religion.

Would you consider the following a spiritual practice?

- I am a Muslim.
- I pray five times a day.
- I read the holy book (*The Quran*).
- I read inspiration literature.
- I sometimes write my thoughts about religion.
- I tape myself or write poetry about some aspects of religion.
- On a continuous basis I explore how to live a more spiritual life.
- I attend some Friday prayers in congregation.
- I apply my religion to be a guideline for my daily life.
- I provide services to my communities in a variety of aspects.
- I review my practices to improve my lifestyle on a regular basis.

- I pray at work. A reminder of being good and obeying God.
- I praise God in the highest and the greatest constantly.

I think that such a practice gave me the strength and the power to be better in everything I do. More specifically:

- Spirituality to me is personal growth.
- It is a commitment to be a better person.

  - Honesty in dealing with others.
  - It helps me to forgive and forget.
  - It reminds me of my duty in the job and at home.
  - It reminds me not to be biased or prejudiced against others.

- It makes me more effective at my job.

  - It constantly reminds me several times a day to be fair and just in dealing with others.
  - It improves my decision-making skills.
  - It improves my listening skills.
  - It helps me to make ethical decisions.
  - It helps me to be more tolerant of others.

- It teaches me how to be open and patient with others.
- My regular prayers every day at certain times make me disciplined. This discipline, in turn, makes me more productive and more effective in my job.

CONCLUSION

Any effort at spiritualism is commendable, especially in this day and age of consumerism and materialism. The test of the ultimate effectiveness of such efforts ought to be the bottom-line question as to what kind of societal structure the desired system seeks to establish, and what kind of individual that societal structure is expected to produce. Muslims believe that Islam offers the ultimate balance among various aspects of human personality, and caters to their demands in a manner that no other system has so far been able to do. Any spiritual exercises that contribute to this balance would be praiseworthy, but anything that interferes with this golden mean may only be an exercise in futility. Spirituality is a big part of people's lives and it is becoming popular in the workplace. Some of the corporate leaders today are more than willing to include spirituality and religion in the workplace. This is a corporate issue that needs to be highlighted. The more that people talk about the subject, the more it is going to be in the public eye.

The divine message calls for reforms and a balance of the soul (spiritual aspects), the mind (intellectual aspects), and the body (social and economic well-being). It all depends on, and must be started with, a clean consciousness and a clean heart. The spiritual part is the basis for everything else. If the conscious mind and heart are not clean, everything will fall apart. The genuine divine message has always taught followers in various times and places to strike a balance between the demands of soul, mind, and body.

REFERENCE

Braham, J. (1999, February 1), "The Spiritual Side" *Industry Week, 248(3)*, pp. 48–56.
Miller, D. Patrick. "The Spirit of 9 to 5." *Yoga Journal.* Nov./Dec. 1997, pp. 73–79.
The San Diego Union-Tribune, "Spirituality on the Job." August 23, 1999.

10

■

Christian Spirituality and Contemporary Business Leadership

André L. Delbecq
Santa Clara University

INTRODUCTION

There is always an interest in how an individual speaker defines spirituality. My definition is:

> The unique and personal inner experience of and search for the fullest personal development through participation into the transcendent mystery.

It always involves a sense of belonging to a greater whole, and a sense of longing for a more complete fulfillment through touching the greater mystery (which in tradition I call *God*). My test of authenticity is the extent to which progress in the spirit of journey manifests itself in loving and compassionate service.

Since Robert Silvers asked each participant to speak from their individual spiritual traditions, I will discuss my interactions with executives in Silicon Valley with whom I have also shared religious reflection in the context of Santa Clara University as a Catholic and Jesuit institution. This is necessarily only my perspective and that of those executives I will report on. Christianity itself speaks with robust and diverse voices. Witness within the Catholic tradition diverse voices—

From the mountains: The Desert Fathers, John of the Cross, and the contemporary Carmelite Thomas Merion
From the valleys: St. Francis and the contemporary Teilhard de Chardin
From the City: Augustine, Aquinas, Ignatius, Newman, and the Contemporary Mother Theresa

There are also the great reformer voices of Christianity: Luther, Calvin, Wesley; black Christian spirituality (King); and feminist voices (Dorothy Day, Rosemary Ruether).

When I first began my intense study of Christian spirituality I was a bit taken aback by the diversity of the Christian voices. Then I reminded myself that God is infinite. So should there not be an infinite variety of voices speaking His language?

There is, of course, the common denominator among all the voices. God is love, and he who abides in God abides in Love and God in him. Love of God and Neighbor rests at the heart of Christian spirituality.

THE INSPIRATION OF BUSINESS LEADERS

Let me forthrightly state that my interest in spirituality in the context of business leadership did not flow from my own inner inspiration. Rather it came from experiencing the intense spirituality of senior executives in Silicon Valley, and their selflessness of service flowing from the richness of their individual inner journeys.

How then do I perceive the Christian message informing executive leadership?

A FEW ILLUSTRATIONS OF THEMES

Robert J. House and I first interviewed many of these executives as part of a leadership study of CEOs dealing with rapid-change environments in the 1980s. As I have come to know these individuals more intimately in subsequent years, there are some common themes from their Christian spiritual tradition which inform their individual journeys as senior executives.

Theme 1. *The Christian perspective on "calling" as an orientation to work that adds a sense of vitality and purpose to their leadership journey.*

The first and overarching theme is that business leadership for these individuals is a calling to service, not simply a job or a career.

They share the pivotal Christian belief that all creation is redeemed and good, and therefore being involved in co-creation through industrial enterprise can be an act of love.

They see their own role and the function of their business enterprise as a form of service, in this case the design and provision of goods or services which meet important societal needs.

Theme 2. *The integration of their spirituality with their work rather than the separation between a "private life of spirit" and a " public life of work."*

These individuals share the "Ignatian" ethos of being contemplatives in action; the Rahnerian notion of finding God in the everydayness of their organizational challenges.

They see business as a dominant social institution at the turn of the 20th century. They are aware that the vast majority of individuals in modern societies find the expression of their individual talents within the private-sector organization, that community will or will not be experienced primarily within these organizations, and that human solidarity will be impacted by the practices of these organizations. Therefore, to them leadership in the private-sector organization is a role worthy of the highest form of servant leadership.

This parallels the Ignatian notion of looking where God is at work at a time in history, and selecting a contemporary institution as a place for service.

LET ME MENTION THREE EXAMPLES

Retailing: The chairman and CEO of a retailing organization who created one of the healthiest organizational communities I encountered during my early years in California. A man growing up in very modest circumstances, he established a major firm to provide quality and fashionable goods at modest prices for people of limited means, and employed and trained individuals with modest social-economic backgrounds to manage his organizations. Within the company he established a culture of generous service to the customer, and a mature and respectful internal organizational ethos among a very diverse work force. He exemplifies the Christian beatitude: clothe the poor, through creating a remarkable corporation that does so, and employs the poor as well.

Data Systems: Another of my heroes is a computer scientist who formed one of the earliest firms providing databases to a variety of consumer and scientific groups. He believed that knowledge should be shared, so a worker in Kenya should have the same knowledge resources as a scholar at Oxford. With enormous courage, overcoming many technical and market obstacles, he created and modeled the potential for sharing information through computer technology truly being a contemporary "educator/missionary" across national boundaries.

Bioengineering: I think of a woman executive in love with biological science, adding an NMA to her credentials in biology, who through creative financing of early-stage bioscience developments was as much of a medical missionary as Albert Schweitzer. She was filled with a passion to eliminate several diseases through her bioscience financial efforts.

Theme 3. *Courage to stay the course and survive with dignity the special challenges of executive leadership which are daunting to the best and the brightest.*

These leaders must continually strive to lead through a vision which is bold and courageous, yet remain flexible in order to accommodate continual change. This calls for detachment from what is comfortable and familiar, often taking them and their organizations into high-risk paths. For many of these executives (often introverts with scientific training in Silicon Valley) this requires excruciating public presence, with constant need to interface with diverse stakeholders.

Through personal reflection and meditation they manage to balance the dangers of over extension and burnout (illustrated by the "hero myths" as described in the work of Sonnenfeld).

In addition, they experience the hypercriticism, public scrutiny, hard times, uneven successes, and many other trials of senior leadership.

TWO EXAMPLES

Environmental Services: My MBA's favorite profile of executive courage is the CEO of an environmental services company twice facing bankruptcy due to changes in legislation and government support, who remained dedicated to developing a breakthrough technology for dealing with automotive emissions. His story of snatching success from the jaws of defeat through rededication and inspiration of his managerial team is one of overcoming the greatest of hardships. His courage to deal with these setbacks and ability to help the management team remain focused on how to solve an important environmental problem is truly inspiring.

Finance Services: A banking executive who created many of the enabling financial structures for both early-phase technology firms and urban reconstruction, who envisioned banking as a way of enacting the great works of mercy. Through his commitment to banking as a calling he managed to sustain his political position through four ownership transfers (in an era of mergers and turbulence) in order to sustain the financial arrangements he had put in place to serve his clients.

THE BONFIRES OF EXECUTIVE VANITY: PRIDE, POWER AND WEALTH

Obviously the story of executive leadership is not always a story of unmitigated goodness. I find mischief and occasionally evil in the executive state as in all institutional sectors. However, for many Christian executives, I perceive and they report that their spirituality provides protection against the many pitfalls of executive leadership.

As identified by executives at a NASDAQ conference, the major cause of leadership failure is hubris. Or as Richard Hagberg, the consultant on leadership failure, writes, pride leads to executive failure because it leads to impatience, an unwillingness to build consensus, the inability to receive criticism, and the unwillingness to endure periods of trial and uncertainty. Humility as a Christian virtue looms large in the stories told by these executives.

CONCLUSION

Let me conclude these brief remarks by pointing out that in the contemporary business context illustrated by these brief vignettes of executives from Silicon Valley, I often listen to executives who tell me they find inner strength and wisdom in their Christian tradition which informs their leadership. It provides them with wisdom to discern and to reach toward noble goals, with contagious passion and courage that captivates their own and the energies of their colleagues, with the ability to sustain concentration and commitment in the face of daunting problems, with discipline which allows them to reduce their own egos and free themselves of debilitation obsessions, and with compassion that leads to a recognition of their own unity with their fellow men in all the stakeholder roles associated with business. For these executives, their spirituality is the integrative force enabling them to engage in business leadership as a form of human service, thus transforming it as part of the path for attaining their own union with The Transcendent Mystery. Nor do they expect that this path will always lead to success, and they are certain it does not allow them to avoid personal suffering. Thus, spirituality is a quiet but powerful force in their lives, not accounted for in most of our current management literature.

Of course I do not claim that only Christian spirituality matters. I have found Taoist Buddhist, Jewish, and Hindu executives with a similar centeredness transforming their leadership, but my task was to speak to Christian tradition, whose impact I find to be a major motivational element in the journeys of many Christian executives.

REFERENCE

Sonnenfeld, Jeffrey A., (1991), *The Hero's Farewell: What Happens When CEOs Retire*. New York, Oxford: Oxford University Press.

11

■

Managing with Ahimsa and Horse Sense: A Convergence of Body, Mind, and Spirit

Grace Ann Rosile
"Horse Sense At Work"

***Note**: Portions of this article are drawn from "Managing with Ahimsa and Horse Sense," published in March 1999 on the web site www.spiritatwork.com.

I have been teaching management courses for 20 years at the undergraduate as well as graduate levels. During this same time, I have been a student of Jain philosophy as presented by Gurudev Chitrabhanuji, as well as a lover of horses. Looking back, I see that these three distinct aspects of my life—the physical, mental, and spiritual—were not integrated very well. It was like three compatible strangers living as me. I even had totally different clothing for each activity.

Then my former husband (also a management professor) and I decided to combine my interest in horses with our business skills. We sold our suburban home and bought a beautiful horse stable with a run-down 100-year-old farmhouse. We spent over 10 years owning and operating a "full-service" horse business.

Soon stories of raising and training horses began to creep into my management lectures. Then one day Gurudev Chitrabhanuji and his Pittsburgh students all met for an enjoyable afternoon picnic at my farm. Everyone loved the closeness to nature and the beauty and gentleness of the horses. I was proud of the loving and peaceful aura I had established throughout my farm. Yet afterward, I began to examine how the standard practices of a horse business might look through the eyes of these people. I questioned how well I had applied Ahimsa and Jain philosophy to my practices with horses and with this business. My current work on "Managing with Horse Sense" emerged from the convergence of these three areas, representing body, mind, and spirit.

This chapter offers some examples of how my horses helped me to develop this integration and see the spiritual in my daily physical and mental work.

HORSE SENSE AND AHIMSA

For me, the term "horse sense" refers to what I learned about life, relationships, and management, from over 10 years of training horses. It is what the horses have taught me. And many of you may know that Ahimsa is the concept embraced by Gandhi, which is at the core of the Jain (from India) philosophy. Ahimsa* (see endnote) comes from a Sanskrit word which means "non-harmfulness." Ahimsa is not a religion; rather it is a daily spiritual practice of enhanced mindfulness and awareness. In the process of living, we cannot help but cause some harm. The spiritual path of Ahimsa asks that I constantly strive to minimize the harm I do in the world.

But what does horse sense have to do with Ahimsa? Horse sense is based upon my ability to understand how my horse thinks and feels. Since a horse does not speak, I had to develop a heightened awareness of subtle cues, body language, and the look in the eye, to know what a horse is "saying." In addition to understanding the horse, I learned to be understood, by using many verbal and non-verbal means of getting my message across to the horse. The skills I developed through this combination of "listening" and "speaking" to horses allowed me to avoid inadvertently harming or frightening, allowed me to build trust, and allowed me to overcome fear (my own and the horse's). Ultimately, I learned to "connect" with horses by establishing a loving, trusting, and understanding environment. This "connecting" goes beyond mere communicating. For me, it is a very spiritual experience, perhaps the essence of spirituality.

I realized my horse-related skills worked with people too, especially when I consciously applied them. This conscious application to human relationships at work can yield the same benefits of greater trust and understanding, and yes, even love, in the workplace.

Here is one story of how my young Arabian stallion Nahdique (pronounced nah deek) taught me something about practicing Ahimsa. He taught me that showing reverence for life can be the simple acknowledgment of that life, and that the absence of that acknowledgment can be very painful to others. It happened like this.

It was during a period when I was even busier than usual, teaching full-time at the university, running my horse business, and training my three Arabian stallions every day. To fit everything in I was riding Nahdique at 6 or 7am. On these chilly Pennsylvania mornings I would enter his stall, put his halter on his head, lead him into the concrete aisle, and tie him in place. I would quickly begin to groom and then saddle him. I began to notice that each day he was becoming more restless, acting like he might kick me, and beginning to snap at me. As he was getting worse, I was getting less patient. We had WORK to do!

One morning I was again issuing another sharp "no!" and I was about to smack him on the neck to get his attention so he could "hear" my message. Suddenly I stopped, and I realized HE had been trying to get MY attention. That morning, an awareness began. I paused to really look at Nahdique. I saw his body, tense and prepared to dodge the slap which he was clearly expecting. I saw his eyes, looking rebellious and resentful. I stopped, went to his right side, and looked into his eye. He watched me warily. I said slowly, "I'm sorry, buddy. I SEE you. I'm glad you're here." I put a hand out, then hugged his neck. I stepped back and saw the anger fade from his eyes, leaving some righteous resentfulness. Then his look said, "well okay, I guess I'll accept your apology." I stroked his neck again, and then he looked calm and content. The "apology" took only a minute. We continued our work with no further problems. After that, each morning I would look in this eyes and feel that connection for just a second. Then I would pat him and say "Hi buddy, how are you this morning?"

One morning a few weeks later, as I walked into his stall I was worried about some other issues. Without thinking about what I was doing, I stood motionless and I sent a mental message, "Hi buddy, can I have a hug this morning?" To my surprise he did something he never had done before. He calmly lifted his head from the hay he was munching and he gently rested his chin on my shoulder.

What did I learn from this? I had wanted that "connected" feeling of wondrous joy at communicating with one of God's most beautiful creations, the horse. In this insidious culture of productivity, speed, and efficiency, I had allowed my work to overshadow the importance of my relationships. Ironically, both the relationship and the work suffered. It took a horse to get my attention, to bring me back to awareness that my ultimate reason for working with horses was to experience that connected feeling. And then, when the relationship worked, the work was better too.

If such small gestures can be so important to "even" a horse, how much more important might they be to a person? Nahdique taught me that in business and in life, Ahimsa can be the simple acknowledgment of a fellow living being. A simple greeting can become a joyous affirmation of the connectedness of all life. One connection at a time is what it is all about. It's just horse sense.

To use horse sense to best promote understanding and enhance spirituality in the workplace, I recommend the following three strategies:

1. That we incorporate direct experience as a preferred methodology, relegating written texts to the role of serving the cause of direct experience
2. That we deepen the centuries-old practice of looking to nature to understand our world from a spiritual perspective
3. That we use horses for the opportunity they offer us, to have a direct experience of Nature, which is a close parallel with interpersonal relationships in the workplace

I will address each of the above three points in turn.

DIRECT EXPERIENCE AS PART OF LEARNING

The concept of "direct experience" was explicitly identified as a component in the theoretical model of learning widely popularized by Kolb and others in the 1960s and 1970s (see Kolb, 1984). However, learning through direct experience is still rather rare in our educational systems.

How can we reap the benefits of direct experience without giving up the value of collective knowledge? I suggest that narratives can serve this purpose.

Narratives are the communication medium of experience. Historically, one thing we see from cultures which are non-literate is that narratives play an important part in their learning and understanding. These narratives are stories, which means they have action, plot, characters, and some underlying theme or "moral" (Boje and Dennehy, 1994). In other words, narratives vicariously convey direct experience.

THE DIRECT EXPERIENCE OF NATURE AS A WAY OF LEARNING

We commonly think of Thoreau when we think of great philosophers who recommended the benefits of a direct experience of the natural environment. One recent study found that most respondents cited time spent outdoors in nature as the most common source of spiritual renewal. Warren Grossman (1999) presents a new twist on this old idea. He suggests that the earth's energy field truly operates as a nourishing mother. He presents evidence that direct physical contact with the earth (for example, standing barefoot on the ground) provides great physical, emotional, and spiritual healing.

Steingard and Fitzgibbons (1999) call for organizational studies in the new millennium to integrate both intellectual and experiential approaches, and to incorporate "a greater understanding of our relationship to the natural world" (p. 537). This relationship would not be based on dominating or transcending the natural world, but rather being an integral part of it, beyond the man/nature false dualism. They call this approach "Integral Organizational Studies."

Ivan Illich (1993) (and many postmodernists, among others) studied the way language has affected our ways of knowing. His book, *In the Vineyard of the Text,* examines some of the ways written language distanced humans from nature and shifted our focus from personal experience, which was personally conveyed, to written texts.

LEARNING, SPIRITUALITY, AND HORSES

We have seen that direct experience offers us something unique and irreplaceable in the learning process. The direct experience of nature is acknowledged to be a common path to greater spiritual awareness. Given that we can learn about humanity and spirituality from nature, I suggest that working with horses provides an opportunity for learning which is spiritually grounded and also uniquely relevant to our relationships in the workplace. I use the language of direct experience (that is, narrative) to offer my experiences in this area. I ask that the reader remember that the value of the story lies in your ability to make it your own. I offer my interpretations only as a starting point, because some of what I learned from these experiences I know I can only convey with you, me, and a horse all present. This I do in my workshops called "Horse Sense" (copyright 1999). These workshops offer experiences with obvious, direct, practical relevance to the workplace, while being personal and spiritual.

People have different definitions of what is spiritual to them. My stories offer personal insights, gained not through some mystical process or spiritual experience but through common daily interaction with horses. If you agree with me that shoveling manure is an enjoyable meditative process (I truly love it), then this is a spiritual experience also. Feeling a connection with a horse as we work together is an experience which is spiritual, physical, mental, emotional, aesthetic, and practical all at once.

Some people may have explicitly spiritual experiences with animals, as reported by Mannes:

> The stories I collected from people who have had spiritual experiences involving animals almost always involved personal insights, often occurring in the most private realm of dreams, and often so personal the storyteller could not even say what the experience meant, only that it was meaningful. (Mannes, 1997, p. 67)

I do not consider my experiences to be directly "spiritual" as such. I cite Mannes' quote here, because my daily work with horses often leaves me feeling that I do not know what these experiences have meant, yet I am completely convinced that they are deeply meaningful. I encourage you to allow yourself the gift of such experiences.

A FINAL STORY

At a conference of prominent academics in the field of discourse and organizational change, I took a big risk and told my "horse stories." The main point of these stories was (and is) to demonstrate the management implications of the best kind of horse and human partnerships. I believe these partnerships work best when characterized by mutual respect, mutual empowerment, and mutual trust. (With horses, you also need mutual liking or love. Whether that is true in human organizations is a story for another time.)

After telling several of my stories, I was responding to questions. A gentleman with a French-sounding accent asked, was I not perpetuating hierarchical notions of worker/manager with my horse/rider analogies, since the horse and rider could never change places? I explained that my main point was exactly the opposite, that only outsiders falsely perceived the rider to be completely dominant; my point was that the partnership was more that of equals. He did not agree. After several attempts to convince him that he had misunderstood my message, the gentleman still argued that I was promoting a managerialist view. Running out of both time and counterarguments, I said "YOU sit on that horse and tell me you are in control!" And everyone laughed.

My final response was not just a clever retort. It reflects the main reason I use my "horse stories." These stories are direct experience. The learning I received from those experiences can be only partially conveyed through language. It is the concrete, physical experience which adds a different dimension to our understanding. When I have told this story to other expert riders, they nod knowingly at that non-horse person's views. They assume a non-rider will not understand what they have learned through experience. Still, many people may be able to vicariously experience the events I recount and gain their own insights. So I work to be better at telling the stories, and I recommend my workshops or your own "field research" for direct learning experiences.

I have always liked what I once heard: that we are not physical beings learning to be spiritual; rather, we are spiritual beings learning to be physical.

I believe we can be physically spiritual.

Horses can teach us some of these lessons.

Note

*Ahimsa, or reverence for life, means respecting the right of all living things to live. For Jains (and for me), it means being vegetarian and not eating meat, fish, or poultry, and avoiding animal products like leather and silk. Ahimsa means non-violence. Practicing Ahimsa means living in such a way as to minimize the inevitable violence we commit every day, thanking even the plants for giving their lives to nourish us. Typically, Jains would not engage in any animal-related businesses. Elsewhere, I have a long explanation of what this means to me as a rider. In brief, such concerns have led me to leave the horse business and to restrict my riding to that which is mutually beneficial to myself and to the horse (we provide exercise for each other). I continue to question my relationship to horses, to make it as non-exploitive as possible.

In the Jain philosophy, the attitude of non-violence must extend also to non-violence in thoughts and beliefs. Thus, Jains do no missionary work. They believe that trying to persuade another that their ideas are wrong does violence to that other person's beliefs. In summary, Ahimsa is not a religion, but is a way of living (and managing) with a heightened awareness of the implications of our actions.

REFERENCE

Boje, D., and Dennehy, R. (1994), *Managing in the Postmodern World*. Dubuque IA: Kendall Hunt Publishers.

Grossman, Warren (1998), *To Be Healed by the Earth*. Cleveland, Ohio: The Institute of Light.

Illich, I. (1993), *In the Vineyard of the Text*. Chicago: The University of Chicago Press.

Kolb, D. (1984), *Experiential learning: Experience as the Soures for Learning and Development*. Englewood Cliffs, NJ: Prentice Hall.

Mannes, Christopher (1997), *Other Creations: Rediscovering the Spirituality of Animals*. New York: Doubleday.

Steingard, D., and Fitzgibbons, D. (1999). "R/E-volution in Organizational Theory: Organizational Science, Organizational Studies, and Integral Organizational Studies" in Biberman, J., and Alkhafaji, A. (eds.), *Business Research Yearbook*, Vol. VI, pp. 534–538.

ORGANIZATIONAL
AND SOCIETAL ISSUES
AND APPLICATIONS

12

■

Integral Sensemaking for Executives: The Evolution of Spiritually-Based Integral Consciousness

John E. Young and Jeanne M. Logsdon
University of New Mexico and University of New Mexico

This article presents philosophy and theory supporting an integral approach to executive sensemaking and problem solving, which is beginning to emerge as a result of the continuing evolution of consciousness. Integral sensemaking is contrasted with the mental-rational approach that has characterized management practice in the industrial and post-industrial eras. The two approaches to sensemaking are applied to the organizational context in five key areas: leadership, strategy formulation, organizational culture, ethical culture, and human resource management. Implications of the evolution of consciousness on management and spirituality and on organizations are discussed.

Key Words: *Spirituality, Integral Management, Sensemaking, Consciousness*

An early version of this manuscript was presented to the Management, Spirituality and Religion (MSR) Interest Group at the 2004 Academy of Management meetings.

Executives today face the daunting task of leading their organizations while facing exceedingly complex problems, including rapidly increasing globalization, war and terrorism, environmental change and degradation, extremism in various forms, accelerating technological change, and social turmoil. Effective executive leadership in such challenging environments requires the utilization of a consciousness capable of embracing differences in a comprehensive and creative unity (Chaudhuri, 1977; Anderson and Anderson, 2001; Torbert and Associates, 2004). This paper suggests that such a consciousness—integral consciousness—is beginning to unfold at the societal level and offers great potential for organizational leaders to cope with extraordinary and multi-dimensional change. The article further suggests that many of the challenges currently facing humankind essentially reflect failures of predominant worldviews or structures of consciousness.

An understanding of this evolution is essential if leaders of contemporary organizations are to enhance their spiritual awareness (Mitroff and Denton, 1999; Cavanagh, 2000; Pauchant, 2002) and attempt to solve the complex and critical challenges they face. For the shift to integral consciousness to occur, executives will need to transform their thinking from the mental-rational structure of consciousness that characterizes contemporary management practice. Scholars too will need to see beyond the mental-rational perspective that grounds much of their research in order to explore the promise of integral consciousness for more effective management in their research.

Specifically, this article focuses on the question, "How will the emerging integral structure of consciousness affect executive sensemaking and problem solving?" We answer this question by first identifying arguments and notable philosophers who support the concept of the evolution of consciousness. Secondly, key characteristics of the current mental-rational and emerging integral structures of consciousness are generally described, compared, and illustrated in the context of executive sensemaking. Next, the mental-rational and integral structures are applied to five key organizational functions, namely leadership, strategy formulation, organizational culture, ethical culture, and human resource management. Finally, we discuss the implications of the evolution of consciousness on management and spirituality and on organizations.

THE EVOLUTION OF CONSCIOUSNESS

The underlying premise of this article is that human consciousness is evolving both collectively and individually, and it has done so in progressive stages over the millennia. The concept of evolution to describe fundamental change is commonplace in many academic disciplines that take a long-term perspective (e.g., biology, cultural anthropology and sociology, astronomy, palaeontology, etc.). However, it has not been applied to management[1], and for a very good reason. The field of management began only in last third of the 1800s with the growth of large-scale private-sector business organizations beginning with the railroads and did not flourish until after World War II (e.g., Chandler, 1977).

The ideas of four major 20th-century proponents of the concept of an evolving human consciousness are briefly described in this section. First, we introduce three pioneers who intuited the notion of the evolution of consciousness: Pierre Teilhard de Chardin, Jean Gebser, and Sri Aurobindo. A brief presentation of the views of Ken Wilber, the most prominent contemporary proponent, follow. Teilhard de Chardin, Gebser, and Aurobindo developed their pioneering perspectives independently of each other in disparate parts of the globe and from different perspectives. They all concluded that the unfolding of the universe is a physically as well as a spiritually evolutionary phenomenon. Wilber, the only one of the four philosophers currently living, synthesized and augmented the work of these as well as other philosophers.

Pierre Teilhard de Chardin

Teilhard de Chardin (1881–1955) was a French Jesuit paleontologist, and the Christian faith was central to his vision and work (King, 1996). He was the first major philosopher in the West to articulate, in a comprehensive manner, that evolution and the sacred identity are correlated (Swimme, 2001). He felt that there is only one truth and that religion and science are two separate avenues toward this truth. As a

---

[1] The population ecology perspective attempts to explain shifts in the composition of organizational populations within industries and geographical regions by using some biological concepts, such as niche, but it has no grand theory of evolution.

result of his view of the complementary relationship between religion and science, he is considered by some as a modern-day analogue of St. Thomas Aquinas (Provenzano, 1993). It has been suggested that in time, during the present millennium, Teilhard de Chardin will be regarded as the fourth major thinker of the Western Christian tradition along with St. Paul, St. Augustine, and St. Thomas Aquinas (Swimme, 2001). Some of his most notable works include *The Phenomenon of Man* (1959), *The Divine Milieu* (1963), and *The Future of Man* (1965).

Perhaps the most significant of Teilhard's propositions was what he called The Law of Consciousness and Complexity. This idea suggests that evolution is a process that is continuously striving to produce increasingly complex creatures with increasing levels of consciousness. He believed that this law was the most fundamental aspect of the universe. Further, he perceived a primordial urge, present in all matter and energy, to combine into structures of increased complexity and consciousness (Provenzano, 1993). Human beings with their capacity for self-reflection represent the highest manifestation of the Law of Consciousness and Complexity.

Regarding the future, Teilhard de Chardin predicted an ultimate convergence of the human race based on knowledge and love. He referred to this point of convergence as the Omega Point. This Point would represent a collectively higher level of consciousness of humankind consistent with the Law of Consciousness and Complexity. According to Teilhard, at this point a conjunction of science and religion will be realized.

Jean Gebser

Jean Gebser (1905–1973), a German cultural philosopher, is considered by some to be one of the major thinkers of the 20th century along with Teilhard de Chardin and Martin Heidegger (Mickunas, 1997). His monumental work *Ursprung und Gegenwart* (1949/53) was first translated into English as *The Ever-Present Origin* in 1985.

Gebser's thesis is that, throughout history, the consciousness structures of humankind have undergone an evolution through a series of mutations that represent fundamentally different ways of experiencing reality (Mahood, 1996). He suggested that human consciousness has transitioned through three stages (the archaic, magical, and mythical)[2] and is currently embedded in the mental stage, which in turn is being challenged by the emerging integral stage. The structures are co-constituents, and each structure is an essential feature of our modern consciousness (Feuerstein, 1987).

The mental structure of consciousness began its emergence between 10,000 and 500 B.C. It became the dominant mode of perceiving reality during the final centuries before the beginning of the Christian era and remains the dominant structure today (Combs, 1996). During the Renaissance (14th to 17th centuries) a particular form of the mental structure, the mental-rational structure, began to flourish in Europe. The mental-rational structure involved the development of a perspectival worldview. This worldview entailed the separation of the ego from the rest of the world or perceived reality (Combs, 1996).

Gebser intuited that an integral structure, a fifth mode of consciousness, has been in the process of unfolding since the beginning of the 20th century. This structure represents a shift toward what he referred to as an "arational consciousness." This arational consciousness is in contrast to the emphasis of rational consciousness in the mental-rational structure. In his interdisciplinary work *The Ever-Present Origin* (Gebser, 1985), he demonstrated the emergence of integral consciousness in numerous fields of art, science, and scholarship.

Sri Aurobindo

Sri Aurobindo (1872–1950) was initially an Indian revolutionary who attained self-realization or enlightenment while in prison and went on to become a pre-eminent philosopher/yogi and evolutionary philosopher. He created a form of yoga practice that he called Integral Yoga, which

---

[2] According to Gebser, the *archaic structure* of consciousness was the first to evolve from the Origin. It prevailed during the prehuman phase of history in an epoch of nonhuman primates. The *magical structure* emerged approximately one and a half million years ago and evolved within our humanoid ancestors (Feuerstein, 1997). This structure dominated until approximately 40,000 B.C. and the emergence of the Cro-Magnon (Feuerstein, 1987). The *mythical structure* coincided with the appearance of *Homo erectus*. The appearance of the Neanderthal, Homo sapiens, and eventually the Cro-Magnon occurred with the evolution of a symbolic universe. While earlier Cro-Magnons are representative of the magical consciousness, later Cro-Magnons (20,000 B.C.–12,000 B.C.) typify the early mythical consciousness.

represents a modern synthesis of the ancient yoga tradition. His magnum opus was *The Life Divine* (Aurobindo, 1990), which appeared serially in India from 1914 to 1919. Integral Yoga practice has the explicit purpose of bringing "divine" consciousness down into the human body-mind and into ordinary life (Feuerstein, 2001).

Aurobindo suggested that the Supermind powers evolution, a steady progression toward ever higher forms of consciousness (Feuerstein, 2001)[3]. Individuals transformed by the Supermind represent the pinnacle of evolution. He felt that the human brain-mind has an innate tendency to go beyond itself to grasp the Supermind or larger Whole. Regarding the notions of philosophy and science, he felt that these fields represented failed attempts of the human mind to grasp the Whole; accordingly, the most the human mind can do is to recognize its inherent limitations and open up to the higher reality of the Supermind.

Aurobindo outlined three stages of both individual and societal evolution (Dalal, 2001): infrarational, rational, and suprarational. The infrarational stage is characterized by individuals and societies reacting on the basis of instincts, impulses, and spontaneous ideas. In this stage, individuals and societies live according to their vital intuitions or their first mental inclinations (Dalal, 2001).

The rational stage of development is characterized by the utilization of individual and group intelligent will that becomes the arbiter of thought, feelings, and actions. The arrival of the rational stage occurs only when a significant portion of a society learns to exercise its rational intelligence actively (Dalal, 2001).

Finally, Aurobindo suggested an individual and societal suprarational stage of conscious development as the next step in the evolution of the human species. He predicted a spiritual age in which a supra-intellectual and intuitive consciousness will manifest in individuals and society at large. Like Gebser, Aurobindo suggested that each of these stages of consciousness will co-exist in different parts of the earth simultaneously as the suprarational stage unfolds.

---

[3] This Supermind resembles Gebser's notion of the Origin.

Ken Wilber

Ken Wilber (1949-present) is considered by some to be one of the most important theorists in the field of consciousness studies and philosophy of mind of our time (De Quincey, 2000). Wilber built upon the work of numerous theorists who recognized the evolutionary development of humankind (Wilber, 1999a). However, he refined the notion of evolutionary development to include four distinct perspectives, which he called quadrants (Wilber, 1999c). From the perspectives of quadrants, individuals are capable of evolving or developing their own levels of consciousness. For example, sages have developed individually throughout human history. However, Wilber suggests that this development of individual levels of consciousness is distinct from the collective development of societal consciousness.

When Wilber elaborated upon the collective development of cultural or societal evolution, he acknowledged Gebser's influence on his thinking by hyphenating his stages of development, incorporating Gebser's language. That is, he used the labels "archaic-oroboric," "magic-typhonic," "mythic-membership," and "mental-egoic" for his stages of social evolution (Wilber, 1999b). According to Wilber, the current challenge facing individuals in Western cultures is to move from a more self-centered first-tier mode of thinking to a more transpersonal, integral second-tier mode of thinking (Wilber, 1999c; Beck and Cowan, 1996). In terms of society at large, he feels that the challenge is to move from the current collective rational level of consciousness, which permeates decision making throughout government and industry in the West, to what he calls the "centauric" level, which would manifest a more integral view held by society (Wilber, 1999c).

The Consensus

The consensus of all of the above scholars is that (a.) humankind in general represents the highest level of consciousness and complexity; (b.) societal and individual consciousness are on an evolutionary trajectory correlated with the evolution of the physical universe; (c.) the evolution of the inner (spiritual) and outer (physical) worlds is driven by the Divine; and (d.) a significant portion of humankind is presently experiencing a transition from one stage of consciousness to another, more "advanced" stage of consciousness (see also Bruteau, 1997, 2001).

In support of the consensus by these four theorists is the work by a number of contemporary scholars across the scientific and cultural spectrum. They have independently examined the concepts of individual and societal evolution of consciousness and concluded them to be accurate portrayals of past human experience and a logical theory of present and future human existence. For example, physicists Capra (1982, 2000) and Bohm (1980) have considered the role of evolution and consciousness as these relate to quantum physics. Goodenough (1998) has considered the role these elements play in biological evolution. Evolutionary psychologists such as Dawkins (1976), Dennett (1995), and Blackmore (1999) have examined the biological, sociological, and psychological evolution of humankind. And spiritual writers such as Hawkins (1995), Tolle (1999), Redfield, Murphy, and Timbers (2002), and Cohen (2002) represent a few of the spiritual writers who have emphasized both the biological and conscious evolution of humanity over time. With the notable exception of authors such as Neal, Lichtenstein, and Banner (1999), Anderson and Anderson (2001), and Torbert (e.g., Torbert and Associates, 2004), few management scholars have incorporated in their work an understanding of structures of consciousness and their significance.

GENERAL CHARACTERISTICS OF MENTAL-RATIONAL AND INTEGRAL CONSCIOUSNESS

The evolution of consciousness refers to the progressive expansion of one's sense of identity from egocentrism to a universal identification with the cosmos or the Absolute. Consciousness can be defined as one's sense of identity that reacts to the visible course of events in reality (Feuerstein, 1987). Currently, humankind is collectively experiencing a transition from one structure of consciousness to another. This cultural, Spirit-led transition is described similarly by each of the above mentioned philosopher-theorists although the structures themselves have been given different names. For example, this transition is said to be from the mental-rational to integral (Gebser, 1985), rational to suprarational (Aurobindo, 1990), rational to centauric (Wilber, 1999c), or partial to wholistic consciousness (Bruteau, 2001).

In this paper, this Spirit-led transition is referred to as a transition from the current mental-rational structure to an integral structure of consciousness. Both of these structures and their general characteristics are presented next. After that, in the following two sections, each structure is then applied to the notion of executive sensemaking and then to five key organizational functions.

The Mental-Rational Structure

According to Gebser (1985), an efficient form of the mental structure of consciousness existed during classical Athenian democracy and in the writings of Plotinus, St. Paul, and St. Augustine. However, the deficient form of this structure, which began to emerge during the Renaissance and persists today, represents a perspectival consciousness. In this structure, one's perspective is fixed. Gebser (1985) referred to this structure as mental-rational. However, this structure has little to do with reason or logic as applied to philosophy, mathematics, or ethics.

The mental-rational structure represents a warped form of rationality that is egocentric and myopic in its divisiveness and destructiveness. The ego can be understood as the "I" that represents the center of one's conscious awareness (Stein, 1998). In the mental-rational structure, in order to arrive at a judgment, one typically begins with an initial reference point anchored by a fixed ego perspective. Then, with reluctance and hesitancy, in order to reach a judgment, one begins to adjust his or her initial estimate away from the initial anchor (Aronson, Wilson, and Akert, 1997). Due to ego fixation, even subsequent judgments remain tied to an initially anchored impression and are rarely sufficiently adjusted away from the initial value as one's tendency is to reinforce one's initially anchored impression.

In the mental-rational structure, one tends to be ego-fixated as one experiences the world to essentially be hostile or antagonistic, something to be conquered (Feuerstein, 1997). Ego-fixity is exemplified as psychological insularity or isolation (Feuerstein, 1997). Other characteristics of this perspectival consciousness include tendencies to adapt isolated, self-centered viewpoints, wrangling, and hairsplitting over trivial differences of opinion (Combs, 1996). During mental-rational thinking, thought processes and perceptions attach themselves to specific objects that can be either abstract or concrete as individuals become attached or cling to their perspectives.

Even at its highest levels, and under the best intentions, this perspectival consciousness tends to be undercut by self-centered egoic agendas and a failure to see beyond one's own perspectival limitations (Combs, 1996). Perspectival consciousness manifests when individuals view their environments through a "grid of partiality" (Bruteau, 2001). Bruteau (2001) suggested that when individuals and other entities are preoccupied with parts or categories, then a partial consciousness is being adopted. She states that a partial consciousness, which engages in analysis by considering "this" as "not that," can be very useful for certain types of analysis. For example, during technological pursuits and in various forms of abstraction, a grid of partiality can be very useful. However, dangers can occur when this form of analysis is carried too far, as when people are mechanistically compartmentalized to fit statistical classes and bureaucratic schedules (Bruteau, 2001). In the mental-rational structure, problem solving tends to proceed linearly by drawing on conclusions from established premises (Puhakka, 1998). Individuals utilizing the mental-rational structure place an emphasis on such notions as power and control, the quest for certainty, and predictability.

The mental-rational structure also has a unique perspective of time. The linear notion of time, moving from the past through the present to the future, is a concept that stems from the mental-rational structure of consciousness. In the contemporary mental-rational mode of consciousness we are preoccupied with time by measuring, living by, not having enough of, and "wasting" it (Feuerstein, 1997). Contemporary mental-rational consciousness is characterized by time anxiety.

The Integral Structure

In the integral structure, one's perspective is fluid. Gebser referred to this structure as "arational consciousness." It is neither egocentric nor myopic; rather, in this structure, one begins ego transcendence (Feuerstein, 1997). In integral consciousness, individuals are not attached to ideas or objects. Instead, integral consciousness is accompanied by a transparent experience of reality, one in which perspective is no longer anchored in the perspectival ego (Combs, 1996). Gebser created the term "waring" (wahren) to refer to category-free perception that is possible when the perspectival ego is transcended (Combs, 1996). Waring is direct and intuitive. Others have referred to this aperspectival waring as "seeing"—a nonlinear, more contemplative and intuitive experience of reality (e.g., Puhakka, 1998). Heidegger (1966) referred to this mode of perception as "meditative thinking."

Seeing or waring neither clings to perspectives nor looks for fundamental truths. Instead, it contemplates forms and interrelationships that are the hidden presumptions of rational thinking. In waring, these hidden presumptions become transparent[4]. Further, seeing is not the same as rational self-reflection. Rational self-reflection represents a capacity for viewing one's own mental processes as an object. However, rational self-reflection also manifests the fundamental subject-object dualist structure present in all mental-rational thinking (Puhakka, 1998). In seeing, the subject-object structure softens and in some instances dissolves altogether (Puhakka, 1998).

Waring requires a presupposed holistic attitude or stance of openness in contrast to an emphasis on parts. This attitude or stance of openness is manifested in a readiness to include all in a given situational context, with the realization that contexts themselves are constantly changing. Bruteau (2001) suggested that a "wholistic" consciousness represents a non-dual awareness in which one can no longer divide the world into "we's" and "they's." She suggests that a wholistic consciousness supercedes and absorbs partial consciousness. Puhakka (1998) has suggested that "seeing" does not proceed linearly by drawing on conclusions from established premises as does ordinary rational thinking, but rather, seeing spreads out spaciously, embracing and pervading rather than seizing or grasping at mental objects. Individuals utilizing integral consciousness are motivated more by love and kindness than by power, control, and the quest for certainty.

The integral structure of consciousness also has its unique perspective of time. For example, integral structure entails an experience of freedom in time (Miller, 1994). Miller (1994) points out how Gebser's idea of time-freedom resembles the perspective of Krishnamurti

---

[4] Wilber (1999c) suggested that individuals begin to acquire the ability for "seeing" at the vision-logic stage of consciousness, the stage preceding the transpersonal levels of consciousness.

(e.g., Krishnamurti and Bohm, 1985) who felt that time is a product of the mind and memory. Krishnamurti felt that for most of us, the past is the present. Miller points out that Krishnamurti's belief in time-freedom does not imply that one is cut off from the past or fails to recognize it, but rather that one's mental processing has no direct connection with the past, that he or she problem-solves free from the conditioning influence of the past.

When individuals experience this vertical mode of time, as opposed to horizontal modes of "clock time," life is experienced as slower, more cohesive, and more energizing than in the world of horizontal clock time (Eberle, 2003; Needleman, 2003). A summary of the characteristic differences between mental-rational and integral structures of consciousness is presented in Table 1.

Depending upon the structure of consciousness of executive leaders, the conclusions they reach regarding organizational challenges and problem solving can vary dramatically. In particular, differences occur regarding how executives make sense of their environments, based upon their underlying structures of consciousness. These differences are explored in the following section.

TWO PERSPECTIVES FOR EXECUTIVE SENSEMAKING

According to the Talmud[5], "we do not see things as they are but as we are" (Walsh, 1998: 41). This wisdom or understanding portends significant implications for contemporary management. It reflects the paradox of "sensemaking" (Weick, 1995) within organizations. Fiol and O'Connor (2003) explain how cognitive approaches to sensemaking tend to treat information processing as disembodied and point out how the human mind is typically ignored in sensemaking research. This paper embraces Fiol and O'Connor (2003) and further explains how the underlying structures of consciousness of the mind influence executive problem solving.

In management practice, all issues, policies, and perceptions are viewed through some sort of lens or frame of reference (e.g., Starbuck

---

[5] The *Talmud* is the designation of the two commentaries on the *Mishnah* (a collection of oral laws by Judah). One commentary was produced in Palestine circa 275 C.E., and the other was produced in Babylonia circa 500 C.E.

Table 1: Summary of Characteristic Differences Between Mental-Rational and Integral Structures of Consciousness

Characteristics	Mental-Rational Structure (Perspectival Consciousness)	Integral Structure (Aperspectival Consciousness)
Status of the Ego	Acute sense of individuation	Diffused sense of individuation
	Ego-fixated	Ego-fluid
	Egocentric, myopic	Ego-transcending
	Psychological insulation, isolation	Psychological accessibility
	Hairsplitting	Open-minded
Domain of Analysis	Focus on parts and categories	Focus on the whole
Processes for Analysis	Linear analysis	Spacious nonlinear analysis
Conceptualization of Time	Horizontal time (Time anxiety)	Vertical time (Time freedom)
Focus of Attention	Attachment to ideas and objects	Non-attachment to ideas and objects
Areas of Concern	Power, control, certainty	Love and kindness
Ontological Manifestation	Subject-object duality present	Subject-object duality begins to dissolve

and Milliken, 1988; Weick, 1995; Bolman and Deal, 1997). Frame of reference or frames organize meaning and motivation as well as subsequent involvement and action (Drazin, Glynn, and Kazanjian, 1999). Sensemaking within organizations takes place when individuals pose to themselves the question, "What's going on here?" with respect to the organization's internal and external environments (Drazin, et al., 1999). This question requires one to categorize environmental stimuli (Harris, 1994). Also, "What does the stimulus mean?" is a second important question for organizational sensemaking (Harris, 1994). The frame of reference an individual applies in a given situational context is a function of his or her structure of consciousness, and one's frame of reference ultimately affects one's sensemaking processes, which in turn significantly impact executive problem solving, decision making, and leadership. Frame of reference influences the selection of environmental stimuli that one believes to be important in a given situational context (Rumelhart and Norman, 1990).

Pre-existing stores of knowledge saved in long-term memory as mental maps or schemas (e.g., Harris, 1994; Weick, 1979) also dramatically influence the effectiveness of one's sensemaking processes (Johnson, Daniels, and Huff, 2001; Rumelhart and Norman, 1990). This article contends that executives' structures of consciousness have a significant effect on how they view their existing stores of knowledge and ultimately their sensemaking processes. How executives interpret or misinterpret threats and opportunities, and how they interpret the past and present, and then formulate expectations about the future are affected by their frames (e.g., Dutton and Jackson, 1987; Abrahamson and Fombrun, 1994) and structures of consciousness. For example, the manner in which strategic leaders effectively formulate and implement strategies and match their strategies to their changing environments determines their organizations' ultimate success (Eisenhardt and Martin, 2000; Johnson, et al., 2001). Accurate perceptions of the environment lead to managerial choices that are more congruent with an organization's environment (Tenbrunsel, Galvin, Neale, and Bazerman, 1996).

Even the most vigilant or mindful executives (Fiol and O'Connor, 2003) formulate dramatically different conclusions depending on their underlying structures of consciousness. Due to the significantly different underlying characteristics of mental-rational and integral structures of consciousness, sensemaking outcomes vary dramatically when the two structures are compared and contrasted. For example, how executives perceive the magnitude, complexity, content, action to be taken, and source of strategic issues (Dutton, Walton, and Abrahamson, 1989) vary depending upon their structures of consciousness. Figure 1 depicts how an executive's underlying structure of consciousness affects his or her sensemaking processes, problem solving, decision making, and ultimate outcomes.

The Mental-Rational Structure

Since the mental-rational perspective is ego-fixated, inherent conflict is generally presumed when stakeholder differences arise. Further, within organizations it is generally presumed that conflict between operating units as well as hierarchical levels is normal. For example, Thomas and McDaniel (1990) and Trice (1993) described what they believed was the natural discord that arises between self-referent teams within organizations. Also, Sutton and Hargadon (1996) discussed

Figure 1:   The Relationship of Structure of Consciousness to Executive Sensemaking Processes

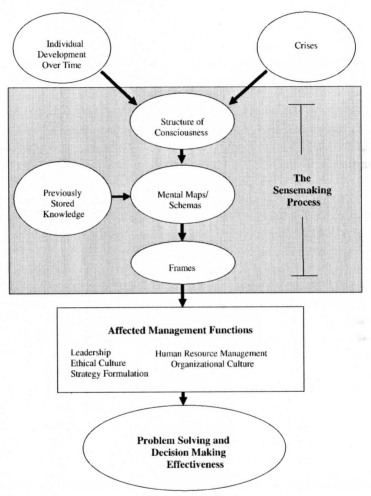

how technicians, as a subgroup within organizations, seek ego-fixated and self-gratifying reputational capital in organizational brainstorming sessions. From the mental-rational point of view, individual, group, and organizational perspectives are "fixed" as individuals tend to develop self-serving attributions regarding their particular circumstances. For example, individuals tend to attribute successful circumstances to themselves, while attributing failed circumstances to the situation (Ross, 1981). Dualities between subject and object are always presumed in the vast majority of the sensemaking literature, which is based on a mental-rational perspective.

From the mental-rational perspective of consciousness, success can be achieved through the mutual accommodation of the perspectives of others (Poole, Gioia, and Gray, 1989). Kegan's (1994) level four describes an advanced form of mental-rational consciousness in which stakeholders recognize the perspectives of others and are willing to accommodate them through compromise. From this point of view, each party is willing to accommodate the perspectives of others while keeping his or her own perspective intact. In the mental-rational mode, there is always a hesitancy with respect to a willingness or a need to reframe mental models or "fixed" individual, group, or organizational perspectives (Drazin, et al., 1999). In the mental-rational structure, individuals tend to seek evidence within their environments that confirm their prior beliefs and pre-existing stores of knowledge as a means of uncertainty reduction (Hogg and Terry, 2000). They tend to ignore disconfirming feedback and instead seek evidence that confirms prior beliefs in the behaviors in others (Hinsz, Tindale, and Vollrath, 1997).

Executives operating out of the mental-rational structure emphasize such notions as power and control, the quest for certainty and predictability, and the feasibility of objectivity in management practice. The mental-rational consciousness stresses control over one's environment. For example, this quest for control over the environment is manifested as an over-obsession for "rational" control over work processes. At its most extreme, this quest was exemplified in the scientific management techniques of Taylor (1960). However, current manifestations of this same obsession may be seen in such practices as the obsessive monitoring of employees through various technologically advanced forms of observation.

Finally, while crises represent disruptive events that may serve as antecedents for reframing, only a new fixed perspective is adopted if the individual remains in the mental-rational structure. In other words, individuals can and do experience frame changes while remaining in the mental-rational mode of consciousness. From the mental-rational perspective, an ability to reconfigure mental models while maintaining an ego-fixated perspective can lead executives and their organizations to dramatic commercial success (e.g., Daniels and Henry, 1998). However, sensemaking from an integral structure of consciousness differs dramatically from sensemaking from the mental-rational approach and is much better suited for the dynamism and complexity of the 21st century.

The Integral Structure

In order to utilize the integral structure of consciousness, one must first become aware of his or her own ego, thereby allowing a fluid ego perspective to emerge at the individual, group, and even strategic organizational levels. Integral consciousness suggests the acceptance of the perspectives of others (as described above in Kegan's level four) as well as malleable self-perspectives. Executives utilizing this mode of consciousness accept change as a given and are willing to change themselves in order to be successful. They are willing to modify their perspectives in order to achieve their ultimate goals or objectives. This process is similar to Torbert's notion of triple-loop feedback or learning (Torbert and Associates, 2004). Integral consciousness does not presume that one's own perspective must invariably remain intact; thus an aperspectival view is adopted. Therefore, this viewpoint presumes an active self-transcendence of the ego during problem solving. This approach is described in Kegan's (1994) level-five stage of development in which the individual ego is capable of malleability during conflict. While success can be conceived as achievement of one's goal or a set of objectives in the mental-rational structure, in the integral structure success is conceived as the capacity to embrace differences in a comprehensive unity in the face of continuous change.

The practice of sensemaking from an aperspectival outlook requires the transcendence of the ego, or ego-freedom. Such transcendence becomes feasible when the mind is cleared of the "incrustations" that life has deposited upon it (Combs, 1996). We define the practice of consistently utilizing integral consciousness during the process of organizational sensemaking and management problem solving as the practice of integral management. Integral management requires a transparent state of consciousness in which everything is seen holistically.

Integral or aperspectival consciousness has the potential to make possible new realms of stakeholder collaboration and other realities in which transparency is the norm. It can facilitate an awareness and authentic understanding of stakeholder values and actions (Waddock, 2002). Integral consciousness unfolds in and through freedom from the ego, the source point in the mental-perspectival consciousness (Feuerstein, 1997). It allows the pursuit of power, control, and certainty to be replaced by the genuine capacity for love and kindness (Combs, 1996).

Integral consciousness begins to emerge as integral management practice when executives begin to see traditional management dualities as wholes. In integral consciousness, executives begin to view their situational contexts through a lens of "nondualism" (Chaudhuri, 1977). For example, some typical artificial dichotomies of management include labor—management, management processes—management outcomes, tangible—intangible, customer—company, competitor—company, company—environment, and so forth. Sensemaking in the mental-rational mode too often sees these phenomena as opposites or antagonists rather than as category-free concepts or entities. Executives utilizing integral consciousness are better prepared to discard their ego-fixated perspectives in order to consider the diverse perspectives of various stakeholders holistically (Hodgkinson and Johnson, 1995; Johnson, Daniels, and Asch, 1998) and in the process formulate their own new perspectives. They are better prepared to change themselves.

Eggert (1998) uses the term "lucid" to describe waring. She suggests that lucidity implies a "gazing upon raw existence without turning away. It is seeing clearly and directly to the depths" (Eggert, 1998: 234). She goes on to suggest that contemplative executives, who utilize integral consciousness in sensemaking, are lucid about themselves, their own neuroses, frailties, and hidden agendas, and they are likewise lucid about others.

Other examples of the emergence of integral consciousness in management practice include Weick's (1995) notion of enactment and the concepts of corporate and global business citizenship (Logsdon and Wood, 2002; Waddock 2002). However, it should be noted that in each of these contemporary concepts, the dualism of an ego-based subject-object analysis remains intact, while in true integral management these dualities are softened or eliminated (Young, 2002).

Sensemaking from an integral management perspective enables executive leaders to utilize waring or seeing that will allow them to be more sensitive to emerging paradigm shifts within their environments (Anderson and Anderson, 2001). Anderson and Anderson detail how "conscious"[6] executives tend to develop insights into emerging paradigms and, as a result, enter their markets as forerunners. Waring executives are consciously aware of their situational contexts, possessing self-knowledge in the sense that they are fully cognizant of their own state of mind and emotions, while simultaneously manifesting a comprehensive awareness of their organization's internal and external environments (Anderson and Anderson, 2001; King and Nicol, 2000).

Executive leaders utilizing integral management in sensemaking employ Gebser's notion of systasis, which is conjoining parts into integrality. While systasis does not discard the mental-rational notion of systems thinking (e.g., Churchman, 1982), it proceeds farther as a "temporic" endeavor to include time in one's understanding of reality. Here, time is experienced as an "acategorical intensity"[7] and not merely as measurable clock-time (Feuerstein, 1987).

Executives utilizing sensemaking from an aperspectival view would, therefore, tend to problem solve in time-freedom. Given appropriate due diligence, this would entail problem solving in the present moment unencumbered by the past or the future.[8] Freeing oneself from the past or the future would lead to less misdiagnosis of critical challenges facing the firm (Johnson, Daniels, and Huff, 2001).

When executive leaders problem solve in this manner, softening or eliminating dualities, their compassion for others is enhanced, and they are more capable of hearing and understanding stakeholder concerns. Integral executives are also more likely to engage in collective sensemaking, such as participation in multi-stakeholder learning dialogues (Calton and Payne, 2003), in order to more fully

---

[6] Anderson and Anderson (2001) distinguish "conscious" managers (who utilize waring or seeing) from reactive managers whose mindsets are rooted in an industrial (or mental-rational) consciousness.

[7] We experience time as an "acategorical intensity" when we succeed in experiencing the "present moment."

[8] Csikszentmihalyi (2003) refers to this experience of time in management practice as one of the eight characteristics of "flow."

grasp the nature of complex and interdependent problems that require the involvement of many parties to solve.

Crises can cause not only frame changes within the mental-rational mode of consciousness, but they can also precipitate a transcendence of ego to an arational mode of knowing (e.g., Neal, et al., 1999). Drazin, et al. (1999) discuss the role of crises in reframing mental maps. They point out that such reframing can occur on a temporary or a more permanent basis. In either case, their assumption is that the sensemaking entity (individual, group, or organization) retains a fixed perspective of consciousness. However, individuals can move to integral consciousness through a gradual process of personal development over time (Leonard and Murphy, 1995), or they can experience individual or organizational crises that can spur their transition to integral consciousness (Beck and Cowan, 1996). Anderson and Anderson (2001) discuss how transformational environmental change, which has a greater impact on organizations than smaller developmental or transitional change, can force executives to abandon ego-fixated perspectives in favor of more fluid self perspectives.

Thus, it is clear that the level of consciousness that executive leaders have attained may influence virtually every aspect of their organizations because of the impacts of consciousness on their mental maps and frames for interpreting facts, trends, relationships, and environments. These differences are manifested in a number of organization functions, which are compared and contrasted from mental-rational and integral perspectives in the next section.

ORGANIZATIONAL FUNCTIONING AND STRUCTURES OF CONSCIOUSNESS

In the 21st century, organizational leaders will be required to collect, understand, and synthesize a variety of information, as well as to understand and appreciate value differences from exceedingly diverse sources in order to solve their problems in a comprehensive and creative manner (Chaudhuri, 1977). In this section, key organizational functions—leadership, strategy formulation, organizational culture, ethical culture, and human resource management—will be compared and contrasted as they are envisioned from the currently dominant mental-rational structure versus the emerging integral structure of consciousness (Young and Logsdon, 2004). The descriptions of integral consciousness in each of the five organizational functions present introductory characteristics to what the authors consider as the practice of integral management.

Leadership

Leadership involves developing a capacity for encouraging the organization's associates to embrace a common vision and shared goals for realizing that vision and for moving forward together in pursuit of the vision and goals. In complex ever-changing environments, leaders must have greater abilities in order to manage higher levels of cognitive complexity (Kets de Vries, 1995).

Mental-rational. In the mental-rational structure, leaders are oriented toward power and control. They are more likely to operate as if in a closed system in which the organization can be separated from the external environment. They are also likely to be transactional leaders and thus rules-oriented, rewarding subordinates for good performance and punishing them when their performance is deficient (Bass, 1990). Executives utilizing this structure tend to lead within the context of parochial domains, frequently emphasizing "us" versus "them" categorizations and perspectives. In particular, mental-rational leaders keep a tight grip on information in order to maintain their power and control, and they are afraid to admit weaknesses or uncertainty.

Integral. Conversely in the integral structure, leaders are more oriented toward a detached empowerment of subordinates (Csiksentmihalyi, 2003). Their actions tend less toward their own self-interest, but rather are for the good of the organization (Collins, 2001) and for the larger community. They are likely to be transformational leaders who can assist in developing a comprehensive and inclusive vision. They tend to provide intellectual stimulation undistorted by egocentrism, individual consideration, and inspirational motivation (Bass, 1990, 1998). Dynamic change is perceived as the source of opportunity.

The integral structure of consciousness fits well with the concept of authentic leadership (Luthans and Avolio, 2003), which moves beyond the traditional conceptualization of transformational leadership. The authentic leader is concerned about the "needs of others, over their own self-interests ... because they are guided by something more important than self-interest, which is to be consistent with their high-end values" (Luthans and Avolio, 2003: 247–48).

Strategy Formulation

Strategy formulation involves developing the capacity for creating various means of achieving the organization's overall goals. Since strategy formulation and decisions about implementation take place at the highest levels within the organization, it is imperative that executives formulating corporate strategies comprehend the interconnected as well as the heterogeneous nature of their operating environments.

Mental-rational. With regard to strategy, executives exemplifying the mental-rational structure tend to examine only the goals and objectives of their organizations, and assess and calculate alternatives based upon net positive returns to their organizations. Executive leaders utilizing this structure display tendencies for maximizing the benefits to their respective organizations and a few stakeholder groups (typically including investors, but not always). Successful executives in this structure understand and focus upon interdependencies within systems (Churchman, 1982). Reflecting Kegan's fourth order consciousness, mental-rational executives are more likely to "lead hierarchically and unilaterally but out of a vision that is internally generated, continuously sustained, independent of and prior to the expectations or directives of the environment" (Kegan, 1994: 227).

Integral. Executives in the integral structure are more comprehensive and seek solutions that encompass a larger perspective for as many stakeholders as possible (Hooijberg and Schneider, 2001).They not only perceive and understand interdependencies within systems, but perhaps even more importantly for formulating contemporary global strategies, they also see and understand interdependencies across systems (Kegan, 1994). Integral executives would tend to be less rigid in terms of maintaining their own points of view and perspectives (Kegan, 1994; Rooke and Torbert, 1998).

Executive leaders operating from an integral or aperspectival structure tend to exhibit a greater appreciation for the comprehensive nature of strategy formulation. A deep appreciation of interconnectedness brings about a wisdom and understanding that realizes that minute fluctuations within a broadly defined situational context can amplify into dramatic changes. The situational contexts for contemporary strategy formulation represent unique sets of dynamic, organically related, mutually determining circumstances. Integral executives see and understand the dynamic milieu in which contemporary strategy formulation takes place. Thus, their structure of consciousness provides their organizations with a strategic competitive resource advantage (Jacobs and McGee, 2001).

Organizational Culture

Organizational culture reflects "the way we do things around here." Organizational culture has included traditional dimensions such as structure, task and technology, rules, procedures, and financial controls as well as shared stories and rituals that communicate fundamental values (Deal and Kennedy, 1982; Martin, 2002).

Mental-rational. Organizations immersed in mental-rational consciousness behave in predictable ways. Executives in this mode have a greater preoccupation with predictability, control, and the feasibility of objectivity in management practice. Thus, organizational structure is likely to be hierarchical with a clear chain of command and performance expectations. Since top-level executives are more likely to use financial reports to judge performance, their subordinates focus on "making the numbers," and implicit organizational norms adjust to facilitate "making the numbers," regardless of what the explicit norms state.

Several other manifestations of the mental-rational perspective are often observed in organizations. Fixed egos tend to use a rigid, inflexible approach to internal bargaining and negotiation for resources. Egocentrism is also reflected in myopic understandings of problems and their solutions as individuals and various hierarchical units vie for their separate goals (e.g., Thomas and McDaniel, 1990; Trice, 1993). In addition, executives tend to maintain a rigid and unbending adherence to rules and operating procedures.

Integral. Organizational culture from an integral perspective provides a context in which parties solving various organizational problems create solutions that they can uphold collectively (Kegan, 1994). The more formalized elements of organizational culture, such as structure, are likely to favor innovative approaches, including flat structures and bottom-up decision making. Integral executives would tend to favor engaging organizational members in jointly formulating a coherent vision, mission, or purpose (Heifetz and Sinder, 1988).

Rather than manifesting a preoccupation with predictability, control, and the feasibility of objectivity, executives exhibit a genuine concern for love and kindness. Shared stories and rituals involve empathy, empowerment, and appreciation for the contributions of all organizational members. In the integral culture, executives who have begun to transcend their own egos are better equipped to modify or change their positions and perspectives during negotiations and bargaining. Finally, rather than rigidly adhering to "rules," integral executives exhibit flexibility and have the capacity to embrace change, paradox, and uncertainty while formulating judgments (Waddock, 2002).

Ethical Culture

The ethical culture of an organization consists of the formal and informal social control factors that shape perceptions of "right" and "wrong" behavior of the organization's employees (Trevino, 1990). Informal elements of ethical culture involve aspects of the socialization process, such as role modeling by superiors and informal organizational norms that support or violate formal ethics statements (Logsdon and Young, 2005).

Mental-rational. Reflecting the mental-rational leader's desire to control events and to operate within a hierarchical and more bureaucratic structure, formal statements of ethical culture are extensive, specific, and rule-oriented (Logsdon and Young, 2005). The legalistic approach may extend to a focus on legal compliance as the appropriate criterion for guiding ethical analysis. The mental-rational consciousness can incorporate conventional expectations, such as contributing to the local community, as long as this helps the organization achieve its goals.

In the mental-rational perspective, ethics training is likely to be addressed in a perfunctory, check-off fashion. That is, as a matter of course, employees are expected to complete a training module on the company's ethics code and policies. Often today, these ethics training modules consist of applying clearly stated rules to a set of typical scenarios, such as whether to lie on one's expense report or pay a bribe.

Integral. From the integral perspective, the criteria for all problem solving, including explicitly ethical challenges, focus on identifying optimal solutions within an ever-changing, complex socio-economic environment. Such problem solving takes into account the impacts on all stakeholders, not just stockholders. In other words, integral ethical analysis considers multiple ethical criteria, including the full costs and benefits to everyone affected by a decision (true utilitarianism), impacts on individual rights and duties, and justice concerns of fair distribution of costs and benefits and equitable treatment among individuals.

Integral executives are likely to be transformational leaders and would, therefore, trust their associates to understand and act on a clear set of ethical values, rather than require a detailed set of ethical rules to be followed in all cases (Logsdon and Young, 2005). They would recognize that ethical principles often exceed legal requirements. In the integral organization, ethics training is likely to be an important component of regular training programs.

Human Resource Management

In the 21st century, addressing human resource challenges requires continual recruitment, selection, training, and re-training, as all managerial processes become virtual, digital, and mobile (Fiorina, 2003). In an era of virtual, digital, and mobile processes, the management of human resources has changed dramatically and permanently.

Mental-rational. Executives operating from this structure will tend to emphasize short-term performance measures such as quarterly earnings, return on investment, stock market values, and so forth. They tend to view personnel as "disposable parts" and are primarily concerned with net positive gains to their own organizations and higher compensation to themselves.

During performance evaluations, mental-rational executives tend to emphasize differences and rankings among individuals and groups of subordinates, along various qualities that have been abstracted from the subordinates as a whole (Bruteau, 2001). In such evaluations, more progressive mental-rational leaders respect and appreciate the "culture of mind" of other organizational members (Kegan, 1994). However, in even the most sophisticated application of the mental-rational structure, executive leaders will continue to maintain a psychological sense of their own wholeness or completeness.

Integral. Executives operating from integral consciousness will tend to seek solutions that consider the long-term competitiveness of their own firms, as well as long-term local and national competitiveness. Therefore, they emphasize training, but perhaps even more importantly in rapidly changing environments, they emphasize the re-training of workers displaced by continually changing technologies. Integral HR executives will co-create with the organization's employees not only optimal career paths for employees but also the futures of organizational units and the organization as a whole. Such partnerships, collaborative, and co-creation are described in Zohar's (1997) quantum organizational model and Mackenzie's (1991, 2004) holonomic organizational framework.

During performance evaluations, integral executives are capable of not only recognizing multiplicities along various dimensions of subordinates, but also they can perceive the union among subordinates and themselves (Bruteau, 2001). In this structure, one initially questions his or her own presumption of wholeness or completeness. Therefore, during performance evaluations, leaders leave themselves vulnerable to their own ego modification and commence such evaluations with an admission of the possibility of their own incompleteness. Such a stance allows executive leaders to evaluate their associates without being defensive or threatened—without having to prove themselves "right."

These five brief analyses of differences in organizational functioning illustrate how profoundly the mental-rational and integral sensemaking perspectives influence what happens within organizations and how organizations operate in the external environment. These five areas are by no means exhaustive but are intended as representative of the fundamental shift in every significant aspect of organizations. Next some spiritual implications of the Spirit-led evolution of consciousness are considered.

SPIRITUAL IMPLICATIONS OF THE SPIRIT-LED EVOLUTION OF CONSCIOUSNESS

Feuerstein defined spiritual as "any value, thought, attitude, impulse, mood, disposition, bodily comportment, or action that refers to, or is expressive of, the native human orientation of self-transcendence" (Feuerstein, 1987: 157). This human aptitude for transcending the self, the ego, is the capacity that makes all religion and all morality possible (Feuerstein, 1987). Wilber (2000) describes transformative spirituality as the transformation that takes place when individuals alter their sense of identity, moving from egocentrism to universal perspectives. The spiritual dimension of the premise set forth here lies in the unfolding of consciousness in which the Origin (Gebser, 1985) or Supermind (Aurobindo, 1990) is becoming more directly accessible to humankind than in any previous period. According to Walsh (1998), an authentic evolutionary theory of consciousness must acknowledge some self-transcendent drive in the cosmos. Currently, this self-transcendent drive is beginning to move an increasing number of people beyond the conventional development of rationality into transrational, transpersonal stages (e.g., Hawkins, 1995; Walsh, 1998). The collective message of the philosophers introduced earlier is that humankind's evolution represents a multi-dimensional process that can fulfill itself only by transcending itself. Further, they suggest that where this premise is ignored or neglected, there is likely to be found individual and collective suffering (Feuerstein, 1987).

There is a spiritual depth to integral consciousness. Each new structure of consciousness elevates humankind to new levels of knowledge and competence. While each new level also carries humankind one step farther in terms of horizontal time from the source of consciousness, the Origin (Combs, 1996), integral consciousness offers humankind's greatest potential for directly accessing the Origin or Supermind.

Facilitating individual access to integral consciousness requires an appropriate disposition or attitude. Attributes suggested by Feuerstein (1997) for developing a disposition favorable for cultivating integral consciousness within individuals are presented in Table 2.

Table 2: Attributes of a Disposition for Cultivating Integral Consciousness*

Prefers ...	Over ...
Quiet and silence	Haste and noise
Spontaneity	Goal-directed thinking
Compassion and loving kindness	Lust for power and manipulation
Inner harmony and balance	Mechanical organizing
Unsentimental tolerance	Prejudice
Authenticity	Blind conformism
Delight in inner growth	Fear of change
Acceptance of life and death	Mere avoidance

* Adapted from Feuerstein (1997).

ORGANIZATIONAL IMPLICATIONS AND FUTURE PROSPECTS

If integral consciousness is to be achieved by humanity at large, rather than by only a few advanced individuals, as has been the case throughout history, then the conscious participation of large numbers of individuals, especially those in leadership positions, is imperative (Feuerstein, 1987). Therefore, we are left with the question, "What can executive leaders do to foster the emergence of integral consciousness, and its associated benefits, within their organizations?" We propose that executive leaders who understand the emerging integral consciousness and begin fostering this consciousness within their organizations have a competitive advantage over competing organizations that are either unaware of or are unable to encourage similar perceptions (e.g., Jacobs and McGee, 2001). In other words, integral consciousness can be conceived as a competitive resource (Barney, 1996; Wernerfelt, 1984) by those firms that possess this perspective (e.g., Neal, et al., 1999).

As suggested within this research, executive leaders can begin transforming their organizations for greater integral awareness by fostering environments in which the attributes listed in Table 2 can flourish. These attributes can be facilitated in organizations in conjunction with their human resource and strategic development activities, as leaders systematically provide their employees with benefits such as time during work hours for regular contemplation; paid or discounted training in meditation techniques (e.g., yoga, qigong, contemplative prayer, etc.); access to spiritual counseling; opportunities for regular gatherings for spiritual discussions; sabbaticals for personal growth; opportunities for volunteer activities during work hours; and instruction in "ego-free" decision making. In other words, progressive leaders should actively develop and promote spiritual health plans in addition to traditional medical health plans for their employees. Progressive executive leaders should offer ample opportunities for their associates to engage in and develop through integral transformative practices (Leonard and Murphy, 1995; Young and Logsdon, 2004).

Organizations imbued with integral consciousness are more likely to exhibit characteristics such as fairness, loving kindness, compassion, serenity and calm, spontaneity and creativity derived from ego-freedom, respect for others, unbiased decision making, and wisdom. As Csikszentmihalyi (2003) suggests, such organizations will represent forums for the practice of "good business." As a result, these organizations are more effective in terms of reaching their goals, but perhaps more importantly, they are more capable of continually modifying their goals to meet situational contexts within their ever-changing environments.

The cultural emergence of integral consciousness requires the coalescence of the Divine with consciousness for both individuals and societies in general. Of particular importance to management practice is the notion that the "joys" associated with power and possession will dwindle over the coming years (Gebser, 1985). Further, the unimportance of these false values will become evident as individuals become aware of their material pseudo-security (Gebser, 1985; Bruteau, 2001). Then the implications for and impacts on executive compensation could be significant.

CONCLUSION

The philosophers discussed at the outset of this paper suggest that when integral consciousness emerges on a large enough scale, when a critical mass is achieved, the future of humankind will be enhanced. It should be noted that this does not imply that all societal problems will be abruptly and magically resolved. Further, according to these philosophers, mental-rational resistance will accompany the full-fledged emergence of integral consciousness from every quarter as entrenched sources of perspectival consciousness seek to prevent the emergence of integral consciousness.

Contemporary executive leaders should be encouraged to foster cultures within their organizations that lead to the transformation of their associates from mental-rational to integral consciousness. The resulting transformations should lead to more effective, more compassionate, therefore, more ethical decision making at all organizational levels.

Integral consciousness and its manifestation in integral executive sensemaking reflect a truly comprehensive perspective of management in that they cover the entire spectrum of human growth and aspiration (Wilber, 1993). Sensory, emotional, mental, social, ethical, and spiritual dimensions are considered in the integral management process. Integral consciousness and the practice of integral management have the capacity to significantly influence the effectiveness of management practice in the 21st century.

Further, the authors believe that an understanding of and appreciation for the differences between mental-rational and integral consciousness have the potential to significantly alter the corpus of contemporary management theory and research. If organizations are to address challenges such as the pressures of economic globalization, conflicting cultural values, social turmoil, health and disease, environmental degradation, and other critical issues facing the world today, they should embrace integral consciousness and integral executive problem solving with an enlightened sense of urgency.

REFERENCE

Abrahamson, E.C. and Fombrun, C. (1994) Macro cultures: determinants and consequences, *Academy of Management Review*, 19, 728–755.

Anderson, D. and Anderson, L.A. (2001) *Beyond Change Management: Advanced Strategies for Today's Transformational Leaders*, San Francisco: Jossey-Bass/Pfeiffer.

Aronson, E., Wilson, T.D. and Akert, R.M. (1997) *Social Psychology,* (2nd ed.), New York: Addison-Wesley.

Aurobindo, S. (1990) *TheLlife Divine*, Twin Lakes, WI: Lotus Press.

Barney, J.B. (1996) The resource-based view of the firm, *Organization Science*, 7, 469–501.

Bass, B.M. (1990) *Bass and Stogdill's Handbook of Leadership: Theory, Research, and Managerial Applications,* (3rd ed.), New York: Free Press.

Bass, B.M. (1998) *Transformational Leadership: Industry, Military, and Educational Impact, Mahwah,* NJ: Erlbaum.

Beck, D.E. and Cowan, C.C. (1996) *Spiral Dynamics: Mastering Values, Leadership and Change,* Malden, MA: Blackwell.

Blackmore, S. (1999) *The Meme Machine,* Oxford: Oxford University Press.

Bohm, D. (1980) *Wholeness and The Implicate Order,* London: Routledge.

Bolman, L. and Deal, T. (1997) *Reframing Organizations,* San Francisco: Jossey-Bass.

Bruteau, B. (1997) *God's Ecstasy: The Creation of a Self-Creating World,* New York: Crossroads Publishing.

Bruteau, B. (2001) *The Grand Option: Personal Transformation and a New Creation,* Norte Dame, IN: University of Notre Dame Press.

Calton, J.M. and Payne, S.L. (2003) Coping with paradox: Multistakeholder learning dialogue as a pluralist sensemaking process for addressing messy problems. *Business and Society,* 42, 7–42.

Capra, F. (1982) *The Turning Point: Science, Society, and the Rising Culture,* New York: Bantam.

Capra, F. (2000) *The Tao of Physics: An Exploration of the Parallels Between Modern Physics and Eastern Mysticism,* (25th anniversary ed.), Boston: Shambhala.

Cavanagh, G.F. (2000) Spirituality for managers: Context and critique. In J. Biberman and M.D. Whitty (Eds.), *Work and Spirit: A Reader of New Spiritual Paradigms for Organization.,* 149–166, Scranton, PA: The University of Scranton Press.

Chandler, A.D. (1977) *The Visible Hand: The Managerial Revolution in American Business,* Cambridge, MA: Harvard University Press.

Chaudhuri, H. (1977) *The Evolution of Integral Consciousness,* Wheaton, IL: The Theosophical Publishing House.

Churchman, C.W. (1982) *Thought and Wisdom,* Seaside, CA: Intersystems Publications.

Cohen, A. (2002) *Living Enlightenment: A Call for Evolution Beyond Ego,* Lenox, MA: Moksha Press.

Collins, J. (2001) *Good to Great: Why Some Companies Make the Leap . . . and Others Don't,* New York: Harper Business.

Combs, A. (1996) *The Radiance of Being: Complexity, Chaos and the Evolution of Consciousness,* St. Paul, MN: Paragon House.

Csikszentmihalyi, M. (2003) *Good Business: Leadership, Flow, and the Making of Meaning,* New York: Viking.

Dalal, A.S. (2001) *Sri Aurobindo: A Greater Psychology,* New York: Jeremy P. Tarcher/Putnam.

Daniels, K. and Henry, J. (1998) Strategy: A cognitive perspective, In S. Segal-Horn (Ed.), *Readings on Strategy.* New York: Macmillan.

Dawkins, R. (1976) *The Selfish Gene,* Oxford: Oxford University Press.

De Quincey, C. (2000) The promise of integralism, In J. Andresen and R.K.C. Forman (Eds.), *Cognitive Models and Spiritual Maps: Interdisciplinary Explorations of Religious Experience.* 177–208, Bowling Green, OH: Imprint Academic.

Deal, T.E. and Kennedy, A.A. (1982) *Corporate Cultures: The Rites and Rituals of Corporate Life.* Reading, MA: Addison-Wesley.

Dennett, D.C. (1995) Darwin's *Dangerous Idea: Evolution and the Meanings of Life*, New York: Touchstone.

Drazin, R., Glynn, M.A. and Kazanjian, R.K. (1999) Multilevel theorizing about creativity in organizations: a sensemaking perspective, *Academy of Management Review*, 24 (2), 286–307.

Dutton, J.E. and Jackson, S. (1987) Categorizing strategic issues: links to organizational action, *Academy of Management Review*, 12, 76–90.

Dutton, J.E., Walton, E.J. and Abrahamson, E. (1989) Important dimensions of strategic issues: separating the wheat from the chaff, *Journal of Management Studies*, 26, 379–396.

Eberle, G. (2003) Sacred *Time and the Search for Meaning*, Boston: Shambhala.

Eggert, N.J. (1998) *Contemplative Leadership for Entrepreneurial Organizations: Paradigms, Metaphors, and Wicked Problems*, Westport, CT: Quorum Books.

Eisenhardt, K.M. and Martin, J.A. (2000) Dynamic capabilities: what are they?, *Strategic Management Journal*, 21, 1105–1121.

Feuerstein, G. (1987) *Structures of Consciousness: The Genius of Jean Gebser*, Lower Lake, CA: Integral Publishing.

Feuerstein, G. (1997) *Lucid Waking: Mindfulness and the Spiritual Potential of Humanity*, Rochester, VT: Inner Traditions International.

Feuerstein, G. (2001) *The Yoga Tradition: Its History, Literature, Philosophy and Practice*, Prescott, AZ: Hohm Press.

Fiol, C.M. and O'Connor, E.J. (2003) Waking up! mindfulness in the face of bandwagons, *Academy of Management Review*, 28, 54–70.

Fiorina, C. (2003) The state of the information technology industry. Speech presented at the Robert H. Smith School of Business, University of Maryland, College Park, MD, October 10. Available from C-Span.

Gebser, J. (1985) *The Ever-Present Origin*, Translated by Noel Barstad with Algis Mickunas. Athens, OH: Ohio University Press.

Goodenough, U. (1998) *The Sacred Depths of Nature*, New York: Oxford University Press.

Harris, S.G. (1994) Organizational culture and individual sensemaking: A schema-based perspective, *Organization Science*, 5 (3), 309–321.

Hawkins, D.R. (1995) *Power vs. Force: The Hidden Determinants of Human Behavior*, Carlsbad, CA: Hay House.

Heidegger, M. (1966) *Discourse on Thinking*, New York: Harper.

Heifetz, R.A. and Sinder, R.M. (1988) Political leadership: managing the public's problem solving. In R. Reich (Ed.), *The Power of Public Ideas*. Cambridge, MA: Ballinger.

Hinsz, V.B., Tindale, R.S. and Vollrath, D.A. (1997) The emerging conceptualization of groups as information processors, *Psychological Bulletin*, 121, 43–64.

Hodgkinson, G. and Johnson, G. (1995) Exploring the mental models of competitive strategists: the case for a processual approach. *Journal of Management Studies*, 31, 525–551.

Hogg, M.A. and Terry, D.J. (2000) Social identity and self-categorization processes in organizational contexts, *Academy of Management Review*, 25, 121–140.

Hooijberg, R. and Schneider, M. (2001) Behavioral complexity and social intelligence: how executive leaders use stakeholders to form a systems perspective. In S.J. Zaccaro and R.J. Klimoski (Eds.), *The nature of organizational leadership: Understanding the performance imperative confronting today's leaders*. 104–131, San Francisco: Jossey-Bass.

Jacobs, T.O. and McGee, M.L. (2001) Competitive advantage: conceptual imperatives for executives. In S.J. Zaccaro and R.J. Klimoski (Eds.), *The Nature of Organizational Leadership: Understanding the Performance Imperatives Confronting Today's Leaders*. 42–78, San Francisco: Jossey-Bass.

Johnson, P., Daniels, K. and Asch, R. (1998) Mental models of competition. In C. Eden and J.C. Spender (Eds.), *Managerial and Organizational Cognition: Theory, Methods, and Research*. Thousand Oaks, CA: Sage.

Johnson, P., Daniels, K. and Huff, A. (2001) Sensemaking, leadership, and mental models. In S.J. Zaccaro and R.J. Klimoski (Eds.), *The Nature of Organizational Leadership: Understanding the Performance Imperatives Confronting Today's Leaders*. 79–103, San Francisco: Jossey-Bass.

Kegan, R. (1994) *In Over Our Heads: The Mental Demands of Modern Life*, Cambridge, MA: Harvard University Press.

Kets de Vries, M.F.R. (1995) If I'm the leader, will anyone follow? A definition of leadership. In M.F.R. Kets de Vries (Ed.), *Life and Death in the Executive Fast Lane: Essays on Irrational Organizations and Their Leaders*. 5–14, San Francisco: Jossey-Bass.

King, U. (1996) *Spirit of Fire: The Life and Vision of Teilhard de Chardin*, Maryknoll, NY: Orbis Books.

King, S. and Nicol, D.M. (2000) Organizational enhancement through recognition of individual spirituality: reflections of Jaques and Jung. In J. Biberman and M.D. Whitty (Eds.), *Work and Spirit: A Reader of New Spiritual Paradigms for Organizations*. 137–148, Scranton, PA: The University of Scranton Press.

Krishnamurti, J. and Bohm, D. (1985) *The Ending of Time*, San Francisco: Harper.

Leonard, G. and Murphy, M. (1995) *The Life We Are Given: A Long-term Program for Realizing the Potential of Body, Mind, Heart, and Soul*, New York: Jeremy P. Tarcher/Putnam.

Logsdon, J.M. and Wood, D.J. (2002) Business citizenship: from domestic to global level of analysis, *Business Ethics Quarterly*, 12 (2), 155–188.

Logsdon, J.M. and Young, J.E. (2005) Executive influence on ethical culture: Contributions from positive psychology, In R. Giacalone, C.L. Jurkiewicz, and C. Dunn (Eds.), *Positive Psychology in Business Ethics and Corporate Social Responsibility in Press*. Greenwich, CT: Information Age.

Luthans, F. and Avolio, B. (2003) Authentic leadership development, In K.S. Cameron, J.E. Dutton, and R.E. Quinn (Eds.), *Positive Organizational Scholarship*. 241–258, San Francisco: Berrett-Koehler.

Mackenzie, K.D. (1991) *The Organizational Hologram: The Effective Management of Organizational Change*, Boston: Kluwer Academic.

Mackenzie, K.D. (2004) *The Practitioner's Guide for Organizing an Organization. Lawrence*, KS: Mackenzie and Company.

Mahood, E. (1996) *The Primordial Lead and the Present: The Ever-present Origin - An Overview of the Work of Jean Gebser,* Campbell, CA: Synairetic Research.

Martin, J. (2002) *Organizational Culture: Mapping the Terrain*, Thousand Oaks, CA: Sage.

Mickunas, A. (1997) An introduction to the philosophy of Jean Gebser, *Integrative Explorations: Journal of Culture and Consciousness*, 4 (1), 8–20.

Miller, W. (1994) A Krishnamurti perspective on integral consciousness, *Integrative Explorations: Journal of Culture and Consciousness*, 2 (1), 36–44.

Mitroff, I.I. and Denton, E.A. (1999) *A Spiritual Audit of Corporate America: A Hard Look at Spirituality, Religion, and Values in the Workplace*, San Francisco: Jossey-Bass.

Neal, J.A., Lichtensein, B.M. and Banner, D. (1999) Spiritual perspectives on individual, organizational, and societal transformation, *Journal of Organizational Change Management*, 12 (3), 175–185.

Needleman, J. (2003) *Time and the Soul: Where Has All The Meaningful Time Gone - And Can We Get It Back?* San Francisco: Berrett-Koehler.

Pauchant, T.C. (Ed.) (2002) *Ethics and Spirituality at Work: Hopes and Pitfalls of the Search For Meaning in Organizations,* Westport, CT: Quorum Books.

Poole, P., Gioia, D. and Gray, B. (1989) Influence modes, schema change, and organizational transformation, *Journal of Applied Behavioral Science*, 25, 271–289.

Provenzano, J. (1993) *The Philosophy of Conscious Energy*, Nashville, TN: Winston-Derek.

Puhakka, K. (1998) Contemplating everything: Wilber's evolutionary theory in dialectical perspective, In D. Rothberg and S. Kelly (Eds.), *Ken Wilber in Dialogue: Conversations With Leading Transpersonal Thinkers.* 283–304, Wheaton, IL: The Theosophical Publishing House.

Redfield, J., Murphy, M. and Timbers, S. (2002) *God and the Evolving Universe: The Next Step in Personal Evolution*, New York: Tarcher/Putnam.

Rooke, D. and Torbert, W.R. (1998) Organizational transformation as a function of CEO's developmental stage, *Organizational Development Journal*, 16, 11–28.

Ross, M. (1981) Self-centered biases in attribution of responsibility: antecedents and consequences. In E.T. Higgins, C.P. Herman, and M.P. Zanna (Eds.), *Social Cognition: The Ontario Symposium.* 1, 305–321. Hillsdale, NJ: Lawrence Erlbaum Associates.

Rumelhart, D.E. and Norman, D.A. (1990) Representation of knowledge. In A.M. Aitkenhead and J.M. Slack (Eds.), *Issues in Cognitive Modeling.* Mahwah, NJ: Erlbaum Associates.

Starbuck, W.H. and Milliken, F.J. (1988) Executives' perceptual filters: What they notice and how they make sense. In D.C. Hambrick (Ed.), *The Executive Effect: Concepts and Methods for Studying Top Managers*. 35–65, Greenwich, CT: JAI Press.

Stein, M. (1998) *Jung's Map of the Soul*, Chicago: Open Court.

Sutton, R.L. and Hargadon, A. (1996) Brainstorming groups in context: effectiveness in a product design firm. *Administrative Science Quarterly*, 41, 685–718.

Swimme, B. (2001) The digitization of the cosmos: An interview with Brian Swimme on Pierre Teilhard de Chardin. Interview by Susan Bridle. *What is Enlightenment?*, Issue 19 (Spring/Summer), 43–46.

Taylor, F.W. (1960) The principles of scientific management, In H.F. Merill (Ed.), *Classics in Management*, 82–113, New York: American Management Association. (First published in 1912).

Teilhard de Chardin, P.T. (1959) *ThePphenomenon of Man*, London: Collins.

Teilhard de Chardin, P.T. (1963) *The Divine Milieu: An Essay on the Interior Life*, London: Collins.

Teilhard de Chardin, P.T. (1965) *The Future of Man*, London: Collins.

Tenbrunsel, A.E., Galvin, T.L., Neale, M.A. and Bazerman, M.H. (1996) Cognitions in organizations, In S.R. Clegg, C. Hardy, and W.R. Nord (Eds.), *Handbook of Organization Studies*. 313–337, Thousand Oaks, CA: Sage.

Thomas, J. and McDaniel, R. (1990) Interpreting strategic issues: effect of strategy and the information-processing structure of top management teams, *Academy of Management Journal*, 33, 286–306.

Tolle, E. (1999) *The Power of Now: A Guide to Spiritual Enlightenment*, Novato, CA: New World Library.

Torbert, B. and Associates. (2004) *Action Inquiry: The Secret of Timely and Transforming Leadership*, San Francisco: Berrett-Koehler.

Trevino, L.K. (1990) A cultural perspective on changing and developing organizational ethics, *Research in Organizational Change and Development*, 4, 195–230, Greenwich, CT: JAI Press.

Trice, H.M. (1993) *Occupational Subcultures in the Workplace*, Ithaca, NY: ILR Press, Cornell University.

Waddock, S. (2002) Leading corporate citizens: Vision, values, value added. Boston: McGraw-Hill.

Walsh, R. (1998) Developmental and evolutionary synthesis in the recent writings of Ken Wilber. In D. Rothberg and S. Kelly (Eds.), *Ken Wilber in Dialogue: Conversations with Leading Transpersonal Thinkers*, 30–52, Wheaton, IL: The Theosophical Publishing House.

Weick, K.E. (1979) Cognitive processes in organizations, In B.M. Staw (Ed.), *Research in Organizational Behavior*, Vol. 1, 41–74, Greenwich, CT: JAI Press.

Weick, K.E. (1995) *Sensemaking in Organizations*, Thousand Oaks, CA: Sage.

Wernerfelt, B. (1984) A resource-based view of the firm, *Strategic Management Journal*, 5, 171–180.

Wilber, K. (1993) Paths beyond ego in the coming decades, In R. Walsh and F. Vaughan (Eds.), *Paths Beyond Ego: The Transpersonal Vision*, 256–266, New York: Jeremy P. Tarcher/ Putnam.

Wilber, K. (1999a) *The Spectrum of Consciousness. The Collected Works of Ken Wilber*, Vol. 1, Boston: Shambhala.

Wilber, K. (1999b) *Up from Eden: A Transpersonal View of Human Evolution. The Collected Works of Ken Wilber*, Vol. 2, 293–680, Boston: Shambhala.

Wilber, K. (1999c) *Sex, Ecology, Spirituality: The Spirit of Evolution. The Collected Works of Ken Wilber*, Vol. 6, Boston: Shambhala.

Young, J.E. (2002) A spectrum of consciousness for CEOs: a business application of Ken Wilber's Spectrum of Consciousness, *International Journal of Organizational Analysis*, 10, 30–54.

Young, J.E. and Logsdon, J.M. (2004) Impacts of evolution of consciousness on organizational functioning: a contribution to positive organizational scholarship. Paper presented at the 11th International Conference on Advances in Management (ICAM), Orlando, FL, March.

Zohar, D. (1997) *Rewiring the Corporate Brain: Using the New Science to Rethink How We Structure and Lead Organizations*, San Francisco: Berrett-Koehler.

13

■

Lessons From Oz: Balance and Wholeness in Organizations

Jerry Biberman, Michael Whitty, and Lee Robbins
University of Scranton, University of Detroit-Mercy, and Golden Gate University

INTRODUCTION

Organizations worldwide have begun to show an increased interest in spirituality and spiritual values (e.g., Brandt, 1996; Galen, 1995; Labbs, 1995; Vicek, 1992). Consultants and business writers are urging organizations to pay more attention to spiritual values (e.g., Bolman and Deal, 1995; Gunn, 1992; Russell, 1989; Schechter, 1995; Scherer and Shook, 1993; Walker, 1989). Perhaps the most mainstream business title bringing the good news is Novak (1996). Novak, a leading conservative Catholic, suggests spirituality is vital to a fulfilling life in business. One scenario which we believe can be achieved shows a harmonic convergence between old values reaffirmed—work as a calling or duty—and an evolving consciousness which has stirred the soul in the modern workplace.

By contrast, authors such as Schaef (1987), Schaef and Fassel (1988), Kets deVries and Miller (1984), and Harvey (1977) described business organizations in the United States as "addictive," "neurotic," and "phrog farms." Tom Peters shifted from discussing "excellent" organizations

(Peters and Waterman, 1982; Peters and Austin, 1985) to contending there are no excellent organizations after the leading corporations he previously had cited as being excellent rapidly deteriorated (Peters, 1987). Leading companies aggressively market their wares while concealing evidence of severely damaged products (from silicone breast implants to asbestos to defective condoms). Global tsunamis in the financial markets leave devastated economies and the starving and unemployed in their wake. The United States subsidizes third world exports of the same tobacco products which bear government health warnings at home. Leaving "things as they are" risks an early end to healthy human enterprise.

While popular organizational consultants such as Stephen Covey (1989) urge inner/outer victory for individual managers in large systems, other leading business writers and leaders recommend a paradigm shift in basic organizational values. Both individual and systemic changes are needed for the future evolution of work on a spiritual plane. Stephen Covey makes great use of story telling in his trainings. In this essay we will take our inspirational lessons from *The Wizard of Oz* (Baum, 1899). On our journey through our work lives we must find ourselves and our true work. We believe there is a sacred dimension to our daily work.

Holistic thinking is a leading metaphor for an integral work culture. We believe that for organizations and individuals the key to spiritual change lies in transformation which must come from within. Using *The Wizard of Oz* as a metaphor, we explain how an organization can balance its intellect, emotionality, and sense of purpose; and we recommend steps organizations can take in each area to achieve this balance.

We then suggest the beginnings of a different organizational paradigm. Preconditions for transformational or paradigmatic shift have been described (Robbins, 1992; Robbins and Stevenson, 1988) as repeated experiences of frustration, hope, and the emergence of a new model. Continuing social, economic, and ecological disasters can be the repeated experiences of frustration which lead to reexamination of basic assumptions. Unlike the single sharp crisis which leads to stronger attempts to implement the same paradigm—"more of the same, harder"—such repetitious experiences provide the foundation for the fundamental reexaminations and massive shifts described in Kuhn's (1970) seminal study and in Gersick's (1991) examination of punctuated equilibrium. Hope is found in the human spirit and activated through such cultural stories as that of Oz. An alternative model, which we describe later, involves questioning the single-pointed pursuit of profit maximization—which requires reexamining organizational processes and values of higher education as well as those of corporations.

A QUESTION OF BALANCE

Every spiritual tradition emphasizes the importance of being in balance or balancing one's energies as a means for spiritual transfor-mation. These energies are often described in terms of "masculine" (or assertive) and "feminine" (or receptive) energies. Examples include the familiar yin and yang symbols, and the (perhaps less familiar) description in Kaballah or Jewish symbolism of the three pillars or columns of masculine, feminine, and center or balanced pillar. This emphasis on balance has found its way into the popular culture through such media as the Karate Kid films (with Mr. Myagi's teaching of, and emphasis on, learning balance, not just in karate but in all of life) and the Star Wars trilogy (with the Jedi philosophy of the force), the various Star Trek television and film series (illustrating balancing emotion and intellect—as illustrated by the interplay of Mr. Spock and Dr. McCoy, and in Data's wanting to express human emotions), and in the music of the Moody Blues (including their "Question of Balance" album). In each case, the balance is of energies, and the balance occurs within each person, so each person has both masculine and feminine qualities within her or himself; the task is to balance these qualities within one's self. The balance and subsequent transformation must be initiated by and performed from within the person, though, paradoxically, this occurs in response to contact with external forces, ideas, or teachings. Organizations too must discover the inner power to balance their energies and to transform themselves into more humane systems.

On this "yellow brick road" to organizational transformation, we have all encountered many cultural, political, and even technological obstacles. Toxic stress, selfish competitiveness, and inequity in the name of profit have created an economic and organizational world out of balance (Shaef and Fassel, 1988). Large systems and organizational processes have been undermined through cultural pathologies, addiction, and shadow. Sadly, the currently dominant paradigm contains much of addiction and shadow.

Chappel (1993) has developed a practitioner's model for integrating values, beliefs, and business. This type of integration is what we mean by organizational balance. Biberman and Whitty (1997) catalog some of the ever-expanding literature on spirituality and organizations. It is also helpful to apply the principles of transpersonal psychology to organizational transformation and the possible future. Readers may wish to refer to Shaef (1987) and LaBier (1989). In addition to the trend in business philosophy, a similar trend is occurring in economics and public policy. This drive for integration, wholeness, and balance applies not only to organizations and systems undergoing constant change but also to global society seeking new paradigms for balanced change. The foremost thinker along these lines has been Korten (1996).

SHARING VISIONS AND EXPERIENCES BY MEANS OF THE METAPHOR OF *THE WIZARD OF OZ*

Telling and retelling the story of *The Wizard of Oz* has allowed our Western/world culture to understand what it is to be a balanced and integrated person. Folk tales often feature insights or some form of morality story for individuals and national cultures. *The Wizard of Oz*, in the book by L. Frank Baum, the MGM movie, and later incarnations, has served this purpose for readers and viewers over the past hundred years. A search by the authors for articles and books using *The Wizard of Oz* theme and story has found books that use the story as a metaphor for personal spiritual growth (Stewart, 1997), for survival as a spiritual orphan (Kolbenschlag, 1988), and to convey the principles of managerial and organizational accountability (Conners, Smith, and Hickman, 1994). Schlesinger (1997) used the Oz fable as a metaphor for helping subordinates to work and learn under different types of bosses. In this article, we intend to expand the metaphor to describe spiritual transformation of organizations at the macro level. Our goal in utilizing the story of *The Wizard of Oz* is to encourage the reader to go beyond securing personal balance at work to explore the steps needed to contribute to organizational balance from the individual in the basic work unit to the macro organization and all its stakeholder environments.

The characters of the Oz story illustrate the strengths and challenges we all face, individually and collectively. We intend to show the necessary choices required to humanize organizations by commenting on the story and major characters of the Oz story.

THE STORY

In this article, we refer mainly to the story and characters depicted in the MGM movie. The story begins in Kansas, where Dorothy yearns to leave her farm home and all of her perceived problems to go far, far away, "somewhere over the rainbow." A tornado sends Dorothy and her dog Toto to the land of Oz, where her house kills a wicked witch and she inherits the witch's ruby slippers. Dorothy meets the munchkins, the wicked witch's more wicked sister, and Glinda, the good witch of the story. No sooner does Dorothy get to Oz than she wants to return to her home in Kansas. She is told the Wizard of Oz can help her: the way to get to the Wizard is to follow the Yellow Brick Road. Along the road, Dorothy and Toto encounter the Scarecrow, Tin Woodsman, and Cowardly Lion. The characters then overcome a series of crises culminating in the killing of the Wicked Witch, the realization the Wizard is a fraud ("humbug"), and a further realization that each character has indeed demonstrated the quality each believed her or himself to be lacking. Finally, Dorothy learns she has always had the power to return home, but had to realize it for herself. We will examine Dorothy and each of the other characters, and their organizational counterparts, in more detail in the next section. In this section, we explore possible interpretations of the story.

On the simplest level, the story can be viewed as an exciting and humorous children's adventure tale, with the moralistic conclusion that "there's no place like home." On the psychological level, the story could be interpreted as a coming-of-age story for Dorothy and her companions or a series of initiation trials to be completed before Dorothy could return home. The story could be further seen as the importance of using all of your abilities (represented by each of the characters Dorothy encounters). Jesse Stewart (1997) described how the story serves a metaphor for balancing energies and reclaiming of personal power, resulting in personal spiritual growth and transformation.

THE UNBALANCED VALUE SYSTEM OF THE MODERN WORLD

The Oz story offers an allegory of the interconnectedness of all things—humankind and the natural world. The human condition stands as a witness and mirror to the natural world. Humankind and its inventions including human organizations are part of the natural world. Organizations and human society are part of the transformational process in much the same manner as individuals. When the Oz characters are out of balance, nature reflects this crisis. Without the tornado, Dorothy would not have learned her lessons. Chaos and crisis are part of all life. Everyone and everything is our teacher. For example, the cowardly lion seems to represent aspects of our self-doubt or low self-esteem. Yet, each of us and our human creations, such as complex organizations, has the potential for empowerment, confidence, and high self-esteem. Organizations—and the researchers who study them and the academics who teach about them—can create a work culture supporting these potentials. Even the animal kingdom has an important role to play in saving the corporate planet through the cultural myth containing animal helpers, guides, and archetypes. Witness the supportive role of Toto and the messages from nature and the spirit kingdoms in the Oz story.

The story could also be looked at as a metaphor for the struggles of modern life and work. On that level, the Good Witch/Bad Witch could be seen to represent the two faces of twentieth century organizational life—on the one hand, bringing the grace of wealth/growth/technology, etc., but often at the expense of humanity, soul, and nature. Work and work structures have brought both light and darkness to humanity.

With the creed of greed threatening both ecology and human justice, it seems humankind has resigned itself to worship the false god of conflict and destruction. Spirituality seems so unscientific. The bad witch seems to have the upper hand. As Shaef and Fassel (1988) demonstrate, organizational pathology dominates office politics. The Wizard is in charge. He (and we mean He) rules via mass media. All the initial coping methods produced rigid rules, paternalism, bureaucracy, and crisis management. These methods, initially useful in creating the economic development of the earlier industrial revolution and checking the earlier liabilities of feudalism and mercantilism, achieved much of their ends. These same methods in a wired world allow heightened control of the munchkins and the other inhabitants of Oz both at work and in politics. Their excesses can lead to a world out of balance.

As crisis mounted, Dorothy and her allies from all walks of life discovered personal transformation led surprisingly to the transformation of organizations and whole systems such as the land of Oz. Perhaps the metaphor of Oz can apply to any system or imposed structure. All reactive management is like the politics of the Wizard. Change steps were needed. Let's examine each of the characters of the story in more detail, and explore counterparts and implications for the organization.

THE CHARACTERS IN "OZ" AND WHAT THEY SYMBOLIZE

Scarecrow. The Scarecrow represents intellect. The Scarecrow, who has no brains, is the problem solver of the story. On the organizational level, an organization that is not using its head does not plan. It usually operates using crisis management. An organization that makes full use of its brainpower uses a balance of rational (left hemisphere) and intuitive (right hemisphere) thinking and problem solving, uses strategic planning, and often finds creative solutions to problems. Change steps to develop this capacity include providing challenges, brainstorming and other creativity techniques, encouraging decision-making opportunities, and group problem-solving sessions including training in statistical process control tools, strategic planning, and team skills. A smart organization thinks with heart and head.

Tin Woodsman. The Tin Woodsman represents emotions. The Tin Woodsman, who has no heart, is the most emotional character in the story. On the organizational level, an organization that is not using its heart runs on bureaucracy, paternalism, and rigid rules, operating as if its mission were purely defined by objectively measured profit maximization. An organization that uses its heart encourages emotionality with celebrations and reward ceremonies. It encourages change by providing challenges, rewards, and recognition, and uses story telling, envisioning, revisiting its mission, and service projects, while providing positive reinforcement and training in communication and conflict management. The organization must discover its soul.

It seeks to discover broader values externally by serving the larger economic and community systems with which it is interdependent, and internally by responding to the needs of its own employees. Soulful leadership is needed for this breakthrough in corporate culture.

Cowardly Lion. The Cowardly Lion represents the will to act. The Cowardly Lion, who has no courage, overcomes his fears to demonstrate great courage in the story. On the organizational level, an organization that has no courage is afraid to take risks, is compliant, and manages by reacting. Argyris and Schön (1976, 1978, 1993) and Senge (1990, 1994) demonstrated that organizational learning requires accepting error as an opportunity to learn, challenging assumptions of the existing paradigm, and acting with a belief in organizational robustness. All of these require courage. An organization that demonstrates courage takes risks, is proactive, and is socially conscious. It encourages change by providing challenging assignments and projects while providing training in survival training, ethics, and social justice.

The Wizard, the two wicked witches, and Glinda each represent an outside agent or external force to which the characters in the story initially attribute the ability to create change, i.e., the ability to exert power over them. The power which is attributed to each of them produces a sense of fear and results in compliance by the inhabitants of Oz. As Connors, Smith, and Hickman (1994) point out, this combination of blame and attribution of power to the Wizard and the witches serves to disempower the other characters in the story, and allows the inhabitants to act as victims who elude accountability. Each of these characters has counterparts in business firms. The balance of rights and responsibility requires vigilance and heightened self-awareness. Trust, integrity, courage, and compassion bring much needed balance to organizational power and politics.

The Wizard. The Wizard represents power in the organization. At the beginning of the story, this power is attributed to a specific magical person, but by its end, the Wizard is revealed to be a "humbug" or fraud, and the power and accountability are reclaimed by Dorothy and her companions. Similarly, on the organizational level, an organization that attributes power to a single charismatic leader disempowers itself in the long run. An organization that reclaims its power and accountability empowers all its internal resources, trusts its processes, and uses empowering techniques such as envisioning and process consultation.

It encourages change by providing experiences and opportunities for spiritual growth, while providing training in self-awareness, community building, creativity, meditation, even the cultivation of basic virtues such as discernment. This will help bring life to work in its full human potential.

The Witches. The witches represent the opposing forces or energies of power that operate in the story, in each of us, and in organizations. At the beginning of the story, these forces or energies are, again, externalized and split, and are attributed to a "good" witch (Glinda) and to two "bad or wicked" witches. By the end of the story, Dorothy and her companions, through their shared experiences in overcoming the challenges they encounter, have reclaimed and balanced these energies within themselves. It is by reclaiming these energies that Dorothy realizes how to use her power and return home. On an individual psychological level, killing the wicked witch represents the psychological work of reclaiming one's "shadow," as Carl Jung called it, or accepting and integrating one's "dark side," or, as John Pierrakos (1987) refers to it, reconnecting one's lower human emotions (like anger and rage) with one's higher or spiritual self. A recurring theme of science fiction and myth is that we need both our so-called good and evil natures in order to be complete persons, and how, indeed, our darker, angrier side often contributes decisively to leadership and action. On the organizational level, such an energy split is manifested in the kinds of organizational defenses and pathology described by Schaef and Fassel (1988) or by Kets de Vries and Miller (1984). An organization can encourage the balancing of its energies by exorcizing its pathologies, while providing training in conflict management and incorporating the self-help philosophy of the various twelve-step programs (Robbins, 1992; Robbins & Stevenson, 1998).

Dorothy. Dorothy symbolizes all the various energies and forces of the story. She reclaims her personal balance and power, resulting in her spiritual transformation. The Oz characters, Dorothy and her friends, achieved inner victory over their darker sides as well as outer victory in attaining their goals. While the changes come from within, it is their integration of their experiences along the path that allows these changes to occur. Organizations need to balance recognition of their inner strengths with responsiveness both to ideas and to shifts in their environments. An organization that undergoes a spiritual transformation will exhibit the characteristics described at the beginning of this article. It will empower all of its members and celebrate their diversity. Its members will feel that they are in balance with their natures and are "home."

CONCLUSION

We hope our use of the Oz metaphor puts a human face on organizational theory. Institutions need to practice self-analysis ["inventory"] just as people do. Evolving organizations need to develop closer relationships with their feelings, culture, intentions, and mission. Learning organizations must take the initiative to evolve toward their highest and most creative possibilities. The recovering organizations at the turn of the century are overcoming much of this pathology in work, inch by inch, day by day. Hopefully, our story telling with the Oz metaphor gives encouragement to courageous leaders from all walks of life to face their witches and confront their wizards and contribute to the spiritual future of work.

L. Frank Baum, the author of *The Wizard of Oz*, was a forerunner of transpersonal psychology in his story telling of trusting the basic goodness of our earthly destinies. He saw humankind weaving back and forth between the wizard and the witch. Our human organizations, which reflect our consciousness in evolution, must contain a balance between masculine and feminine, the light and dark, levity and gravity —all with the final aim of partnership in creation. For the organizational psychologist or cultural anthropologist, the non-integrated soul of the modern organization is represented by the Scarecrow, the Tin Man, and the Lion. The combination of these outside "higher powers" and the higher self resulted in positive evolution to solutions on the yellow brick road. The oncoming organizational myth makers, heroes, and heroines will be those who balance the dualities of work life with the organic destiny of the human enterprise. We believe the unfolding of a servant heart within future business leaders will produce the organizational consciousness necessary for a breakthrough to a new business paradigm. How might they apply these perceptions to the modern business firm? Moving along the path from organizational addiction to organizational transformation and developing work processes where people matter is a spiritual journey. In this journey the firm comes to recognize not just its particular mission but a broader mission of serving humanity, ourselves. Thus, this new work paradigm is one of balance, which likely will require deviations from the "lower" objective of profit maximization.

Without spirituality the normative goal of business is profit, an objective which has shown demonstrable effectiveness in increasing industrial output. In this paradigm income distribution is only a side effect, wagged by the output maximization goal. While the lack of attention to distribution is recognized (e.g., regulations to deal with the internal and external diseconomies and moral hazard), such adjustments fail to fully correct specific effects and deal weakly with the perception of profit as the proper legitimate goal. The impact of such a one-pointed goal, which readily comes to be seen as the goal rather than just a means to an end, expands. Concepts and behaviors based on the goal of profit maximization become embedded in organizational cultures and in the measures used in academic research to evaluate management techniques.

From the multiple goals advanced for spirituality, an increase in variety seems requisite just as Dorothy found multiple characteristics necessary in her journey home. Multiple criteria, rather than the single criterion of profit or profit's cousins, growth, and market share, are required. Spiritual alternatives mean widening the focus of business objectives including recognizing different and potentially conflicting criteria for, on the one hand, production, and, on the other, distribution. A set of more extensive normative criteria helpful for widening our concepts of the purpose of business can be found in the schema of Russell Ackoff (1981). Maintaining that we are a species in search of ideals, he contends we have developed five recognizable foci (with each corresponding body of theory and academic disciplines in parentheses) as follows: Truth (Science), Beauty (Aesthetics), The Good (Ethics, Philosophy), Plenty (Economics), and Justice (Law). The ideals are the governing variables, the indicators of success, of the associated disciplines. Management is not included in Ackoff's list of disciplines; the prevailing paradigm we have discussed seems to imply that the purpose of business, its ideal, is simply Plenty, the domain of economics. Profit becomes a constraint, a necessary condition to achieve multiple objectives, rather than a single varied objective to be maximized. Even with multiple criteria, the problem of balance remains. Focusing on any of these ideals without attending to the others produces a bad result. Only Good and Justice (distribution) produces the problems of socialism with a potential for equity, but, as recently seen, too little to distribute, and the sterility of "socialist realist art." Only Truth produces science, but not necessarily sufficiency or ethics or fairness. Only Beauty produces neither food nor social concerns nor a search for truth—including medical progress. And only Plenty (abundance) produces an ugly, unjust society with little attention to truth or compassion.

Robbins (1992) suggests how a balanced firm might look with semi-autonomous units of limited size, minimal coercive pressures, recognition of error as a source of learning, and other characteristics. The Brazilian firm, Semco, which fits many of these characteristics, went from near financial disaster in 1980 to a position as Brazil's largest food-process machinery manufacturer and one of Brazil's fastest-growing companies in 1988, and, despite recent difficulties in Brazil, continues to thrive (Semler, 1989, 1995). Spirituality seems based more on questions than on proscriptive answers—the search for meaning in the ordinary business of life. Without spirituality the normative purpose of business is profit. If we choose to develop more spiritual organizations, we must use multiple criteria such as those suggested in Ackoff's model and develop organizational designs which support such criteria. This new paradigm contains many of the features of the Oz story in which all the characters have an awakening.

Both individuals and organizations work best with awakening, joy, meaning, and commitment in the work process. Richards (1995) calls this a centered organization—one which will produce environments where commitment is the norm, where people strive to be perceptive, receptive, and expressive and where people are involved in work that is congruent with the requirements of their own spirits and souls. Dorothy and her friends learned we are born with this potential if we only can wake up to its reality in our lives.

As the post-modern organization struggles to turn chaos into creativity, it is coming to grips with the necessity of integrating its soul and spirit. Dorothy and the dynamics of spirit may herald the coming of a new work community. A basic workplace spirituality can be the common ground for the new work community. Working people and human evolution itself are constantly seeking meaning, purpose, and a sense of contribution to work life. Reframing the meaning of work has the support of the servant leaders worldwide, who see that a life of service best fits the basic human need for relevance, recognition, meaning, and self-transcendence. Jesse Stewart (1997) is convinced that our human culture has the map for the modern spiritual journey. This journey runs through all of life at every level. In an age of economics where corporations rule the world, this journey has a most important passage through the world of work. From this universal folk tale and modern morality play, maybe we may some day reinvent work and transform human organizations in a way that will make the world more humane. We believe the experiences of the Scarecrow, Tin Woodsman, and Cowardly Lion, along with Dorothy and Toto, represent the challenge to everyone on this planet. We have the ability not only to heal ourselves but also the organizations within which we work.

We all have the opportunity to be servant leaders of the next breakthrough of human organizational evolution. There is a certain urgency for humanity to develop the consciousness needed to meet the new and diverse challenges arising on the planet. As they neared the Emerald City, Dorothy and her "fellow travelers" said to each other, "Well come on then. What are you waiting for?" "Hurry! Hurry!" "You can't rest now—we're nearly there" (Stewart, 1997, p. 174).

REFERENCE

Ackoff, R. (1981), *Creating the Corporate Future*, John Wiley & Sons, New York.

Argyris, C. (1993), *Knowledge for Action: A Guide to Overcoming Barriers to Organizational Change*, Jossey-Bass, San Francisco.

Argyris, C., and Schön, D. (1976), *Theory in Practice: Increasing Professional Effectiveness*, Jossey-Bass, San Francisco.

Argyris, C., and Schön, D. (1978), *Organizational Learning: A Theory of Action Perspective*, Addison Wesley, Reading, MA.

Baum, L. (1899), *The Wizard of Oz*, Random House, New York.

Biberman, J., and Whitty, M. (1997), "A postmodern spiritual future for work," *Journal of Organizational Change Management 10 (2)*, pp. 130–188.

Bolman, L., and Deal, T. (1995), *Leading with Soul: An Uncommon Journey of Spirit*, Jossey-Bass, San Francisco, CA.

Brandt, E. (1996), "Corporate Pioneers Explore Spirituality: Peace," *HR Magazine*, Vol. 41, No. 4, April, p. 827.

Brisken, A. (1996), *The Stirring of Soul in the Workplace*, Jossey-Bass Publishers, San Francisco, CA.

Canfield, J., and Hansen, V. (1996), *Chicken Soup for the Soul At Work: 101 Stories of Courage, Compassion and Creativity in the Workplace*, Health Communications, Deerfield Beach, FL.

Chappel, T. (1993), *The Soul of a Business: Managing for Profit and the Common Good*, Bantam, New York.

Connors, R., Smith, and Hickman (1994), *The Oz Principle: Getting Results Through Individual and Organizational Accountability*, Prentice Hall, Englewood Cliffs, NJ.

Covey, S. (1989), *The Seven Habits of Highly Effective People*, Simon and Schuster, New York.

Fisher, R., and Ury, W. (1981), *Getting to YES: Negotiating Agreements Without Giving In*, Houghton Mifflin, Boston.

Galen, M. (1995), "Companies Hit the Road Less Traveled," *Business Week*, No. 3247, 5 June, p. 824.

Gersick, C. (1991), "Revolutionary Change Theories: A Multilevel Exploration of the Punctuated Equilibrium Model," *Academy of Management Review*, Jan. 1991.

Glanz, B. (1996), *Care Packages for the Workplace: Little Things You Can do to Regenerate Spirit at Work*, McGraw Hill, New York.

Gunn, B. (1992), "Computeruism: Ideology with a Sustainable Future," *Futures*, Vol. 24, No. 6, July/August, pp. 559–575.

Harvey, J. (1977), "Organizations as Phrog Farms," *Organizational Dynamics*, Spring 1977, American Management Association, New York.

Heerman and Barry (1997), *Building Team Spirit: Activities for Inspiring and Energizing Teams*, McGraw Hill.

Kets de Vries, F. R., and Miller, D. (1984), *The Neurotic Organization*, Jossey-Bass, San Francisco, CA.

Kolbenschlag (1988), *Lost in the Land of Oz: Befriending Your Inner Orphan*, Crossroads, New York.

Korten, D. (1996), *When Corporations Rule the World*, Berrett Koehler, San Francisco, CA.

Kuhn, T.(1970), *The Structure of Scientific Revolutions*, University of Chicago Press, Chicago, IL.

Labbs, J. J. (1995), "Balancing Spirituality and Work," *Personnel Journal*, Vol. 74, No. 9, September, pp. 60–76.

LaBier, D. (1989), *Modern Madness: The Hidden Link Between Work and Emotion*, Addison Wesley, Reading, MA.

Novak, M.(1996), Business as a Calling: Work and the Examined Life, *The Free Press*, New York.

Peters, T. (1987), *Report Card on American Competitiveness: Are There Any Excellent Companies?*", Tom Peters Group, Palo Alto, CA.

Peters, T., and Austin, A. (1982), *A Passion for Excellence*, Warner Books, New York.

Peters, T., and Waterman, R. (1982), *In Search of Excellence*, Harper and Row, New York.

Pierrakos, J. C. (1987), *Core Energetics: Developing the Capacity to Love and Heal*, Life Rhythms, Mendicino, CA.

Richards, D. (1995), *Artful Work*, Berkeley Books, Berkeley, CA.

Robbins, L. (1992), "Designing More Functional Organizations: The 12 Step Model," *Journal of Organizational Change Management*, 1992, Vol. 5., No. 4.

Robbins, L., and Stevenson, W. (1998), "Counter-Intuitive Approaches to Leadership: Implications of 12-Step Methodologies for Leadership Education," *Journal of Management Systems*, Vol. 10, #2, p. 27–42.

Russell, P. (1989), "The Redemption of the Executive," *Leadership and Organization Development Journal*, Vol. 10, No. 3, pp. i–iv.

Schaef, A. W. (1987), *When Society Becomes an Addict*, Harper & Row, San Francisco, CA.

Schaef, A. W., and Fassel, D. (1988), *The Addictive Organization*, Harper & Row, San Francisco, CA.

Schechter, H. (1995), *Rekindling the Spirit at Work*, Barrytown, Ltd., Barrytown, NY.

Scherer, J., and Shook, L. (1993), *Work and the Human Spirit*, John Scherer Associates, Spokane, WA.

Schlesinger, Les (1997), "It Doesn't Take a Wizard to Build a Better Boss," *Handbook of the Business Revolution Fast Company*, Boulder, CO, p. 20–25.

Semler, R. (1989), "Managing Without Managers," *Harvard Business Review*, September–October 1989, p.76–84.

Semler, R. (1995), *Maverick*, Warner Books, New York.

Senge, P. (1990), *The Fifth Discipline: The Art and Practice of the Learning Organization*, Currency/Doubleday, NY.

Senge, P., et. al. (1994), *The Fifth Discipline Fieldbook*, Doubleday, New York.

Stewart, J. (1997), *Secrets of the Yellow Brick Road*, Sunshine Press Publications, Hygiene, CO.

Vicek, D. J. (1992), "The Domino Effect," *Small Business Reports*, Vol. 17, No. 9, Winter, pp. 21–25.

Walker, R. G. (1989), "The Imperative of Leaders to Create Leader," *Directors and Boards*, Vol. 13, No. 2, Winter, pp. 21–25.

14

.

Integrating Spirituality into Management Education in Academia And Organizations: Origins, a Conceptual Framework, and Current Practices

Sandra King, Jerry Biberman, Lee Robbins, and David M. Nicol

California State Polytechnic University, Pomona, University of Scranton, Golden Gate University, and Frostburg State University

INTRODUCTION

Spirituality engenders questions more than normative prescriptive answers. As such, it is better approached in formative rather than summative terms. We suggest a simple but comprehensive definition of spirituality—*the search for meaning in the ordinary business of life.* Thus, our goal in this paper lies not in judging the practice or assessing the literature of spirituality in the managerial environment, but in exploring aspects of the topic to raise questions and increase attention to relevant issues.

The first section suggests factors that appear to be producing increased interest in spirituality for businesses and among managers, drawing upon the literature in spirituality and work and an empirical survey. The survey of academics, managers, and consultants was conducted to determine the extent to which the topic of spirituality is of growing interest in the workplace, and why. The second section explores other frames that may be more consistent with today's spiritual concerns. In the third section, we demonstrate how course design and pedagogy can support the development of a spiritual dimension in the organizational workplace.

ROOTS OF RISING INTEREST IN SPIRITUALITY IN THE WORKPLACE

A growing interest in the relationship between spirituality and the prospect of a healthy, productive workplace is increasingly evident in the broad spectrum of attention being devoted to this topic. In a relatively short time frame, it has become the central focus in such diverse locales as academic conference sessions (e.g., the national meeting of the Academy of Management), an extensive array of paid workshops, published texts, and the syllabi of university courses. Within academia, we have seen the topic of spirituality included in sections of a wide variety of courses and, less frequently, as stand-alone course offerings. A scan of the internet reveals numerous web sites addressing spirituality and the workplace, while a topical review of the literature quickly demonstrates the heightened interest in this topic. This groundswell of interest is driven by the tentative exploration of the question: Is the incorporation of spirituality in the workplace, in fact, of potential benefit? The application of spirituality in the workplace is increasingly the object of discussion among consultants, academics, and the business community (Neal, Lichtenstein, & Banner, 1998). What seems to be driving this interest? A review of the literature suggests the answers to be multi-faceted, a function of the level of analysis—be it the environment external to the organization, the organization, or the individuals in the organizations.

External Environment: Organizational and Individual Levels

We are living in a world characterized by an accelerating rate of change (Vaill, 1989), one in which individuals often feel as though they are unable to achieve a sense of balance and stability in their lives.

Through technological innovation, we have access to instant communication and previously unfathomable masses of information requiring us to process increasing amounts of data. Often, this produces information overload and consequent anxiety (Russell & Evans, 1992).

Fifty years ago, families typically stayed in one place for all of their lives. Today, a large portion of the population has become transient, with the consequent loss of connection to communities, extended families, and, often times, their religious anchors. Concurrently, relieved of many of the external anxieties previously associated with war or economic depression, growing up in a work environment that supports fragmentation and specialization, baby boomers have focused on individual achievement (Briskin, 1996). Without the linkages present in the past, individuals often look to their immediate families and/or to their work for a sense of connection to others (Conger, 1994). Increasing change, unsettling overload, community fragmentation, and disconnection characterize the largest percentage of our working population—the baby boomers, who are reaching the age at which individuals often experience mid-life crisis (Neal, 1997). Not surprisingly, as baby boomers reach mid-life, their drive for achievement and the associated consequences are often subjected to scrutiny in an effort to assess merit and meaningfulness.

On the organizational level, we have witnessed the downsizing and restructuring of numerous organizations with the consequence that many employees have been laid off (Noer, 1993; Pulley, 1997). Not only is there a sense of loss for those who have been laid off, but also an intense residual element of uncertainty and fear within the organization. Though the layoff may create an opportunity for some, for others, it is a disaster. For both those directly affected and their wary colleagues it prompts reexamination of their lives and their organizational duties.

Briskin (1996) suggests that the legacy of focusing on efficiency, being driven by pursuit of profit maximization, has diminished corporate sensitivity to the core human values of its members. In such a climate, individuals often find it difficult to perceive meaning in their work. Many organizations fail to establish and/or maintain a sense of collective purpose, prompting individuals to be disinclined to exercise initiative, instead becoming dependent on the managerial hierarchy to make all decisions. By not providing individuals with a sense of purpose in their work, organizational creativity is suppressed, if not eliminated

(Mitroff et al., 1994). The individualistic emphasis of our society is reflected in a desire for personal accomplishment and the freedom to pursue it. Unfortunately, this drive often conflicts with the organization's efforts at control, thereby contributing to a sense of distrust within organizations (Conger, 1994). The absence of trust has created unproductive competition between individuals, organizational departments, and the employer and employee. Ironically, in organizations initially constructed to achieve a common purpose, the breakdown and fragmentation of individual relationships within them actually creates a lack of community and a dysfunctional work environment. In order to rectify the problems and counter the fragmentation that has occurred, various types of team management processes have been implemented. Many individuals, however, feel the processes merely create an illusion of involvement (Argyris, 1993). In essence, many organizations often fail to walk their talk (Richards, 1995; Secretan, 1997). This results in widening the distance between the organization and its members.

In order to compensate for their sense of deprivation within the organizational setting, many, particularly at the managerial levels, are looking to the spiritual in their quest for meaning. For example, Jerry Harvey (1996) recently observed that when he asks CEOs about their prayer life, they often become so engrossed in the conversation that they will offer to drive him to the airport to continue talking until the last minute.

For many leaders, the growing distinction between religion and spirituality has also created an opening for finding a way to implement spirituality in the workplace. With this latitude, a number of businesses (e.g., Mary Kay, Service Master, Tom Chapell, and Chick-Fil-A) are attempting to integrate spiritual values as the foundation for their corporate mission (Conger, 1994). The turmoil of organizational change, employee alienation, and the absence of collective purpose prompt interest in integrating spirituality into the workplace to enhance organizational performance. At the individual level, a variety of factors have prompted the increased focus on spiritual connections. Individuals have an innate thirst for understanding and direction, heightened in times of confusion and uncertainty. Management theorists (e.g., Mary Parker Follet and Abraham Maslow) have argued that individuals are driven toward self-actualization. A sense of discomfort arises from the discrepancy between an individual's potential capability and the level of work in which s/he is engaged, impelling her/him to search for spirituality in the workplace (King & Nicol, 1998). Even as individuals achieve positions of leadership, thereby fulfilling material (and even ego) goals, they are beginning to acknowledge that they need more— driving organizations toward attentiveness to issues of value, meaning, and spirituality.

To supplement and refine the perspective of our review of the literature, we conducted a survey of academics, managers, and consultants to confirm the growing interest in the topic of spirituality in the workplace, as well as the reasons for such interest. The survey was distributed through academic conferences and an on-line snowball (networking) technique. It requested that the respondents describe: (1) how and why they became interested in the topic of spirituality in the workplace; (2) whether they are aware of a growing interest in this area in general; (3) what factors they believe are driving it; and (4) how they have formally, or informally, included the topic of spirituality in any of their classroom and/or training sessions. To develop a greater understanding of how individuals are integrating spirituality into their courses, we also collected syllabi from those respondents who were offering a course in management and spirituality and/or incorporating the topic in other courses. Over fifty people completed our exploratory survey. We found that the predominant theme mentioned from our respondents was that their interest in spirituality in the workplace was derived from their personal spiritual evolutionary experience and a desire to integrate their personal and professional lives. This is not inconsistent with Maslow's hierarchical perspective. With increasing affluence and the widespread satisfaction of "lower-level" needs in Western societies, individuals are inclined to progress toward self-actualization, and with that, confront what constitutes meaning in their lives. Thus, their emerging spiritual values, whether theological or psychological, become blended into their work life. Most of the participants wrote about how the process was a natural evolutionary one.

A majority of the participants reported an increased interest, both among their colleagues and their students, in the topic of spirituality and management. Many believe this increase has occurred as a direct result of societal insecurity. For example, many of the participants mentioned that the world was becoming more "messed up" (e.g., increasingly rapid rate of change, increased information and technology overload, loss of family life and community, general loss of security). In addition, there were a number of individuals who suggested that the large number of baby boomers reaching mid-life, beginning to reexamine their work life, are driving the increased interest in spirituality in the workplace. These "boomers" are increasingly questioning the meaning of their work, with the consequent search for work that will enable them to integrate their personal values within their work in the organization.

A predominant number of the academic respondents reported that they are including spirituality in their teaching, either formally or informally. A review of the syllabi and the course titles makes it immediately evident that the topic of spirituality and work is being integrated into courses through a number of different avenues. Among the more explicit course titles were: HRD: Spiritual Values; Self-Leadership; Ethical, Moral, and Spiritual Issues of Management; and HRD: The Meaning of Work. Although some conduct entire courses in spirituality and management, the majority report incorporating the concepts within the context of more established courses. To assist in this effort, many are using recent texts that have been written on the topic of spirituality in the workplace. Many remain unsure as to how to effectively implement it in their management courses.

THE SPIRITUAL PERSPECTIVE: ITS LEGITIMACY IN THE WORKPLACE

Although the survey and literature demonstrates strong interest among academics and managers to integrate spirituality and work, we believe a major impediment remains. Managers need a clear framework for spiritual leadership and decision making, distinguishing between activities that are and are not "spiritual." Discussions of management and spirituality are addressed primarily at the individual level. Today, texts, articles, and conferences addressing management and spirituality help incline individuals toward a recognition of critical uncertainties, of unresolved issues. Managers are prompted to bring their inner spirituality, their concerns for value and meaning, through the doors of their offices, rather than leaving them at the enterprise gate. However, without a framework of organizational theory, such arguments may fail to persuade, or, on the other hand, may persuade those inclined to zealotry that will then run roughshod over those with differing beliefs. Less is said at the organizational level. Increased attention to a conceptual framework for choosing directions for the spiritually attentive business enterprise is needed. To begin, we might inquire into the basic assumptions in the current paradigm of business. In this paradigm, what is the purpose of business organizations? In the still prevailing hierarchical firm, power and decision making are concentrated at the top and trickle down through delegation. Priorities, reward structures, agendas of discussion, and data selected to guide decisions all depend upon certain basic assumptions and assumed purpose. When asked about purpose, leaders of firms can proudly respond by pointing to their carefully crafted *Mission Statement,* which generally fails to address the responsibility of the business as a social system. Rather, the purpose is declared in the categorization of the firm as being "for-profit," without further qualification. Though some hold profits to be the sole objective, others suggest that profits should be conceived solely as an enabler for businesses to fulfill their social obligations. The purpose, as argued by economists from Adam Smith to Milton Friedman, is to fulfill the desires of the marketplace, wherein profit is but the mechanism driving the invisible hand.

In the current era, growth and market share have been accorded preeminence as objectives. Instead of focusing on the extent to which the firm has successfully provided value to its stakeholders, we tend to embrace these markers of magnitude, embracing the narrow and quantifiable, rather than the holistic and qualitative. This does not bode well for encouraging organizational innovation, for supporting employee development, for promoting actions that serve the social good, etc. When market share or growth, or "the bottom line," are used as the sole or primary measures of success, we implicitly reinforce the perception that they are the only ultimately worthy ends to be pursued. Rather, we need to acknowledge that organizations serve multiple stakeholders, not just the stockholders. As such, they must balance competing ends to achieve a common success. Hence, being socially responsible, fostering participative decision making, responding to changing consumer demands, and operating profitably is all necessary and appropriate for success; yet none is sufficient by itself. We do not exist in a vacuum, though we may perceive that to be the case in the short term. For too long, we responded to only one of our stakeholders. Now we must acknowledge and be responsive to the needs of others.

Of course, we are habitual animals. Hence, we tend to assess our progress in the form of past measures. Thus, we ask if increased worker satisfaction, heightened productivity, or enhanced creativity resulted in an increase in market share. R&D in firms is functionally evaluated not for its contribution to human welfare, however laudable medical research, for example, might seem, but for its contribution to the welfare of the firm as measured by profit or growth. These approaches to assessment of research, innovation, or general effectiveness are further promulgated in textbooks and classrooms, reinforcing the paradigm for succeeding generations of managers.

Are these criteria sufficient to produce better societies? Will these criteria decrease suffering? Are these the criteria we need? Despite optimism about the invisible hand reinforced by recent comparative production successes in market economies (at least until the recent "Asian crisis"), longings and recognition of the need for something more are increasingly evident. As John Dunning (1998) points out, cooperation must play a larger role in the "global capitalism" of the current era. As the problem of production becomes less pressing, problems of distribution, of equity, of natural and person-created beauty rise in relative importance. Profit, as the guiding mechanism for the invisible hand, has become inadequate.

Choosing different measures of business success would mean that research, practice, and business education would produce different processes for firms, and different content, and perhaps an educational process, in our business schools. Spirituality seems more about questions than about prescriptive answers—*the search for meaning in the ordinary business of life.* If we choose to develop more spiritual organizations, we must use multiple criteria and develop organizational designs that can support such criteria. Further work is needed, but a critical beginning is to recognize both the limitations and the enormous impact of using profit alone as the criterion of success.

BRINGING SPIRITUALITY IN THE WORKPLACE
INTO THE CLASSROOM

We will now examine how the needs driving the interest can be taught to students who will be the future leaders for our businesses. At the end of the 20th century, a new paradigm for business management and business education has been emerging in response to the world business community's need for a different educational product. The main components of this emerging new paradigm for business education, as well as for business management, include a need to connect people's public selves with their personal or private selves. As Parker Palmer (1998) suggests in *The Courage to Teach*, leaders of any kind—including teachers—must begin to find ways to teach the whole person, to consider intellectual, emotional, and spiritual needs, as well as the practical demands of career training. In our recent survey of management educators, finding work that integrates the whole self was mentioned from both students' and teachers' perspective. The inclusion of spirituality and spiritual techniques in management higher education parallels similar trends that are occurring in schools at all levels in several countries—including medical schools (Mangan, 1997), seminaries (Niebur, 1997), public schools in the United Kingdom (Neumark, 1997), and in undergraduate psychology of women classes (Power, 1995). Tools and techniques which enhance a person's ability to become self-aware, to learn and to grow, have been increasingly accepted in business training (Senge, 1990). These new ways of learning require business educators to revamp their approaches to include psychological and spiritual approaches to classroom teaching. The content areas in which spirituality at work can be, and has been, discussed include self-awareness, decision-making, power and politics, ethics, creativity, intuition, problem solving, stress management, leadership, and diversity.

In the course of personal and professional development, the authors have studied techniques and have been experientially involved in a variety of spiritual disciplines—such as Jesuit spiritual exercises of Ignatius of Loyola; the Kaballah; and Vipassana Buddhist, Hindu, and Chinese philosophy and meditative and prayer techniques. We have found the regular practice outside of our classrooms of some spiritual discipline (yoga and tai chi) to serve as a ground for our classroom innovations. Our experiences with these spiritual traditions have demonstrated the similarity underlying all of the spiritual or mystical traditions, regardless of their religious background (Biberman & Whitty, 1997).

Despite differences in culture and specific language or terminology used, the philosophies of all of these spiritual traditions describe spiritual transformation, the awareness and experience of one's higher self, and the interconnectedness of all people with each other and with divine creator, source, or energy. The second author of this paper teaches management courses at a religious institution. The religious nature of the institution provides a natural lead-in and context for him to raise spiritual issues within his classes. He is able to show how the spiritual philosophies of the traditions described above parallel the emerging new paradigm of personal empowerment and group collaboration in business and organizations. We have shared with our students the spiritual teachings and philosophy from mystical traditions of the major world religions, including teachings from Ignatius of Loyola, Buddhist, Hindu, and Chinese philosophy, Zen and Taoist readings, vedic wisdom, Kaballah and Jewish mysticism, and Catholic and other Christian readings. Specific processes and techniques that have been used in class include: explaining the benefits of, and then teaching, various kinds of prayer, relaxation exercises, meditation (including mantra meditation), journalizing and other writing, active imagination, guided imagery, drawings, spiritual exercises, hatha yoga and other stretching, tai chi, breathing exercises, music, dance, and movement.

Two of the authors have used Lee Bolman's and Terrences Deal's text, *Leading with Soul*, as the basis for class discussion and papers in a MBA and EMBA courses. This book describes the personal journey and organizational impact of a CEO's search for meaning. Our use of spiritual techniques and philosophies in our teaching has met with acceptance, not only from our students, but also from our colleagues and superiors. In our experience the use of spiritual philosophies and techniques can lead to physical, cognitive, and spiritual benefits for both teacher and student, on both the individual and class levels. It can also lead to a transformed classroom climate. Classroom meditation has been observed by both the authors to produce increased physical relaxation in our students, as well as anxiety and stress reduction. Cognitively, we believe it enhances mental clarity, empathy, stamina, and confidence. In addition, the use of creative visualization, movement, drawing, music, and story telling in our classes has enabled our students to learn to trust and use their intuition and to improve their creative problem-solving abilities. Examination of alternatives to the single-variable profit model of corporate success has created lively discussion and considerable interest from students, examining a wider range of behaviors and the potential for increased congruence between organizational goals and their individual searches for meaningful work.

As for explicit spiritual benefits, as a consequence of the authors' experiences related to the classes, our students have reported experiencing an expanded sense of wholeness, a renewed sense of purpose and meaning in their lives, and a sense of well-being predicated on contact with their essential natures. A great benefit we have observed when using spiritual philosophies and techniques, has been the transformation of the class climate into that of a learning community. We have observed behavioral changes in our students and in the classroom climate consistent with concepts typically found in models of learning organizations (Senge et al., 1994), such as dialogue; attention to raising questions and to experiment; openness and trust; and consensus seeking. We would argue that a company experiencing similar behavioral changes would become less structurally constrained, more inclusive, less committed to power distance, more holistic, and more process-oriented (focusing on both the means and the ends). To that end, spiritually attentive organizations might be: emotional, smaller, and place emphasis on the role of work organizations as communities as well as production systems.

CONCLUSION

Through heightened understanding of the driving forces underlying interest in the linkage of spirituality and management in the workplace, we can begin to uncover the implications for our role as educators. In this is the prospect for developing a framework that will provide the basis for a new organizational framework. Our review of the literature, in conjunction with our own research, suggest, that the sources that are driving the need for change are multi-faceted, associated with different levels of analysis—be it the environment external to the organization, the organization itself, or the individuals that make up the organization. Although the survey and literature demonstrate strong intentions among academics and managers to bring spiritual perspectives to classrooms and work organizations, we believe that a major impediment remains in the lack of a clear framework to do it. In order to address the issue, we have noted the limitation of the singular focus characterizing blind adherence to the bottom line, or alternatively, growth or market share.

Finally, we have listed and briefly discussed teaching methods and techniques derived through our research and extensive experience. Through our own experience, and a review of the syllabi that we have gathered, we have suggested specific content areas, as well as techniques, in which spirituality at work can be discussed. We have also described anecdotal results and benefits that we have observed resulting from the use of these philosophies and techniques. We have only provided an initial probe into what we hope will become a major body of knowledge related to spirituality in the workplace. It is our belief that by fostering an education perspective that includes attention to spirituality in the workplace, we will not only help to produce a healthier society, but will unleash phenomenal energy and creativity for individuals and the organizational environment.

REFERENCE

Ackoff, R. L. (1981), *Creating the Corporate Future.* New York: John Wiley & Sons.

Argyris, C. (1993), *Knowledge for Action: A Guide to Overcoming Barriers to Organizational Change.* San Francisco: Jossey-Bass.

Biberman, J., & Whitty, M. (1997), A post-modern spiritual future for work. *Journal of Organizational Change Management,* 10(2), 130–136.

Bolman, T., & Deal., T. E. (1995),*Leading with Soul : An Uncommon Journey of Spirit.* San Francisco: Jossey-Bass.

Briskin, A. (1996), *The Stirring of the Soul in the Workplace.* San Francisco: Berrett-Koehler.

Conger, J. (1994), *Spirit at Work: Discovering the Spirituality in Leadership.* San Francisco: Jossey-Bass.

Covey, S. (1989), *The Seven Habits of Highly Effective People: Restoring the Character Ethic.* New York: Simon and Schuster.

Dunning, J. (1998), Presentation: Capitalism at Golden Gate University. San Francisco, CA, Nov.

Harvey, J. (1996), Conversation at the George Washington University; Washington, D.C.

King, S., & Nicol, D. (1998), Individual and organizational change: Jacques and Jung's contribution to spiritual growth. In Biberman, J., & Alkhafaji, A. (Eds.), *Business Research Yearbook: Global Business Perspective: Vol. 5* (pp. 803–807). Michigan: McNaughton & Gun.

Mangan, K. S. (1997, March 7), Blurring the boundaries between religion and science/medical school programs on the healing role of spirituality. *Chronicle of Higher Education*, 43, 14, 26.

Mitroff, I. I., Mason, R. O., & Pearson, C. M. (1994), Radical surgery: What will tomorrow's organizations look like? *Academy of Management Executive*, 8(2), 11–21.

Neal, J. (1997), Spirituality in management education: A guide to resources. *Journal of Management Education*, 21(1), 121–139.

Neal, J., Lichtenstein, B., & Banner, D. (1998, August), What matters most in transformation: Economic and spiritual arguments for individual, organizational and societal change. Paper presented at the meeting of the Academy of Management, San Diego, CA.

Neumark, V. (1997, February 14), Cards on the table. *Times Educational Supplement*, 201, S1.

Niebur, G. (1997, April 12), At Jewish Theological. *New York Times*, 25, 146.

Noer, D. (1993), *Healing the Wounds: Overcoming the Trauma of Layoffs and Revitalizing Downsized Organizations*. San Francisco: Jossey-Bass.

Palmer, Parker (1998), *The Courage to Teach: Exploring the Inner Landscape of a Teacher's Life*. San Francisco: Jossey-Bass.

Power, R. (1995, Summer–Fall), A class that changes lives.*Women and Therapy*, 16, 2–3.

Pulley, M. L. (1997), *Losing Your Job–Reclaiming Your Soul*. San Francisco: Jossey-Bass.

Richards, D. (1995), *Artful Work*. San Francisco: Berret-Koehler.

Roth, G. (1997), *Sweat your Prayers*. New York: Jeremy Tarcher.

Russell, P., & Evans, R. (1992), *The Creative Manager*. San Francisco: Jossey-Bass.

Secretan, L. H. K. (1997), *Reclaiming Higher Ground*. New York: McGraw-Hill.

Semler, R. (1989, September–October), Managing without managers. *Harvard Business Review*, 76–84.

Semler, R. (1995), *Maverick*. New York: Warner Books.

Senge, P. M. (1990), *The Fifth Discipline: The Art and Practice of the Learning Organization*. New York: Doubleday.

Senge, P. M., et al. (1994) *The Fifth Discipline Fieldbook: Strategies and Tools for Building a Learning Organization*. New York: Currency, Doubleday.

Vaill, Peter (1989), *Managing as a Performing Art: New Ideas for a World of Chaotic Change*. San Francisco: Jossey-Bass.

15

■

Linking Community and Spirit: A Commentary and Some Propositions[1]

Sandra A. Waddock
Boston College

"Conscious community concern is at the heart of human morality." – Frans De Waal, *Good Natured* (1996)

Economists have tried to tell us for years that what matters most is the economy, economics, money, and of course the things that money can buy. As the 1996 election refrain went, "It's the economy, stupid!" The only thing that really matters (in this view) is self-interest and personal gain. This slogan translates to the organization level as "maximize shareholder wealth." Make as much as you can as quickly as you can. Get the goods and forget the good. Common good? What's that and what's it got to do with me?

But we know better. It's *not* "the economy, stupid." Not really. Or at least not only. Other things also matter, whatever the economists say. For example, one other thing that matters is developing community, that is, caring, belonging, trust, working with others in a joint enterprise

---

[1] This paper is based on a presentation entitled "Community Matters Most," given in an all-academy symposium entitled "What Matters Most in Management Scholarship: Nature, Community, Spirituality, and Character," 1998 Academy of Management Annual Meeting, San Diego, CA.

that is bigger than oneself, that makes a contribution, and allows us to co-exist in our world successfully. This paper will argue that even in an individualistic society such as the United States, some form of community is important. Community, however, is built on collaboration and not just competition, and derives from the fundamental symbiosis or interdependency that biologists now tell us that organisms have with other organisms. It is premised not solely on independence and autonomy, or dependence and hierarchy, but as well on connectedness and a healthy *inter*dependence. Expressed this way, developing community is an exercise of spirituality. It is part of what Wilber (1996) calls the "left-hand" side, the internal, expressive side of life, as opposed to the external, empirically measurable and observable aspects of the world. Community is a part of organizational life that, like other "left-hand" elements like feelings, aesthetics, intuition, awareness, and meanings, has been largely ignored or discounted, in their collective expressions.

The term *society* implies community at its essence. In this use, community implies care, joint meanings, mutuality, and commonality of purpose, of history, norms, and values. It is community in this sense, I argue, that people need to fully develop as human beings, to be integrated wholes and for our societies to be integrated wholes. It is this sense of community that needs to be valued if we are to reintegrate the expressive and consciousness elements of being with the empirically observable. Yet it is exactly these subjective and intersubjective aspects of community that are too frequently ignored in our objectivist mindset. This paper will explore the importance of creating a sense of community that inspires individuals' commitment to a set of goals encompassing the common as well as the individual good. By implication, this enhancement of community allows for a degree of spirituality in our common enterprises.

We are in the United States, as numerous scholars have pointed out (e.g., Lodge, 1975; Bellah et al., 1985), individualists. Yet it may well be a deep sense of loss or absence of community (and an attempt to understand that loss) that has made Robert Putnam's 1995 "Bowling Alone" the most cited article in recent history. Despite the decline of formal associational activities documented by Putnam, Wolfe (1998) finds that people *do* find or build community in a variety of places, especially in the modern world through work organizations. Indeed, a dissertation based on the data in Wolfe's study (Poarch, 1997) finds that work organizations are replacing other types of communities in many Americans' lives. So even if people in the United States have started bowling alone or do watch too much television (Putnam, 1995, 1996), they still care deeply about creating communities that help shape meaning and purpose in their lives. They—we—still seek engagement and involvement not just with self, not just with the "goods," but with others.

In direct contradiction to the need to evoke community at work, however, there is now significant evidence that many organizations, especially businesses, are experiencing diminished capacity to build successful communities and meaningful work. Layoffs, downsizings, re-engineering, and restructurings of all sorts combine in a devaluing of locational communities, not to mention community among employees. These activities are visible features of the modern corporate landscape, highly rewarded by Wall Street and the business press. Further, despite years of attention to "participative management," the quality "revolution," and decentralization to "empower" employees, too frequently jobs are still structured to provide the most control for management and the least for those who actually perform the work. And now there are numerous virtual organizations where people interact less frequently than in traditional organizations, where telecommuting, temporary offices, and contingent workers are becoming all too common means of cost containment. These shifts arguably occur at some cost to community.

Forces in the global economy thus work in direct contrast to Poarch's (1997) finding that with the loss of other types of community found in earlier years in churches, neighborhoods, and civic organizations, people now develop their sense of community at and through work. Processes of modernization and industrialization have vast potential to shift community dynamics as developing nations attempt to become "world class" (Kanter, 1995) without regard for the impacts of those globalization processes, their inherent materialism, and the homogenization of values and culture on local community (see also Korten, 1995; Barber, 1995).

Given the global realities described briefly above, it may well be an imperative that our institutions, market-based, public, and civil, recognize and deal with this need for community and spirit if they hope to be successful in the future and tap the best of human energies. Perhaps because many companies are not prepared to overtly acknowledge community's importance to their own success and even survival, many people seem to be experiencing a tremendous loss of community. Many people live in suburbs, not knowing their neighbors, working 50–60 hours a week in what is too frequently meaningless work, where "face time" is as important as real contribution, and where pressure to do more substitutes for teamwork. This loss of community relates back to a perceived loss of civil society in a nation characterized as having been "wilded" or as having become a "corporation nation"(Derber, 1992, 1998). Others, looking globally, suggest the term "McWorld" (Barber, 1995) to indicate the homogenization and cutthroat competition characterized by a "race to the bottom" (Korten, 1995; Henderson, 1996) resulting from wage and low-cost producer wars (Greider, 1998) imposed by forces of globalization (Kanter, 1995). This dynamic may be somewhat counteracted by strenuous, but unfortunately not always friendly or civil, attempts to sustain or develop a form of community that one scholar has labeled "Jihad," which represents a form of struggle to sustain community identity (Barber, 1995). Further, these countervailing forces exist in a world that is increasingly "one" whether we are ready or not (Greider, 1998).

INTEGRATING THE UNOBSERVABLE

Generally speaking, issues such as spirituality, emotion, and community have received little attention in management thinking, research, and practice, at least until quite recently. Attention has largely been placed on analytical and readily quantifiable subject matters, particularly those that can be expressed in monetary, or at least quantifiable, terms. In fact, as suggested above, in many cases community may be being systematically destroyed in the modern corporation's effort to compete in what appears to be a constantly changing, highly competitive, and even chaotic environment, where dog-eat-dog competition appears to rule over the "softer" elements of living (cf. D'Aveni, 1994). As management scholars, teachers, and consultants hoping to influence practice, it is time that we ask why so little attention has been paid to people's need for community and spirit in our modern organizations.

Part of the answer lies in the "Cartesian split" (Overton, 1998) that characterizes much of Western thought. This split has brought us the distinction between mind or spirit and body, between the ineffable and what Westerners perceive as the "real," or, alternatively, between the subjective and the objective, the material and immaterial. In some respects, we may have reached the point where we can scarcely believe in the reality of anything, such as consciousness or community, that cannot be empirically measured, touched, tasted, or seen. Yet consciousness and subjective matters of all sorts, as Wilber (1996) points out, things that are of the "spirit" broadly conceived, are not measurable or physical things. If the essence of things such as community is to be shared at all, they must somehow be interpreted in words (or other ways) shared between at least two people (Wilber, 1996). These things of spirit, such as community, are things we cannot measure. Because what gets measured is what gets attention, they have been given short shrift in management thought. Yet as anyone who has ever experienced community, felt a strong emotion, had an idea or a dream knows, the fact that these things are of the "spirit," of the "heart," or of the "head," does not make them any less real—or valuable—than the material goods pursued so vigorously in the modern world.[2]

"Crits" or critical theorists and others have argued, as I am arguing here, that we need to bring back into our thinking what has been called the "ghost in the machine," the presence of consciousness and collective energy that is not readily quantifiable or observable. In research, in teaching, and in decision making, this is the "I" and "we" of deliberate choices, of questions to ask and answer, of perspectives that shape the "realities" explored. In research, it is, if we acknowledge it, the reason why we choose "this" subject rather than that one: because at some level the question tugs at our minds, hearts, and souls. This "I" and "we," the subjective, brings altogether different subject matter to our attention than does positivist science, focusing as it does on the objective ("it" and "its" [Wilber, 1996]) generally permits, embedding the consciousness of the researcher directly into the work. If we wish to know something fully, we need to explore all four realms (Wilber, 1996).

---

[2]Thus, this paper is an essay and commentary rather than traditional empirical research, in part because it presents an argument and a set of ideas rather than a set of "findings."

In Western science, we are most familiar with the objective and inter-objective elements, i.e., the exterior-individual or "it" dimension typically measured in the hard sciences, and the exterior-collective dimensions or "its" addressed generally in the social sciences. We are less familiar with and tend to ignore in Western studies, the subjective and inter-subjective elements, the interior-individual "I" in which consciousness, emotion, sensations, perceptions, ideas, and spirituality are to be found, and the interior-collective "we" where cultural identities are found (Wilber, 1996).

Using a logic of both/and rather than our more typical either/or, we can perhaps accommodate all four realms of "knowing." The great contribution of the critical theorists is (whatever other limitations their work might have) to make us aware, in the words of Wilber (1996, p. 8), that:

> [T]he so-called "empirical" world is in many ways not just a *perception* but an *interpretation*. . . . [T]he allegedly simple "empirical" and "objective" world is not simply lying around "out there" waiting for all and sundry to see. Rather the "objective" world is actually set in subjective and inter-subjective contexts and backgrounds that in many ways govern what is seen, and what *can* be seen in that "empirical" world.

Recognition of *both* the subjective (and intersubjective) and objective (and interobjective) contexts suggests that a profoundly different way of experiencing our worlds—as organizations, and in our teaching, research, and management practice—is needed to honor all of these domains. As Wilber (1996, p. 9) indicates:

> The fact that both of these approaches—the exterior and the interior, the objectivist and the subjectivist—have aggressively and persistently existed in virtually all fields of human knowledge ought to tell us something—ought to tell us, that is, that both of these approaches are profoundly significant. They both have something of incalculable importance to tell us. And the integral vision is, beginning to end, dedicated to honoring and incorporating both of these profound approaches in the human knowledge quest.

We have with our organizations and in most of our teaching and research about management honored primarily the objective, empirically observable "realities," ignoring the subjective and inter-subjective. The rising popularization of "spirituality" in organizations suggests increasing recognition of the need for more integrative approaches.

So, if we hope to influence teaching, scholarship, and practice, and if community is one of the elements on the subjective side of life that reflects spirit, then we need to make it acceptable in our teaching to build small communities, e.g., of inquiry (Fisher and Torbert, 1995) or practice (Wenger, 1998), where spirit and community can flourish. Common enterprise may allow and even encourage communities of practice (Wenger, 1998) to evolve within business organizations so that people within them can cope with today's complexities.

Such an integrated approach allows the expression of individual meanings, feelings, beliefs, aspirations, hopes, and dreams as acceptable elements of organizational life and allows for the feelings of working collaboratively that create a sense of community. Bringing mind, heart, soul, and body into union, individually and collectively, validating subjective as well as objective, can help our enterprises, public and private, acknowledge the importance of community as a basis on which success, even survival, is built.

The first half of this paper has attempted to make the connection between spirituality and community, and to show why management thought has devoted little attention to such issues. Now I would like to develop three propositions about community. The goal is to move management thinking slightly toward a more holistic integrative management that can serve both organizations and societies well into the 21st century, and, as well, incorporate elements of community into organizational life.

WE ALL SEEK COMMUNITY AND CONTRIBUTION

The first proposition is that people need and want to belong to communities where they can make meaningful contributions that build a better world. This, I believe, is a fundamental human—and humane—need too frequently ignored. Many people discover that beyond a certain point more money isn't going to make their lives better, that there are other important things to which they need to pay attention. Getting more goods doesn't result in common goods or even family goods. These discoveries are at least in part realizations about the core importance of community, of relationship, of integration into something meaningful in people's lives, arguably, of spirituality. Of course, such longings may be expressed as framed here largely in privileged societies where people actually move beyond survival and subsistence levels. But then community may be the essence of less privileged societies, where living in tightly integrated units is essential to day-to-day survival, where the Cartesian split is not made. In more developed societies, we have different opportunities and constraints as we live and work largely through managed enterprises of various sorts.

As humans we are aware, conscious. Awareness at its essence makes us want to understand our context, to be part of something that goes beyond ourselves. Once our basic needs are met, as well as in the communal struggle to meet those needs, we seek something higher, beyond ourselves. That something higher finds its expression in community.

Modern organizations, particularly business organizations, however, too frequently fail to provide that "something higher," though there is evidence that those that do generate significant success (e.g., Collins & Porras, 1997). Turned off to work that is at its roots meaningless and in some cases even unethical, many people opt out of their organizations psychically, turning their productive energy and attention to family, civic matters, or self-development. Too many of those who remain engaged are engaged in an endless pursuit of "more," more material goods, more things. Community, where it can be found or created, can be a countervailing force to the stress, isolation, and anomie that characterizes organizations that have cut out too much of what was community in their efforts to become competitive.

Arguably, community, caring, being with others who care, working toward or being in something bigger than us, becomes as important as having more of the goods that are pervasive in developed societies globally. Arguably, it is the positive experience of community that brings out the best in us, that allows us to develop our own sense of connectedness, even of spirituality, that uncovers our deepest values and allows the expression of those values—and that counts for the organization and society as well (the dark side of the power of this experience, of course, is its capacity to imprison and subjugate). From the positive perspective that resonates well with the findings of Collins and Porras's *Built to Last*, Anderson recently noted pointedly:

> Community also provides a necessary counterpoint and precedence to financial goals, since it has a different appeal to basic needs, motives, and instincts; it

enlarges the range of each person's competence, control, initiative, and commitment, which are root causes of economic success.... By itself, shareholder wealth provides an incomplete sense of identity and uniqueness, and does not motivate long-term creativity the same way community does. Coupling strong communities with high economic performance comes closer to assuring the overall health of the organization. Business success is grounded in a stable organization community. (1997, p. 34).

The question is: How and when will our business organizations recognize this fundamental fact of existence and structure themselves to accommodate these needs so that they are better in tune with the needs of the societies and stakeholders they serve? To the extent that community is built within our major organizations, they will have positive values that serve the needs of society. Hence the next proposition.

PROSPERITY IS PREMISED ON COMMUNITY

The second proposition is that organizational prosperity and even survival depend on organizations' capacity to build in structures and caring relationships that permit people to make meaningful contributions and fulfill the fundamentally spiritual need for community. Collins & Porras' (1997) seminal work on visionary companies again sheds some insight into this proposition. How much more meaningful would work and organizational life be if people were able, in fact, to bring their whole selves into work, to engage in personal "projects" (Freeman & Gilbert, 1988) in which they truly believed and that provided a source of shared purpose and identity? Isn't that, in fact, exactly what those visionary companies have in some respects accomplished? These organizations have not only survived long term but have greatly prospered in doing so. Further, recent work on stakeholder relations of these visionary companies (Graves & Waddock, 1998) suggests that they also pay more attention than their less visionary counterparts to primary stakeholders. One implication may be that because of the strength of their value systems and the roles that values play in developing a shared participation in enterprise development, visionary companies also do a better job at building community.

This proposition, then, raises a question. Do most business organizations today encourage people to meet their personal needs, to create meaning in their work? I suspect that the answer is no, probably because they are afraid of the anarchy that might result (and people may be afraid of the power of that total—even totalitarian—commitment).[3] But in the decentralized web structures that have evolved in today's technologically connected organizations, meaning and connectedness, that is, community, arguably get created by the "glue" provided by vision, values, and culture. This "glue" allows people to form their own purposes, hopefully in congruence with those of their employing enterprise. And that congruence: (1) avoids anarchy; and (2) provides the potential for autonomy (decentralization, empowerment) within a context aimed at common goals that simultaneously holds the enterprise together through shared meanings and community spirit.

Let us take an example. What could be more "anarchic" than a university with its front-line personnel, the professors, each pursuing his/her own individual research, teaching, and perhaps personal agenda (Weick, 1976). Yet universities are not really anarchies. Classes get taught and faculty do work together in the common enterprise of creating and disseminating knowledge, each by her own lights. Faculty form themselves into communities of inquiry (Fisher & Torbert, 1995) internally within their universities through research and teaching projects and externally through professional associations. Other "communities" form within departments and colleges, as well as at the institutional level, each creating its own sense of meaning and coherence through the work being done. Business organizations are, arguably, moving closer to this model of organizing. Consider the emergence of web-like structures, electronic connectedness, highly decentralized structures, and multiple strategic and tactical alliances. These elements combine in entrepreneurial subunits to enable employees to get the work done in a flexible, fractal-like set of structures held together primarily by the vision and values of common purpose.

The proposition is that survival and success depend on community, caring relationships, and appropriately supportive structures, yet we find organizations devolving into decentralized units, purportedly managed by empowered employees. The rationale for the proposition is that empowered and autonomous individuals need to be held together by

[3]I am grateful to Bill Frederick, University of Pittsburgh, for this insight which developed in an extensive e-mail discussion prior to a symposium at the Academy of Management, where early versions of these ideas were shared.

some sort of "glue" if they are to be productive for the organization or a community. Vision and values can create meaningful work within these autonomous units, and serve as a source of glue, and the contributions of employees at work can be acknowledged and recognized. This decentralized pattern, as we see it evolving, thus puts significant demands for performance on the empowered and relatively autonomous units, and even on individuals. Yet it also dramatically shifts both the fundamental hierarchical and power relationships toward a fundamentally more collaborative model. What it does to community is more debatable, for unless the vision and values promote positive association with the enterprise, people are likely to become more fragmented, more separated from each other. Positive values, arguably, can draw people into community; positive visions can unite them and provide that very sense of community that risks being lost in the empowerment process.

Perhaps here lies the fundamental reason that I disagree with Collins & Porras' (1997) conclusion that the content of the core ideology of firms doesn't matter: I think the content of core values does matter greatly. If we are to be able to "manage" people toward authentic goals with which they can actually agree, if their own dreams and visions and purposes and actions are to fit into those of the enterprise, collaboration and community are needed at multiple levels: person to person, group or team, organizational, and society to society. Working together toward common goals permits meaning and community to evolve. From shared meaning, from accomplishment, from common tasks a sense of community and spirit develops.

For example, if we looked at Philip Morris (despite that many, including me, would object to the marketing and selling of tobacco products), what we see are values that can be termed end values (Burns, 1978): the right to personal freedom of choice, winning, individual initiative, merit-based opportunity, and hard work and continuous self-improvement. These are values that people of character can buy into and that create a common culture and set of goals within an enterprise like Philip Morris. (This notion assumes, of course, that employees allow themselves to forget that what they are doing is actually selling products that kill people, which has to create authenticity—character— problems for some people at least.) Thus, the values also create a common core around which people join together in work. When shared, they create community spirit and a spirit of community.

Think of the generative power that could be released if organizations were able to incorporate wholeness, authenticity, shared meanings, and end values, and really give people equality, power, efficacy to serve the "common good" as well as profits. Then we wouldn't have to ask people to destroy their spirituality or character (their integrity, i.e., their capacity for integrated wholeness) or their communities or nature for that matter by making decisions that they know are unethical, harmful. Decisions that they would not make if their own kids were the ones being hurt in the interests of efficiency—or economizing, or power aggrandizement (Frederick, 1995). Then perhaps we (people) could be happier making our meanings with less of the "goods" and more of the "good" however we define it in community, spiritually, integratively.

COLLABORATION GENERATES COMMUNITY—AND SUCCESS

The third and perhaps most controversial proposition states that we need collaboration as much as, and perhaps more than, competition to survive as the interconnectedness of the world grows more apparent. The dominant management, business, market paradigm is one of cutthroat competition, even hypercompetition (D'Aveni, 1994), which is now being touted as a desirable way to force communities to become "world class" (Kanter, 1995). The logic of this perspective seems embedded in a sort of amoral winner-take-all competition or race (to the bottom, (Korten, 1995, and Henderson, 1996), among others, would suggest).

Eisler (1988) suggests that dominator societies and models of human interaction with which we are all too familiar today overtook societies that were premised in partnership and collaboration. Halal (1996) indicates that a new paradigm of organizing will bring more democracy to the workplace, partially through collaborative interactions with (vs. on) stakeholders. When, how, can we begin to take this new type of understanding and the role—the importance—of community and collaboration to our students, to societies, and to individuals/managers operating in the world? That's a puzzle.

Stakeholder theory (Freeman, 1984) helps somewhat because it is relational, especially when it is framed in terms of mutual collaboration and interaction, rather than in terms of a focal company that will somehow "manage," i.e., dominate, its stakeholders. In this view, stakeholder relationships involve entities embedded together in a web or interwoven context where the actions of any one person affect all the others (see also Capra, 1995). Despite the emergence of such relational and web-based ideas, the problems of fragmentation and atomization go deeply into our Western roots: we atomize relationships, looking for fundamental parts that don't exist, rather than focusing on the relationships themselves, which actually are the system; we focus, that is, on what is observable and empirical rather than what is intrinsic and related to awareness, meanings, or consciousness. And somehow, we have focused on dominance and competition, one outdoing the other, when it is cooperation—symbiosis—that forms the interstices of both meanings and relationships.

There is a countervailing view to the fully Darwinian "survival of the fittest" logic that generally prevails. This perspective would suggest that it is symbiosis, mutuality, or in organizational terms, collaboration and *inter*dependence on which success is built (Capra, 1995; Maturana and Varela, 1988). And this mutuality occurs at the biological, individual, organizational, and societal levels. This perspective contradicts the dominant values of business of aggressive competition, particularly related to power aggrandizement, and a market logic based on economizing and efficiency (Frederick, 1995). Yet this perspective, which is partially based on what Frederick (1995) terms the set of ecologizing values, suggests that success is achieved within a framework of interlinked, mutually supportive, and interdependent entities. Thus, natural scientists tell us quite directly that life derives from processes of symbiosis—collaboration and community—at least as much as from competition, as the philosophers would have it, "red in tooth and claw."

Symbiosis acknowledges interdependence among each other, a fundamental element of community. What holds community together, arguably, are the cultural norms and shared values, particularly end values (Burns, 1978). End values, I believe, provide the possibility of creating collective spirit—community and connectedness—by giving us something to believe in collectively, to work toward, a higher end, creating a sense of community. This sense of community is based on common interests, goals, and experiences together. The experience of collaboration and sharing needs to be structured so that it is safe for personal expression, so that people are allowed to share and not be punished for sharing, so that community based on authenticity can actually be built. That building process is fragile, I think, easily disrupted by old patterns, hierarchies, power differences, the need for the domination of some by others, competition, and opportunistic personal or organizational agendas.

Think, for a moment, of the traditional hierarchically structured "dominator" (Eisler, 1988) model of organization (and most modern societies). Imagine working on an assembly line or in the tortures of a clothing sweatshop. How many of us would then be able to live out our passions or create meaning in our work, be it spirituality or community? We do the bidding of others in such jobs, bringing very little of our whole selves to the work. Still, there are those rare individuals who rise above their circumstances and exhibit qualities of self-expression, fulfillment, and meaning, and create community around them, no matter what their work.

Csikszentmihalyi (1997), for example, suggests in his book *Finding Flow* that it is entirely possible to live daily life in what he terms "flow." He describes "Joe," an assembly-line worker who created a meaningful work environment by learning everything about all the machines and becoming a tremendous resource for his co-workers. Creating meaning and community that inspires and brings out the best in others—and by extension in organizations—thus can be done. Living this way requires a spirit and a passion that eludes many people, resulting in what Henry David Thoreau (in *Walden*) termed a life of quiet desperation! The very success of the visionary companies over long periods of time (Collins & Porras, 1997) attests to the survival and prosperity value associated with creating this sense of togetherness and community in companies, helping people to focus their energies on meaningful contributions to the work of the collectivity. Thus, the critical question is how can we transform our organizations so that more—all—of them permit this kind of individual self-expression, yet retain the context of the larger enterprise's meaning, purpose, and goal achievement? Creating these types of enterprises really pushes the edge of the both/and logic identified as crucial in the built-to-last companies (Collins & Porras, 1997).

Despite this evidence, one does have to wonder about anarchy if everyone really were able to pursue individually meaningful and community-based work. The world might then (another proposition?)

be full of self-efficacious individuals who didn't need or want to be dominated by those who viewed themselves as superior by virtue of their position, power, or access to resources. Such an evolution would potentially generate real democracy in the workplace. Yet success in such democratically based organizations would, necessarily, result not from cutthroat competition but from cooperation and collaboration with other democratically based enterprises and units. Mind, heart, body, soul, all together—seeking a degree of integration, wholeness, rather than fragmentation; moving out of the Cartesian dualism that has so affected Western thinking.

CONCLUSION

If we want to create meaning in our own lives and want to help our students, clients, and managers create meaning and passion in theirs, then (my guess) we need to do much more to tap into their emotional and spiritual sides than the analytical approaches that dominate management education now allow. Living with passion in organizations requires bigger meanings and purposes, aimed at something beyond the "goods" contained in dollars and products, and something of the common good that is engendered in relationships of care and community, commonality, among all stakeholders in an enterprise. That is the goal of bringing spirituality—and community—into the work-place.

REFERENCE

Anderson, C. (1997), "Values-based Management," *Academy of Management Executive*, 11 (4): 25–46.

Barber, B. (1995), *Jihad vs. McWorld*. Times Books/Random House, New York.

Bellah, R. N., Madsen, R., Sullivan, W. M., Swidler, A., and. Tipton, S.M. (1985), *Habits of the Heart: Individualism and Commitment in American Life*, Harper & Row, New York.

Burns, J. M. (1978), *Leadership*. Harper Torch Books, New York.

Capra, F. (1995), *The Web of Life*, Anchor Doubleday, New York.

Collins, J. C., and Porras, J. I. (1997), *Built to Last: Successful Habits of Visionary Companies*, HarperBusiness, New York.

Csikszentmihalyi, M. (1997), *Finding Flow: The Psychology of Engagement with Everyday Life*, Basic Books, New York.

D'Aveni, R. (1994), *Hyper-Competition: Managing the Dynamics of Strategic Maneuvering*, The Free Press, New York.

Derber, C. (1992), *Money, Murder, and the American Dream: Wilding from Wall Street to Main Street*, Faber and Faber, Boston, MA.

Derber, Charles (1998), *Corporation*, St. Martin's Press, New York.

De Waal, F. (1996), *Good Natured: The Origins of Right and Wrong in Humans and Other Animals*, Harvard University Press, Cambridge, MA.

Eisler, Riane (1988), *The Chalice and the Blade: Our History, Our Future*, HarperCollins, San Francisco, CA.

Frederick, W. C. (1995), *Values, Nature, and Culture in the American Corporation*, Oxford University Press, New York.

Freeman, R. E. (1984), *Strategic Management: A Stakeholder Approach*. Basic Books, New York.

Freeman, R. E., and Gilbert, D. R. (1988), *Corporate Strategy and the Search for Ethics*, Prentice-Hall, Englewood Cliffs, NJ.

Fisher, D., and Torbert, W. R. (1995), *Personal and Organizational Transformations: The True Challenge of Continual Quality Improvement*, McGraw Hill, London, England.

Graves, S. B., and Waddock, S. A. (1998), "Beyond Built to Last . . . An Evaluation of Stakeholder Relations in 'Built to Last' Companies," Boston College Working Paper.

Greider, W. (1998), *One World, Ready or Not: The Manic Logic of Global Capitalism*, Touchstone Books, New York.

Halal, W. E. (1996), *The New Management: Bringing Democracy and Markets Inside Organizations*, Berrett-Koehler, San Francisco, CA.

Henderson, H. (1996), *Building a Win-Win World: Life Beyond Global Economic Warfare*, Berrett-Koehler, San Francisco, CA.

Kanter, R. M. (1995), *World Class: Thriving Locally in the Global*, Simon & Schuster, New York.

Korten, D. (1995), *When Corporations Rule the World*, Berrett-Koehler Publishers, San Francisco, CA.

Lodge, George C., and Vogel, Ezra F. (1987), *Ideology and National Competitiveness: An Analysis of Nine Countries*, Harvard Business School Press: Boston, MA.

Maturana, H. R., and Varela, F. J. (1988), *The Tree of Knowledge: The Biological Roots of Human Understanding*, Revised Edition, Shambala, Boston, MA.

Overton, W. (1998), "Developmental Psychology: Philosophy, Concepts and Methodology," In R. M. Lerner (Ed.), *Theoretical Models of Human Development*. Vol. 1, *Handbook of Child Psychology* (5th edition), Editor-in-Chief: William Damon, Wiley, New York.

Poarch, M. (1997), "Civic Life and Work: A Qualitative Study of Changing Patterns of Sociability and Civic Engagement in Everyday Life." Boston University Doctoral Dissertation.

Putnam, R. D. (1993), *Making Democracy Work: Civic Traditions in Modern Italy*, Princeton University Press, Princeton, NJ.

Putnam, R. D. (1995), "Bowling Alone: America's Declining Social Capital," *Journal of Democracy*, January 6 (1): 65–78.

Putnam, R. D. (1996), "The Strange Disappearance of Civic America," *The American Prospect*, 24, Winter 1996 [http://epn.org/prospect/24/24putn.html].

Reich, R. (quote on society and economy).

Waddell, S., and Brown L. D. (1997), "Fostering Intersectoral Partnering: A Guide to Promoting Cooperation Among Government, Business, and Civil Society Actors," *IDR Reports*, Vol. 13, No. 3, 26 pp.

Weick, K. E. (1976), "Educational Organizations as Loosely Coupled Systems," *Administrative Science Quarterly*, March, Vol. 21, No. 1, pp. 1–11, 19.

Wenger. E. (1998),*Communities of Practice, Learning, Meaning, and Identity*, Cambridge University Press, New York.

Wilber, K. (1996), *A Brief History of Everything*, Shambala Publications, Boston, MA.

Wolfe, A. (1998), *One Nation After All: What Americans Really Think About God, Country, Family, Racism, Welfare, Immigration, Homo-sexuality, Work, The Right, The Left and Each Other*, Viking Press, New York.

Wood, D. J. (with Laquita Blockson, Craig Caldwell, Kim Davenport, Harry Van Buren). "Field-Mapping: Business School Approaches to Corporate Involvement in Community Economic Development." Unpublished Report to the Ford Foundation.

THE POSSIBLE FUTURE

Dawn

by Tom Brown

An infant bursts
From mother's womb,
Broad smiles illuminate the room.
Each birth a chance to celebrate:
Youth, aglow, anew!
Once more, a precious fireball rises,
Shimmering above the morning dew.

Who you are, what you do,
Each day's a dawn
If you stay true:
The fire's deep down inside of you.

Your days blazed fast
When you reprise,
How few the dawns
Since the dawn of you:
The day your lips spoke ooh;
The day you tiptoed through;
The day you learned in school
The thought you never knew.

Who you are, what you do,
Each day's a dawn
If you stay true:
The fire's deep down inside of you.

First dream first friend first kiss first fight
First job first home first speech first flight:
Every alpha, each aurora,
Those flags you made and flew,

In your mind, now folded carefully,
Locked away . . . they're you!

Who you are, what you do,
Each day's a dawn
If you stay true:
The fire's deep down inside of you.

Ticking ever older,
You ache; you mourn; you fear.
Life's quest? A welled-up tear?
All those dawns behind you:
Mere ghosts of greatness now;
Fleeting flecks of fire,
Smothered in the snow.

If mankind's urge is forward:
Ideas, then as now, the glue;
If your own emanations
Have shaped the life you grew;
If you yearn to peel away,
To find once more the new;
Then go again to where you've been:
It's *right there*, though out of view.

Who you are, what you do,
Each day's a dawn
If you stay true:
The fire's deep down inside of you.

—from *The Anatomy of Fire: Sparking A New Spirit Of Enterprise*
by Tom Brown © 2000 by MANAGEMENT GENERAL
http://www.mgeneral.com

16

■

A Postmodern Spiritual
Future for Work

Jerry Biberman and Michael Whitty
University of Scranton and University of Detroit-Mercy

INTRODUCTION

A number of writers are predicting the end of work as we know it
and a bleak jobless future as we head into the twenty-first century
(e.g., Korten, 1995; Lerner, 1994; Rifkin, 1995). This article seeks to
provide a more hopeful and humane paradigm for the future of work—a
model based on spiritual guidelines and principles. In this article we
will explore what these spiritual guidelines and principles might be and
contrast them with the prevailing modernist paradigm. We will then
explore how these principles could be applied to produce shared power
in organizational settings.

THE CHANGING NATURE OF WORK

There certainly appears to be evidence that the kinds of jobs that most
employees have grown used to having for more than the past 50 years
are either changing dramatically or are disappearing entirely. Employees
can no longer look forward to lifetime employment with the same
organization, to eight-hour work days, or to generous benefit packages.

ACKNOWLEDGEMENTS
An earlier version of this paper was presented at the annual meeting of the International
Academy of Business Disciplines in Orlando, Florida, April 1997. Many thanks to Krista
Kepler for her assistance in preparing the article.

Management theorists are predicting that the workers of the future will need to demonstrate to organizations how they can add value to the organization, that workers can look forward to doing this continuously with a number of organizations over a period of less than 20 years (Bridges, 1994), and that this will require continuous skills training and reeducation (Coates et al., 1990; Gordon et al., 1994). Academicians and professionals alike are noticing the increased stress and uncertainty that workers are already encountering as organizations downsize and demand ever-increasing amounts and hours of work from those workers who survive in the organization (Schor, 1993).

Many of the organization theorists who have predicted the above occurrences also claim that the future will provide many exciting opportunities for workers who are flexible and who can demonstrate they add value to organizations (e.g., Harari, 1993). They also point to a shift in organization structure and governance from the hierarchical mechanistic monolithic organization to smaller, more organic structures consisting of empowered leaderless work teams (Coates et al., 1990; Overholt, 1996). Such organizations could provide opportunities for professional development and empowerment of workers at all levels of the organization.

In this article, we contend that both scenarios of future work derive from a modernist paradigm of work that has been the prevailing paradigm for the past 100 years.

TWO CONTRASTING PARADIGMS

MODERN PARADIGM

Most organizations have been designed and managed for the past 100 years using a paradigm based largely on a logical and mechanistic paradigm—a paradigm that values reason and "scientific" principles—that Boje and Dennehy (1994), among others, have called modernism, and that Fox (1994) has called the machine-era paradigm. The paradigm assumed that people can be scientifically measured and categorized based on intellectual and other characteristics they possess, and that certain people are meant to be leaders while others are meant to be followers—or other variations of superior versus inferior—and that organizations, and indeed the whole world, run on rational laws that, once discovered, dictate the only correct way for the organization to run. This paradigm has given rise to such organization practices as scientific management, employment testing, and job instructional training, and to an approach to management that this paper will call "autocratic paternalistic stewardship."

In this paradigm, rational decision making and logical thinking are encouraged, and emotions are to be avoided. Another major component of this paradigm is the belief in scarcity of resources—that is, that all resources, including financial and human resources, exist in finite quantities, and possession of a resource by one person or unit implies its unavailability to other persons or units. This belief has led to such personal and organization practices as competition, political manipulation, "padding" of budget requests, empire building, and lack of trust and cooperation between persons and units. In addition, this paradigm leads to a belief that the person or organization is separate from other persons or organizations, and that preservation of the self, even if it is at the expense of the other, is paramount to survival.

SPIRITUAL PARADIGM

Organizations and their executives both in Japan and in the USA are beginning to show an interest in spirituality and spiritual values (e.g., Brandt, 1996; Galen, 1995; Labbs, 1995; Vicek, 1992). A number of organizational writers are urging organizations and their members to pay more attention to spiritual values and spirituality (e.g., Bolman and Deal, 1995; Gunn, 1992; Russell, 1989; Schechter, 1995; Scherer and Shook, 1993; Walker, 1989).

Some authors have related spirituality to organizational learning processes. Mingin (1985), for example, describes how information-based technology will lead to "spirituality oriented fundamental abstractions." Vail (1985) proposes a "process wisdom" explanation of organizational transformation that involves four elements—grounding in existence, appreciation of the openness of the human spirit, understanding of human consciousness, and an appreciation of the spirituality of humankind. Hawkins (1991) relates the spiritual dimension in learning organizations to Gregory Bateson's concept of double-loop Level III learning.

Interest in organizational learning and creative thinking has also led to the increased use of certain spiritual practices—particularly meditation—among organization members, and an increased interest in intuition and whole-brain thinking in organization decision processes (e.g., Agor, 1989). Increasing numbers of executives and managers are turning to various types of meditation and spiritual disciplines as a way of coping with stress and for finding meaning in their turbulent work environments (Dehler and Welsh, 1994) and in dealing with recovery from job loss (Byron, 1995).

At the same time that organizations and managers are paying more attention to spirituality and to whole-brain thinking and learning, global competition and other conditions are bringing about increased attention to team development and employee empowerment.

When one examines the various descriptions of organizations using work teams (e.g., Levine, 1994), one is struck by the similarity of the values, behaviors, and processes that emerge from these teams to those described in relation to spirituality, creativity, and organization learning. Indeed, Poe (1991) points out that the Japanese, with their knowledge of Zen Buddhism, understood Deming's Plan-Do-Study-Act (PDSA) cycle as a spiritual discipline. As employees master this PDSA discipline, they continually trade information with each other until individual wisdom fuses into a powerful group intelligence. Poe says that excessive reliance on logic and reason led many Westerners to misunderstand this aspect of Deming's theories. Similarly, Fort (1995, p. 16) describes how total quality management's emphasis on fulfilling the needs of customers and stakeholders is a contemporary managerial articulation of what Pope John Paul calls solidarity, or the goodness of understanding the self in terms of the self's dialectical relationships with others. Fort asserts that "this expresses an overlapping wisdom that grounds a spirituality of connectedness in all aspects of life, including business."

What do these emerging trends have in common? It is our contention that they represent a postmodern management paradigm that is emerging—one that emphasizes spiritual principles and practices, as opposed to the current prevailing modern management paradigm.

Rose (1990) describes a new paradigm that is beginning to develop among managers and executives which incorporates ideas from quantum physics, cybernetics, chaos theory, cognitive science, and Eastern and Western spiritual traditions. It contains two main components—everything is seen as being interconnected, and there is a focus on empowering people. Rose attributes the vogue for Japanese management techniques, the spread of technology, and the spread of idealism as fueling the trend. Fox (1994) describes many of these same characteristics as depicting what he calls the green (sheen) era of Creation as Sacrament paradigm. James Redfield (1993, 1996) has summarized many of the components into the ten insights described in the Celestine Prophecy and the Tenth Insight, and Deepak Chopra (1994) has distilled the spiritual laws involved in this paradigm (from the Indian Vedic tradition perspective) into the Seven Spiritual Laws of Success.

It is our contention that this paradigm is continuing to emerge and will become more widespread in future years, and that the existing stress that managers and organizations are experiencing may actually produce the catalyst for organization spiritual transformation, in ways similar to that in which personal crises have led to personal spiritual growth and transformation (Grof and Grof, 1989).

THE TWO PARADIGMS CONTRASTED

The two paradigms can be contrasted on both the individual manager and organization level.

On an individual level, persons who ascribe to the modern management paradigm would be expected to have rigid attitudes and beliefs about the nature of themselves, other managers, their superiors, and their subordinates (similar to what McGregor described as Theory X), and a set pattern of behaviors in dealing with each of them. They would also be likely to establish and follow specific procedures or rules of behavior for themselves and others, and be resistant to change. They would attempt to base their decisions purely on logic and reason, and would frown on the use of intuition and the display of emotion. Their scarcity belief would be likely to lead to their not trusting other people, to the use of win-lose tactics in dealing with conflict situations, and to using a variety of power and political tactics to secure their own power base. They would also have a hard time delegating power to others.

Persons operating from a spiritual paradigm perspective would be open to change, have a sense of purpose and meaning in their life, appreciate how they are connected with a greater whole, and have individual understanding and expression of their own spirituality. In contrast to a scarcity belief, they possess what has been referred to as an "abundance" mentality—a belief that there are abundant resources available to all, so that there is no need to compete for them. They would also be more likely to trust others, share information and work in concert with teams and co-workers to accomplish mutual objectives, and empower their co-workers and people below them in the organization hierarchy. They would be more likely to use intuition and emotions in reaching decisions. They would also be more likely to use win-win collaborative strategies in conflict situations.

Organizations that operate from the modern paradigm possess rigid, bureaucratic structures and hierarchical chains of command. They are more likely to use formal communication channels and have very formal policy manuals and procedures for every activity and job title in the organization. They are more concerned with following policies and procedures than in pleasing either internal or external customers. The belief in scarcity of resources leads to competition between organization units for budget, personnel, and other resources, and leads to politics and power struggles between units.

In contrast, organizations that operate from the spiritual paradigm would be expected to have flatter organization structures and a greater openness to change. Their belief in abundant resources would lead to greater interconnectedness and cooperation between organization units, and empowerment of workers at all levels of the organization. Rather than believing in the preservation of the self at all costs, these organizations would be more concerned with existing in harmony with their environment, and would thus be more supportive of the ecology and environment, and more concerned with meeting the needs of internal and external customers. These organizations would be more likely to encourage creative thinking and the working together of organization units to establish and accomplish mutually agreed-on mission statements and objectives for the organization.

THE SHIFT TO THE SPIRITUAL PARADIGM

It is important to point out that the characteristics we described above of persons and organizations operating from a spiritual paradigm perspective are not new. Many of the concepts advocated date back to the human relations movement of the 1950s, and organization development professors and consultants have been advocating many of these concepts for at least 40 years. What is new about these recent developments, however, is that they appear to be emerging from a different overall paradigm, and that environmental conditions are causing them to emerge much more rapidly than ever before.

It is our contention that the human relations movement, organization development, and its attendant concepts developed as a reaction to the prevailing modernist paradigm, and existed within it, rather than trying to create a new paradigm. Thus, the proponents of the human relations movement and organization development accepted most of the underlying tenants of the modernist paradigm—such as the belief in the scientific method—as true and as fact, and then attempted to use the methods of that paradigm to call for what were largely cosmetic changes in the way organizations were managed.

As we asserted earlier, we predict that more and more organizations and their workers can be expected to shift to this new spiritual paradigm in the coming years. This shift is not only likely to occur for the reasons Boje and Dennehy (1994) and others cite as pushing organizations into postmodern practices, but also because of the shift in the consciousness of workers and managers at all levels of organizations that is already beginning to occur as workers and managers seek to find more meaning in their work.

SPIRITUALITY AND SHARED POWER

What the employee of the twenty-first century will need more than training is the opportunity to control more fully his or her economic destiny. This desired sense of control can only come with an expanded awareness. Part of this heightened consciousness is soulful or implicitly spiritual (Schechter, 1995). Spirit in the workplace can lead to greater kindness, fairness, even industrial democracy, also known as co-management or power sharing. An invitation to co-manage is an important step away from well-intentioned paternalism. An empowered employee increases the organizational strength and competitive energy necessary for global survival. The greatest empowerment comes from heightened consciousness of our highest self. This higher self is ultimately aware that the purpose of life and work is spiritual as well as material (Fox,

1994). The balance or integration of these two aspects will enhance the effectiveness of organizations and the people within them. This trend will expand in the century to come. Rekindling the spirit in work is not only good business but also subconsciously sought after by workers and managers alike.

REKINDLING THE SPIRIT OF COMMUNITY IN WORK

Organizational soul and the spirit of the workforce have been too often ignored or neglected. Nonetheless, the history of economic reform movements and the thread of social justice in philosophy and religion have long called for a basic change of heart in human behavior. This has always implied a more communal approach to organizational theory and practice as well as a more humanistic psychology for individual behavior. These democratizing concepts were often introduced by social democrats in alliance with unions. Liberal religion supported these community-building reforms.

Spirit-based organizational theorists might profit from further interdisciplinary research into aspects of all major work reform movements of the last 200 years. With the rise of modernism came a heightened materialism that marginalized sharing and caring. Industrialism weakened community and sidelined religion. Employees were often excluded stakeholders. Now a post-industrial age yearns for community and spiritual nourishment in both personal and organizational terms. Selfishness seems dysfunctional to many global thinkers. Only by reinventing work from the inside out will individuals acquire a sense of deeper purpose in work.

In the postmodern future, humankind's eternal search for meaning will require not only reinventing work and the workplace but also a renewed sense of the deepest intentions behind human activity. Spirit-based organizations might also profit from such an arrangement. Cooperation may be good for people's sense of shared destiny and good for the future of organizational culture.

SHARED POWER

Employee ownership and community involvement in partnership with local and regional employers could evolve into an advanced form of comanagement where all stakeholders share power with spirituality, forming the common ground for cooperation. The individual would be respected in a work world that values diversity and cooperativeness. The organization would recognize its global stewardship of all its resources. Environmental impacts for the long run would include not only the planet but also the spirit which gives it life and ultimate meaning.

A NEW WORK COMMUNITY: SPIRIT AT WORK

A basic workplace spirituality can be the common ground for the new work community. The philosophy of participation adopted from the team concept model can be expanded in the twenty-first century to involve human unity and higher consciousness as well as continuous improvement. This may require a fuller understanding that management makes decisions that have far-reaching impacts on the spiritual lives of employees. Work life reaches into the very soul of all working people. Employees in touch with their spirituality seek to have more input into those decisions. Rekindling the spirit in work will deepen these efforts. The final step would be a corporate attitude of servant leadership toward all stakeholders. Visionary groups such as the Greenleaf Center for Servant Leadership and the Noetic Sciences Institute have path-breaking conferences and workshops designed to encourage new paradigms in business. These groups believe that shared power will ensure that the future "borderless world" values diversity, embraces pluralism, and provides global servant leadership. Workplace unity and high purpose can create a service-learning atmosphere which will result in high standards, adequate competitiveness, and an agile business system for the century to come. A deepened form of organizational stewardship could evolve from reforms in organizational decision making.

SOUL AT WORK

Working people and human evolution itself are constantly seeking meaning, purpose, and a sense of contribution to worklife. These needs are best served and deepened when a spiritual paradigm frames the intentions of all stakeholders. Real human nourishment is provided by the soulful organization.

The postmodern work organization can transform the purpose and meaning of work without excluding employee stakeholders. During the rest of our professional lives we can teach the wisdom and skills of organizational harmony and evolving. Reframing the meaning of work has support of the servant leaders worldwide who see that a life of service best fits the basic human need for relevance, recognition, meaning, and self-transcendence. The *Journal of Organizational Change Management* has become an academic source for new thinking on matters related to a people-centered approach to the future of work.

REFERENCE

Agor, W. H. (1989), *Intuition in Organizations*, Sage, Newbury Park, CA.

Boje, D. M., and Dennehy (1994), *Managing in the Postmodern World: America's Revolution Against Exploitation*, 2nd. ed., Kendall/Hunt, Dubuque, IA.

Bolman, L. G., and Deal, T. E. (1995), *Leading with Soul: An Uncommon Journey of Spirit*, Jossey-Bass, San Francisco, CA.

Brandt, E. (1996), Corporate pioneers explore spirituality: peace, *HR Magazine*, Vol. 41, No. 4, April, pp. 82–87.

Bridges, W. (1994), *JobShift: How to Prosper in a Workplace Without Jobs*, Addison-Wesley Publishing Co., Reading, MA.

Byron, W. J. (1995), Spirituality on the road to re-employment, *America*, Vol. 172, No. 18, pp. 15–16.

Chopra, D. (1994), *The Seven Spiritual Laws of Success: A Practical Guide to the Fulfillment of Your Dreams*, Amber-Allen Publishing, San Rafael, CA.

Coates, J. F., Jarratt, J., and Mahaffie, J. B. (1990), *Future Work: Seven Critical Forces Reshaping Work and the Workforce in North America*, Jossey-Bass, San Francisco, CA.

Dehler, G. E., and Welsh, M.A. (1994), Spirituality and organizational transformation: implications for the new management paradigm, *Journal of Managerial Psychology*, Vol. 9, No. 6, pp. 17–26.

Fort, T. L. (1995), The spirituality of solidarity and total quality management, *Business and Professional Ethics Journal*, Vol. 14, No. 2, Summer, pp. 3–21.

Fox, M. (1994),*The Reinvention of Work: A New Vision of Livelihood for Our Time*, Harper San Francisco, San Francisco, CA.

Galen, M. (1995), Companies hit the road less traveled, *Business Week*, No. 3427, 5 June, pp. 82–84.

Gordon, E. E., Morgen, R. R., and Ponticell, J. A. (1994), *Futurework: The Revolution Reshaping American Business*, Praeger, Westport, CT.

Grof, S., and Grof, C. (Eds.) (1989), *Spiritual Emergency: When Personal Transformation Becomes a Crisis*, Jeremy P. Tarcher, Los Angeles, CA.

Gunn, B. (1992), Competruism: ideology with a sustainable future, *Futures*, Vol. 24, No. 6, July/August, pp. 559–579.

Harari, O. (1993), Back to the future of work, *Management Review*, Vol. 82, No. 9, September, pp. 33–35.

Hawkins, P. (1991), The spiritual dimension of the learning organization, *Management Education and Development*, Vol. 22, No. 3, Autumn, pp. 172–187.

Korten, D. C. (1995), *When Corporations Rule the World*, Kumarian Press, Inc., West Hartford, CT, and Berret-Koehler Publishers, Inc., San Francisco, CA.

Labbs, J. J. (1995), Balancing spirituality and work, *Personnel Journal*, Vol. 74, No. 9, September, pp. 60–76.

Lerner, S. (1994), The future of work in America: good jobs, bad jobs, beyond jobs, *Futures*, Vol. 26, No. 2 , March, pp. 185–196.

Levine, L. (1994), Listening with spirit and the art of team dialogue, *Journal of Organizational Change Management*, Vol. 7, No. 1, pp. 61–73.

Mingin, W. (1985), The trend toward being: what's after the information age? *ReVISION*, Vol. 7, No. 2, Winter-Spring, pp. 64–67.

Overholt, M. H. (1996), *Building Flexible Organizations: A People-Centered Approach*, Kendall/Hunt Publishing Company, Dubuque, IA.

Poe, R. (1991), The new discipline, *Success*, Vol. 38, No. 6, August, p. 80.

Redfield, J. (1993), *The Celestine Prophecy: An Adventure*, Warner Books, New York.

Redfield, J. (1996), *The Tenth Insight: Holding the Vision*, Warner Books, New York.

Rifkin, J. (1995), *The End of Work*, G. P. Putnam and Sons, New York.

Rose, F. (1990), A new age for business? *Fortune*, Vol. 122, No. 9, 8 October, pp. 156–164.

Russell, P. (1989), The redemption of the executive,*Leadership and Organization Development Journal*, Vol. 10, No. 3, pp. i–iv.

Schechter, H. (1995), *Rekindling the Spirit at Work*, Barrytown, Ltd, Barrytown, NY.

Scherer, J., and Shook, L. (1993), *Work & the Human Spirit*, John Scherer & Associates, Spokane, WA.

Schor, J. B. (1993), *The Overworked American: The Unexpected Decline of Leisure*, Basic Books, New York.

Vail, P. B. (1985), Process wisdom for a new age, *ReVISION*, Vol. 7, No. 2, pp. 39–49.

Vicek, D. J. (1992), The domino effect, *Small Business Reports*, Vol. 17, No. 9, Winter, pp. 21–25.

Walker, R. G. (1989), The imperative of leaders to create leaders, *Directors and Boards*, Vol. 13, No. 2, Winter, pp. 21–25.

Citations

Chapter 1: "Diapers to Car Keys: The State of Spirituality, Religion, and Work Research," by Charles Fornaciari and Kathy Lund Dean. This article originally appeared in the *Journal of Management, Spirituality and Religion*, vol. 1, No. 1, 2004, pp. 7–33.

Chapter 2: "Integrating Spirituality at Work: An Interview with Ken Wilber," by Thierry C. Pauchant. This article originally appeared in the *Journal of Management, Spirituality and Religion*, vol. 1, No. 1, 2004, pp. 113–131.

Chapter 3: "Towards a Spiritually Integral Theory of Management," by David S. Steingard and Dale E. Fitzgibbons. This article originally appeared in the *Journal of Management, Spirituality and Religion*, vol. 1, No. 2, 2004, pp. 145–175.

Chapter 4: "The Growing Interest in Spirituality in Business: A Long-Term Socio-Economic Explanation," by Len Tischler. This article originally appeared in the *Journal of Organizational Change Management*, Vol. 12, No. 4, 1999, pp. 273–279.

Chapter 5: "Spirituality at Work: An Overview," by Dan Butts. This article originally appeared in the *Journal of Organizational Change Management*, Vol. 12, No. 4, 1999, pp. 328–331.

Chapter 6: "Festivalism At Work: Toward Ahimsa in Production and Consumption," by David M. Boje. This article originally appeared in *Work & Spirit: A Reader of New Spiritual Paradigms for Organizations*, Biberman and Whitty, 2000. (Scranton, PA: University of Scranton Press), pp. 77–94.

Chapter 7: "Religion in the Workplace: Correlates and Consequences of Individual Behavior," by Nancy E. Day. This article originally appeared in the *Journal of Management, Spirituality and Religion*, vol. 2, No. 1, 2005, pp. 104–133.

Chapter 8: "Spirituality for Managers: Context and Critique," by Gerald F. Cavanagh. This article originally appeared in the *Journal* *of Organizational Change Management*, Vol. 12, No. 3, 1999, pp. 186–199.

Chapter 9: "What Does Spirituality Mean to Me?," by Abbass F. Alkhafaji. This article originally appeared in *Work & Spirit: A Reader of New Spiritual Paradigms for Organizations*, Biberman and Whitty, 2000. (Scranton, PA: University of Scranton Press), pp. 77–94.

Chapter 10: "Christian Spirituality and Contemporary Business Leadership," by Andre L. Delbecq. This article originally appeared in the *Journal of Organizational Change Management*, Vol. 12, No. 4, 1999, pp. 345–349.

Chapter 11: "Managing With Ahimsa and Horse Sense: A Convergence of Body, Mind, and Spirit," by Grace Ann Rosile. This article originally appeared in *Work & Spirit: A Reader of New Spiritual Paradigms for Organizations*, Biberman and Whitty, 2000. (Scranton, PA: University of Scranton Press), pp. 77–94.

Chapter 12: "Integral Sensemaking for Executives: The Evolution of Spiritually-Based Integral Consciousness," by John E. Young and Jeanne M. Logsdon. This article originally appeared in the *Journal of Management, Spirituality and Religion*, vol. 2, No. 1, 2005, pp. 67–103.

Chapter 13: "Lessons From Oz: Balance and Wholeness in Organizations," by Jerry Biberman, Michael Whitty, and Lee Robbins. This article originally appeared in the *Journal of Organizational Change Management*, Vol. 12, No. 3, 1999, pp. 243–255.

Chapter 14: "Integrating Spirituality into Management Education in Academia and Organizations: Origins, a Conceptual Framework, and Current Practices," by Sandra King, Jerry Biberman, Lee Robbins, and David M. Nicol. This article originally appeared in *Work & Spirit: A Reader of New Spiritual Paradigms for Organizations*, Biberman and Whitty, 2000. (Scranton, PA: University of Scranton Press), pp. 77–94.

Chapter 15: "Linking Community and Spirit: A Commentary and Some Propositions," by Sandra A. Waddock. This article originally appeared in the *Journal of Organizational Change Management*, Vol. 12, No. 4, 1999, pp. 332–344.

Chapter 16: "A Post-Modern Spiritual Future for Work," by Jerry Biberman and Michael Whitty. This article originally appeared in the *Journal of Organizational Change Management*, Vol. 10, No. 2, 1997, pp. 130–138.